P. Adventures

Russell Punter

Illustrated by Christyan Fox

Reading Consultant: Alison Kelly
Roehampton University

Contents

Chapter 1

The return of Captain Spike

On the edge of Rotters' Isle stood a prison for pirates. No one had ever escaped from the fortress's doomy dungeons.

The most famous prisoner was wicked Captain Spike. He was so mean, even the other pirates hated him.

Sneaky Spike just couldn't stop stealing. From the day he arrived, things went missing...

On Monday, Cut-throat Craig's pocket watch disappeared...

on Tuesday, Roger Redbeard's silver earrings vanished in the night...

and on Friday, Sidney Skull couldn't find his gold locket.

5

No one knew who the thief was. But Spike's cell mate, Bobby Bones, noticed the Captain's bag getting fuller.

When Spike wasn't creeping around, he was showing off to the other prisoners.

"No jail can hold me," he boomed. "I'll be out of this smelly rat hole within a month."

Bobby Bones had had enough of the loud-mouthed Spike.

"I bet you'll be back in prison in twenty-four hours," he jeered.

"Oh yes?" growled the Captain. "What do you bet?"

"This!" cried Bobby, holding up a crumpled piece of paper.

"If you stay out for more than a day, I'll send you my treasure map," Bobby offered.

Spike's one piggy eye sparkled with greed.

8

"Address it to the Spyglass Inn," said Spike, with a grin. "It'll reach me there."

"If you fail," said Bobby, "I get everything in your bag."

Spike stroked his bushy beard thoughtfully. "You're on!"

That night, while his cell
mate was asleep, Spike stole the
map from under Bobby's pillow.
Then he quietly unlocked the
cell door with a fat, brass key.

"I'll bet the jailer hasn't
even noticed this is missing,"
Spike chuckled to himself.

Sneaking past the guards,
Spike crept out of the prison
and down to the dock.
Minutes later, he was sailing
out to sea in a stolen boat.

Free at last!

Spike couldn't wait to find
Bobby's treasure. The map
had directions to Spoof Island.
Using the stars to guide him,
he sailed through the night.

Excitedly, he took a shovel from his bag. "Bobby Bones was a fool to trust me," he growled.

Then the double-crossing pirate plunged the shovel into the sand and began digging...

deeper...

and deeper...

and deeper...

Spike felt the sand move
beneath him. "This is it!" he
gasped. With a final thrust, he
slammed the shovel in.

15

Spike tumbled down in a
mass of rubble, landing with a
bump. As the dust settled, he
stared around in disbelief.

16

"Welcome back, cell mate!" shouted Bobby Bones.

Stupid Spike had fallen for Bobby's trick. He had sailed around Rotters' Isle and was back where he started.

Chapter 2

Pirate of the Year

The final of the Pirate of the Year contest was about to begin. Pirates from around the world had gathered to watch.

18

Only two contestants were left – Captain Blackheart and Billy Booty. The winner would take home a chest full of treasure.

Ye scoreboard

Blackheart   Billy

RULES

1. Cheating is expected. (Just don't get caught!)

2. Pirates **must** protect each other against danger.

They had four tasks – and the first was a race. Each pirate had to sail his ship around Skull Island and back.

19

An ear-splitting boom from
a cannon started them off. The
pirates raised their anchors
and the ships left port.

Billy and his crew took an
early lead. By the time the
ships were out of sight of the
judges, they were way ahead.

But sneaky Blackheart had
a trick up his ragged sleeve.
"Alright lads," he barked.
"Out with the secret weapons!"

Flaps opened in his ship's
hull and ten oars shot out.
Blackheart's crew began
rowing as fast as they could.

"That's cheating," yelled Billy, as Blackheart raced by.

"Remember rule one, Booty Brain," laughed his rival.

As the judges came within view, Blackheart's men pulled in their oars. Moments later, they sailed back into port.

"I win!" cried Blackheart.

Blackheart   Billy
1   **0**

For the next task, each pirate had to dive down to the sea bed and bring up a silver chest.

Blackheart gave Billy a hug. "Good luck, matey," he said.

The pirates plunged into the water and dived to the depths.

Spotting a chest, Billy tucked it under his arm.

23

But as he headed back, he was surrounded by hungry sharks. In the struggle to escape, he dropped the chest.

Billy had to come up for air. Seconds later, Blackheart surfaced holding a chest.

"Bad luck, Shark Bait," he snorted.

Blackheart	Billy
2	0

As Billy trudged ashore, he felt something slimy in his pocket. It was a smelly sardine. "So that's why Blackheart hugged me," he thought.

He knew the sharks would come after this fish.

Parrot training was the third task. The pirate with the most talkative bird would win. Billy's parrot, Mimi, went first.

"Beat that, Blackheart," said Billy proudly.

"Ha!" scoffed his opponent. "Wait until you hear my bird Hook Beak."

Hook Beak was declared best bird. The judges hadn't realized one of Blackheart's crew was doing all the talking.

Blackheart poked Billy in the tummy. "You may as well go home now," he said, with a grin.

Everyone sailed to Skull Island for the final task. Each pirate was given a map. The first to find their buried treasure chest would win.

Blackheart's Map

N

12 paces north
22 paces west
14 paces north
9 paces west

X

Start

Billy's Map

N

21 paces north
15 paces east
17 paces north
16 paces east

Start

Billy looked at his map. Something about it didn't seem right. But there was no time to hesitate.

The pirates paced out their routes. Blackheart was so slow at counting, Billy was soon ahead.

...fifteen, sixteen...

...seventee...
OUCH!

But Billy's eyes were on the map – not where he was walking.

He marched straight into a rock pool full of angry crabs.

"Someone added six extra paces to my map," thought Billy. "And I bet I know who."

"Found it!" came a grizzly cry from across the island.

Ha, harr..!

Blackheart had dug up his chest. He ran back to the start to show the judges. Suddenly he felt his legs being sucked down.

"Help!" he yelped. "I'm stuck in quicksand. I'm sinking fast."

Billy raced across the island. "Grab this!" he cried, snapping a branch from a palm tree.

As the gloopy sand dragged him down, Blackheart reached for the branch.

Billy used all his strength to pull his rival to safety.

The pirates who'd gathered around gave a loud cheer.

"Well done, Billy," they cried.

"I still won the task," sneered the ungrateful Blackheart.

"One point for Blackheart," agreed a judge. "But five bonus points to Billy for saving his life. So Billy is Pirate of the Year!"

Blackheart Billy
4   5

Chapter 3

The cabin boy's secret

Harriet Hill helped her parents
run a sheep farm by the sea.
They were poor, but happy.

One day, a stern-looking man
stomped up to the farmhouse.
"It's Sir Rollo Pinchly, the
sea trader," Mr. Hill whispered
to Harriet.

Pinchly flung a tiny bag of
coins at Harriet's dad. "I want
to buy this place," he bellowed.
"We love Curly Fleece Farm,"
said Mr. Hill. "We'll never sell."

Pinchly's face went scarlet. "No one refuses me," he roared, storming off. "I want this land for a new dockyard. And I'll get it somehow..."

The next day, disaster struck. The Hills woke to find that their sheep had vanished.

"We're ruined," sobbed Mrs. Hill. "Now we'll have to sell."

"I won't let Pinchly take our home," said Harriet. "I'll find a job in town and earn some money to buy more sheep."

Harriet packed some clothes and kissed her parents goodbye. But when she got to town, there were no jobs anywhere.

Harriet had almost given up, when she saw a sign by a ship in the docks.

Cabin boy wanted – apply The Salty Seadog

"I need that job," thought Harriet. She hid behind some barrels and put on...

 a pair of shorts...

 a headscarf...

and a long, stripy shirt.

Minutes later, she was in the captain's cabin. "I want to be a cabin boy," she said gruffly.

"What's your name, lad?" asked Captain Cutlass.

"Um... Harry," replied Harriet, nervously.

"Hmm," said the captain, cautiously. "You're a bit skinny, but you're hired."

Once she was at sea, Harriet found life rather strange.

She and the other sailors were taught about...

 sword fighting...

lock blasting...

 and making people walk the plank.

She soon realized that *The Salty Seadog* was no ordinary boat – it was a pirate ship!

39

One morning, a
cry came from a
pirate high in
the crow's nest.

SHIP AHOY!

"Her deck's full of cargo,"
added the lookout excitedly.

"Let's board her and grab it,
lads!" cried Cutlass. "You stay
and steer the ship, Harry."

Harriet watched the pirates go to work. They swung across to the other ship...

 chased its crew...

and tied them up.

But the pirates' luck was about to run out.

A heavy sail whooshed down
from above and swamped them.

Harriet gasped when she
saw who'd dropped the sail
— Sir Rollo Pinchly.
"Nobody steals from
me," he snarled, as he
untied his crew.

42

The pirates were locked in a cabin. "I'll have to rescue them," thought Harriet.

When Pinchly and his crew went below, Harriet swung across.

She slid back the bolt on the cabin door and freed her friends.

Well done Harry.

"Back to the *Seadog*, boys,"
hissed Cutlass.

Suddenly, Harriet heard a
familiar noise coming from
a crate. She peeked inside.

The noise alerted Pinchly
and his crew. "Hands off my
cargo!" he growled at Harriet.

"I recognize those curly coats," fumed Harriet, pulling off her headscarf. "Those are my dad's sheep."

Harriet told her story. Cutlass looked furious. At first, Harriet thought he was mad at her for pretending to be a boy.

45

But it was Pinchly who felt the pirate captain's rage.

"You scurvy scoundrel!" he boomed. "Even a pirate never steals from poor folk."

Pinchly's sailors knew nothing about the theft.

"Shame on you, Pinchly!" said one. "Give her sheep back!"

"Let's take him home for trial," shouted another.

"What about Cutlass and his crew?" asked a third.

"Don't take the pirates," begged Harriet. "After all, they did help find my sheep." Pinchly's men agreed.

"Three cheers for Harry!" the pirates cried, and made her a lifelong member of *The Salty Seadog* crew.

47

Series editor: Lesley Sims

This edition first published in 2007 by Usborne Publishing Ltd.,
Usborne House, 83-85 Saffron Hill, London EC1N 8RT, England.
www.usborne.com
Copyright © 2007, 2006 Usborne Publishing Ltd.

Stories of
Mermaids

Russell Punter

Illustrated by
Desideria Guicciardini

Reading Consultant: Alison Kelly
Roehampton University

Contents

Chapter 1

The ghostly galleon

Harmony lived with her
mother at the very bottom
of the ocean.

They were so poor they could only afford a tiny cave. This was cramped, dark and very cold. It froze their fins and took the shine off their scales.

Harmony tried to keep up their spirits by singing beautiful songs. Her voice was so enchanting that passing fish had to stop and listen.

One day, Harmony's mother woke up shivering all over. She was covered in blue spots and her tongue had turned purple.

Harmony rushed to find Dr. Finley.

Say ahh.

"Your mother is very sick,"
he whispered to Harmony,
"The only cure is polkadot
seaweed, taken twice a day for
one week."

"Where can I find that?"
asked Harmony.

"That's the problem," replied
Dr. Finley. "It only grows in
the Pirates' Graveyard."

"Oh no," gasped Harmony. "Not that spooky place full of sunken pirate ships?"

"I'm afraid so," replied the doctor.

"They say it's haunted by the ghost of Gingerbeard," said Harmony with a shiver. "He was the fiercest pirate to sail the Seven Seas."

7

The thought of visiting the graveyard filled Harmony with fear, but she had no choice. Minutes later, she was swimming nervously between the creepy wrecks.

Harmony searched countless ships without luck. She had almost given up hope, when she saw something spotty sticking out of a rusty old cannon.

Found it!

Suddenly, a terrifying figure appeared from nowhere.

Yahahahaha!

Harmony yelped in fright. It was Gingerbeard's ghost.

10

"Come to steal my treasure, eh?" snarled the pirate.

"No," cried Harmony. "I just need the polkadot weed to cure my mother."

A likely story, fish features.

"I don't believe you," cackled Gingerbeard. He grabbed Harmony roughly and locked her in a cabin.

"No one gets their hands on my gold," screamed the ghost. With that, he shimmered off to patrol the top deck.

What will happen to my mother now?

Harmony felt terrible. She tried to cheer herself up by singing, but all her songs came out sounding sad.

12

Harmony's lovely voice
floated around Gingerbeard's
ship. No matter where he went,
the pirate could hear her.

However hard he tried,
Gingerbeard couldn't drag
himself away from the
mermaid's tragic tunes.

As each day passed, he began
to feel as sorry for Harmony as
a tough old pirate can.

After a week of the singing,
Gingerbeard had had enough.
"I can't take any more!" he
sobbed. "Please just go home
and take this chest with you."

15

Harmony swam home as fast as she could and opened the chest.

Polkadot weed floated out, along with handfuls of coins.

Harmony's mother was cured and, thanks to Gingerbeard's gold, they moved into a warm and cosy new cave.

Chapter 2

The missing pearl

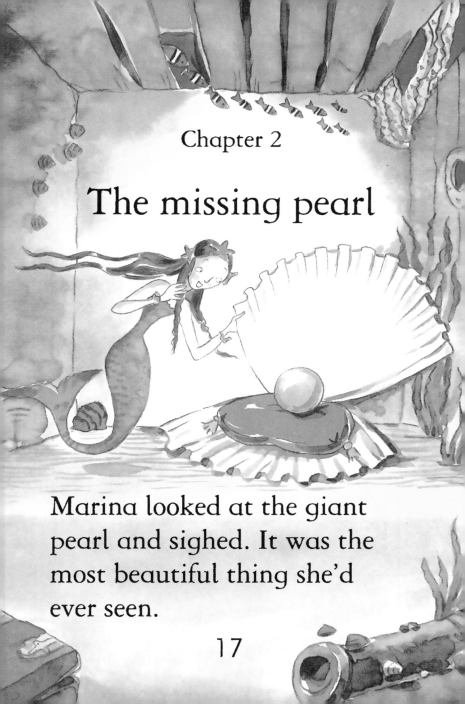

Marina looked at the giant pearl and sighed. It was the most beautiful thing she'd ever seen.

According to legend, anyone who owned the pearl would never grow old and could swim the oceans forever. Sharks guarded it day and night.

Okay, Toothy – time to lock up.

Right-o, Razor.

Giant
Pink Pearl

VIEWINGS DAILY
9am - 5pm

The magical pearl was first prize in King Neptune's Great Seahorse Race.

The event was part of the
king's one-hundreth birthday
celebrations. Marina was sure
that she and her seahorse
Swish could win.

Marina had been preparing
for months with Scuba, her
trainer.

"Make sure Swish has an
early night," she told him.

As Marina swam off, a sneaky-looking pair peeked out from behind a rock.

"Our slowcoach of a seahorse won't stand a chance against Swish," whispered Sid the squid. "And Marina is the ocean's best rider."

20

The mermaid by his side
flicked her tail and gave a
wicked smile. "We'll see about
that," she said.

"What are you going to do,
Storm?" asked Sid.

"I have a plan that can't
fail," she replied. "That pearl is
as good as ours."

Next morning, the seahorses and their riders lined up for the big race.

Marina gently stroked Swish's neck. "You can do it, boy," she whispered.

Storm looked across smugly
at Marina. Then she turned
and winked at her trainer.
Sid winked back and swam
away.

What are those
two up to?

The prawn starter lowered
his flag and they were off.
Soon, Swish and Marina
were way ahead of the others.

Go Marina, go!

As Marina passed the reef, a cloud of thick, black ink shot out in front of her. Quick as a flash, Swish leapt over the top.

Whoops!

Marina lost hold of the reins as Swish sailed over the ink cloud. The others, spotting the hazard ahead, swerved quickly past.

"Lucky you're such a good jumper, Swish," said Marina as she took the reins again.

As they raced off, she just spotted an inky tentacle dart back into the coral.

They soon caught up, and were neck and neck with Storm as the finish line came in sight.

With a final burst, Swish sped forward to win.

Everyone clustered around to congratulate Marina. Everyone except Storm, that is. She was busy whispering something to Sid, who slithered off quickly.

Three cheers for the winner!

A few minutes later, they were all in the cabin of the old shipwreck for the prize-giving ceremony.

But they were in for a shock.
The pearl had gone.

The shark guards searched
everywhere, but the pearl was
nowhere to be seen.

"It must have been stolen!"
cried Scuba.

"But how?" asked Toothy, the
guard. "This room was locked."

The second guard pointed to a tiny porthole. "That's the only other way in and out."

"But it's too small to get the pearl through," said Sid.

"Then it must have been taken before we locked up," said Toothy.

"Who was the last one alone with the pearl?" asked Storm, with a glint in her eye.

Toothy pointed a fin at Marina.

I'm innocent!

"She only took part in the race so we wouldn't suspect her," sneered Storm.

"Yeah," added Sid, waving his tentacles. "She only won by chance."

Marina desperately tried to think of a way to prove her innocence. Suddenly, Sid's dirty tentacles gave her an idea.

"I think the pearl is still in this room!" she cried, pointing at a pile of old cannonballs. She frantically rubbed each one with her seaweed necklace.

32

"Look! This one isn't a cannonball at all," she declared.

"The pearl!" gasped the crowd.

"Covered in squid ink!" added Marina, staring at Sid.

Gulp!

"She made me do it!" cried Sid, pointing at Storm. "I had to disguise the pearl so Storm could collect it later."

"Shush, you stupid squid!" yelled Storm. But it was too late. The two crooks were led away and Marina was presented with her magical pearly prize.

Chapter 3

The dancing mermaid

Coral loved living under the sea. She raced dolphins and sealions.

She swam
with schools
of shimmering
sardines...

she teased
sharks...

Z z Z Z

and spent
the summer
splashing in
the surf.

But Coral had a secret wish.
She wanted to dance.

Every evening, she watched
the humans whirling and
spinning at the dance hall.
She longed to join in.

Coral looked down sadly at her tail. "How can I dance without legs?" she sighed. "I'd give anything to change my flippers for feet."

As she swam past Neptune's palace, Coral had an idea. "Perhaps the king can help me!" With a thrust of her tail, she darted inside.

38

Coral entered the throne room nervously. Her tummy felt as if it was full of butterfly fish.

"And what can I do for you, young lady?" boomed the king.

"W...well your majesty," Coral began, "I'd like some legs please."

"Legs?" repeated the puzzled king. "Mermaids don't need legs."

Coral told the king about
her secret wish. At first, he
looked doubtful, but Coral
begged and begged.

Please, your
majesty.

Hmm...

"I will grant your wish for
one week," he said. "Then you
must decide whether to keep
your legs or your tail."

Coral wanted to dance more
than anything, so she agreed.
King Neptune pointed his
magical trident at Coral's tail.
A sparkling swirl shot out...

and the next
thing she knew,
Coral was
standing on
the beach.

She tried to run to the dance hall. But her new legs took some getting used to...

Oops!

Wooah!

Ooh!

After a lot of practice, Coral walked into the hall. The crowd began to whisper. Who was the beautiful stranger with silky, golden hair?

Soon she was swept off her
new feet by a handsome
young fisherman called Dan.

They spent all
night gliding
and whirling
around the
floor.

Coral had never been so
happy. But she soon found
that life on land wasn't as
good as it looked.

Walking was a lot more tiring than swimming...

fish weren't so much fun when they were stuck in a bowl...

and Coral's tail had never felt as sore as her feet.

Dancing with Dan was the only thing that made it worthwhile.

44

Coral told Dan her amazing
secret. A week later, they went
to the rocks to meet the king.

Neptune rose from the waves.
"So, what is your decision?"
he asked Coral. "Legs or tail?"

Coral had missed her ocean
home more than she had
enjoyed dancing. But she had
fallen in love with Dan.

"Legs," she murmured faintly.

The king looked at Dan.
"And which do *you* think she
should choose?" he asked.

Dan was in love with Coral,
but he'd seen how sad she was
on land. "Tail," he said.

Coral was heartbroken by
his reply. But the king smiled
wisely and whispered another
question in the fisherman's ear.
Dan grinned and nodded.

"I think I have the solution," said the king and he lifted his trident. A magical cloud streamed around the pair.

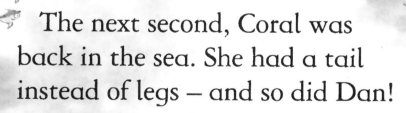

The next second, Coral was back in the sea. She had a tail instead of legs – and so did Dan! "Let's try underwater dancing," said Coral. And they swam off, hand-in-hand.

Series editor:
Lesley Sims

This edition first published in 2007 by Usborne Publishing Ltd.,
Usborne House, 83-85 Saffron Hill, London EC1N 8RT, England.
www.usborne.com
Copyright © 2007, 2005 Usborne Publishing Ltd.

48

The
Secret
Garden

Frances Hodgson Burnett

Adapted by
Mary Sebag-Montefiore

Illustrated by Alan Marks

Reading Consultant: Alison Kelly
Roehampton University

Contents

Chapter 1

Contrary Mary

In the scorching heat of a garden
in India, Mary Lennox stamped
her foot. "Fetch me a drink
NOW!" she ordered.

Instantly, servants rushed to
obey. Meanwhile, Mary began
to make a pretend garden, sticking
flowers into the hot dry earth.
"It looks all wrong,"
she muttered.

Glancing up, Mary saw a
beautiful woman strolling past,
surrounded by an admiring group
of army officers.

"Mother!" cried Mary. She rushed forward, but Mrs. Lennox brushed her daughter away, as she always did.

It was Mary's last glimpse of her mother. Over the next few days a terrible fever, cholera, swept through her parents' house.

Her mother and father died, along with many of their servants.

Mary, shut away in the nursery, never caught the cholera. But she was left all alone in the world.

After that, Mary was passed around like a package between her parents' friends, until a letter came from her uncle, Mr. Craven.

Misselthwaite Manor,
Yorkshire, England

Dear Mary,

I have made arrangements for you to come to England and live at Misselthwaite Manor. My housekeeper, Mrs. Medlock, will meet you in London and escort you here.

I'm afraid I won't see you for some time as I have to travel to Europe on business.

Yours sincerely,

Archibald Craven

"No one cares what I want," Mary thought, but she had nowhere else to go.

Chapter 2

The strange house

Several weeks later, Mary was sitting in a cold carriage, opposite the stern-looking Mrs. Medlock.

"What's that whooshing noise?"
Mary asked, as they drove across a
bleak landscape.

"It's the wind howling across the
moor," Mrs. Medlock replied.

"What's a moor?" asked Mary.

"Miles of empty land – and the
manor is right in the middle of it."

"I hate it already," thought Mary.

"How many servants will I have?" she asked.

Mrs. Medlock looked shocked. "I don't know how it was in India," she said, "but here you'll take care of yourself."

They arrived late at night. Mrs. Medlock marched Mary across a huge hall, up steep stairs and along twisting corridors.

"Your bedroom," she announced,
at last, flinging open a door. "You
must stay here, unless you're going
outside. On no account must you
go poking about the house."

As soon as Mary stepped into the
room, Mrs. Medlock shut the door
and hurried off.

11

Mary looked around. It was not
a child's room. Tapestries hung on
the walls and in the middle stood a
vast four-poster bed.

12

Outside the wind howled like a
lonely person, as lonely as Mary.
Then another noise pierced the
wind – a far-off sobbing sound.

13

"That's not the wind," Mary thought. "It's a child crying. Who is it?"

She was itching with curiosity, but she didn't dare disobey Mrs. Medlock. Finally, worn out from her journey, she fell asleep.

Chapter 3

A robin and a key

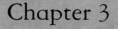

The next morning, Mrs. Medlock
bustled into Mary's room with
her breakfast.

"Ugh!" exclaimed Mary, looking
at the porridge. "What's that? It
looks disgusting. I won't eat it."

15

Mrs. Medlock sighed at the pale, skinny child, swamped by the big bed. "Just drink your milk then," she said, "and you can go out."

"Don't want to," retorted Mary.

"Well, if you don't, you'll be stuck in here and there's nothing to do inside," snapped Mrs. Medlock.

Mary took a while to get dressed – she'd always had servants to dress her before – but finally she was ready.

Mrs. Medlock showed her the way to the gardens and she wandered out, past wintry flower beds and trees clipped into strange shapes.

The only person she could see was an old man digging.

"Who are you?" demanded Mary.

"Ben Weatherstaff," he growled.

"What's in there?" Mary asked, pointing to a crumbling, ivy-covered wall behind them.

"Ah," said Ben. "That's the secret garden. Mr. Craven shut it up."

"Why?" asked Mary.

Ben looked sad. "It was Mrs. Craven's special garden and she loved it. But she died and the master was so unhappy, he buried the key and went away."

As he spoke, a robin flew up to Ben. His wrinkled face creased into a smile.

"There's no door," Ben went on, "but that doesn't stop this one."

The robin cocked its head to the side and looked at Mary. Enchanted, she whispered, "Will you be friends with me?"

"So..." Ben murmured. "You can be friendly. You sound just like Dickon talking to his animals."

20

"Who's Dickon?" asked Mary.

"He's the brother of a maid here," said Ben. "Dickon can grow flowers out of stones and charm the birds. Even the deer love Dickon."

"I wish I could meet him!"

But Ben was growing impatient. "Run along now," he said. "I've got work to do."

The robin flew off. Mary followed him. "Please, robin, show me the way to the garden," she begged.

The robin chirruped and hopped up and down on the ground.

"He's telling me something," thought Mary. She scrabbled in the soil and saw, half-hidden, a rusty ring. Picking it up, she saw it wasn't a ring at all. It was a key.

It's the key to the secret garden!

Chapter 4

Dickon

Every morning, Mary
jumped out of bed, ready to
search for a way into the garden.
"I have the key," she told herself.
"I just need to find the door."

Mrs. Medlock noticed a change in her. "She looks downright pretty now, with her rosy cheeks," she thought. "She was so plain and scrawny at first."

One day, as the winter trees were beginning to blossom and the wind came in sweet-scented gusts from the moor, the robin fluttered down and hopped along beside Mary.

Mary never knew if what happened next was magic. A gust of wind lifted up a patch of ivy to reveal an old wooden door. Mary put her key in the lock, turned it with both hands and pushed. Slowly, the door creaked open...

She was inside the secret garden!
It was a mysterious place — a
hazy, frosty tangle of rose branches
that trailed the walls and spread
along the ground.

Hundreds of green spiky shoots
thrust up through withered grass.
"It isn't completely dead,"
she whispered. "I am glad."

The shoots looked so crowded that she began to clear spaces around them. The robin chirped, as though pleased someone was gardening here at last.

Mary worked for hours. "It must be lunchtime," she thought, hungrily. "I'd better go in, before Mrs. Medlock starts looking for me."

Racing back after lunch, she noticed Ben talking to a curly-haired boy, with a fawn by his side. As the boy walked away, he played a tune on a rough wooden pipe.

Shyly, Mary went up to him. "Are you Dickon?"

"I am," he grinned. "And you're Mary. Ben told me about you."

He looked so friendly and kind,
Mary felt she could trust him.
"Can you keep a secret?"

Dickon chuckled. "I keep secrets
all the time. If I told where wild
animals live and birds make their
nests, they wouldn't be safe."

30

"I've found the secret garden,"
she said quickly. "I think it's mostly
dead. I'm the only person who
wants it to live. Come and see."

She led him through the ivy
curtain and Dickon looked around,
amazed. "I never thought I'd see
this place," he murmured. "It's like
being in a dream."

31

He scraped a rose branch
with his pocket knife. "There's
green underneath," he said.
"These roses are alive.
Some dead wood needs
cutting, that's all."
Mary danced
around the garden
in delight.

"It'll be a fountain of roses, come summer," said Dickon. "We'll add more plants too – snapdragons, larkspur, love-in-a-mist. We'll have the prettiest garden in England."

"Will you really help?" asked Mary. She could hardly believe it.

"Of course," he replied. "It's fun, shut in here, waking up a garden."

Chapter 5

A cry in the night

Every day they worked in the garden. "I don't want it too tidy," Mary decided. "It wouldn't feel like a secret garden then."

"It's secret, sure enough," said
Dickon. "Look – the robin's
building a nest. He wouldn't do
that, unless he felt safe."

"I feel safe and happy here,
too," Mary confided. "But I used
to be angry all the time. Nobody
liked me."

Dickon's fawn nuzzled Mary's hand and he laughed. "There's someone who likes you," he said. "So does the robin and so do I."

That night, lying in bed, Mary heard the wind rage.

"I don't hate it now," she realized.

She thought of the wild animals
on the moor, snuggled in their holes,
protected from its blasts.

Suddenly, she was alert, listening.

"There's that noise again," she
thought. "Crying. It's not the wind.
Where's it coming from?"

Gripping her bedside candle, she followed the sound down shadowy passages, until she reached a door with a glimmer of light beneath.

Quietly, she opened the door. A fire burning in the grate threw a dim light onto a huge carved bed. In the bed was a boy, sobbing. Dark eyes stared from an ivory-white face.

"Are you a ghost?" he whimpered.

"No," said Mary. "Are you?"

"I'm Colin Craven," said the boy.

Mary gasped. "Mr. Craven's my uncle. I'm Mary Lennox."

"Well, Mr. Craven's my father," said Colin.

Mary looked at him in astonishment. "Why didn't Mrs. Medlock tell me about you?"

"I don't let people talk about me," Colin said, "because I'm going to die."

Mary was horrified. "What's wrong with you?"

Colin sighed. "I'm weak."

"You won't die from that," Mary scoffed.

"And my father doesn't even care," Colin went on, as if he hadn't heard. "He hates me because my mother died when I was born. He can't bear to look at me."

"Just like the secret garden," Mary said.

"What garden?"

"Your mother's garden," Mary explained. "Your father shut it up after she died."

"I'll have it unlocked,"
Colin announced grandly.
"No!" cried Mary.
"Why not?"

"Then *everyone* would go in it. It
wouldn't be a secret any more!"
"Never mind," said Colin, fretfully.
"I'll never see it anyway."

"Yes you will!" argued Mary.
"You go outside, don't you?"

"Never," said Colin. "I can't cope
with cold air. Don't forget I'm dying."

Mary felt he was rather proud of
this and she didn't like it. "Don't
talk about death all the time,"
she said. "Think of other things."

Her voice dropped to a whisper.
"Think of the sun and rain and
buds bursting into flower. Think
of new green leaves. Think of the
secret garden, coming alive…"

Gradually, Colin's eyes closed,
and Mary crept away.

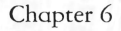

Chapter 6

The magic of the garden

The next morning Mary had to see if she'd dreamed it all. She burst into Colin's room and pulled back the curtains, flooding the room with sunlight.

47

Colin sat up in bed and smiled.
"I've just realized," he said.
"We're cousins!"

They were talking so loudly they
didn't hear Mrs. Medlock come in.

"I told you not to go poking
around," she shouted at Mary. "Go
back to your room *at once*."

"No," Colin ordered. "I like her.
I want her to stay with me."

"She'll tire you out," said Mrs. Medlock. "Come along, Mary."

"DO WHAT I SAY!" screamed Colin. "Leave Mary and get out."

"Yes, dear," said Mrs. Medlock, trying to sound soothing. She'd promised Mr. Craven she would never upset Colin. Hurriedly, she withdrew.

"You're horribly bossy," said Mary. "I used to be like that, when I lived in India. But I'm trying to change now."

"Why shouldn't I give orders?" snapped Colin. "I'm master of this house when Father's away."

Mary got up to leave.

"Don't go!" pleaded Colin, all trace of bossiness gone from his voice. "I don't want to be alone."

"I'll be back later," Mary promised. "I have a friend I want you to meet."

A few hours later, Mary and Dickon crept into Colin's room.

"You've been ages," complained Colin, scowling at them.

"Say hello to Dickon," said Mary. "I want you to come out with us. I want to show you a secret."

"The garden?" guessed Colin. Mary nodded.

"I'll come," he decided and rang a bell to summon Mrs. Medlock.

"I'm going outside," he stated.
"Bring my wheelchair. And tell
everyone to keep away."

"Are you sure, dear?" she asked,
anxiously. "You'll catch cold."

"Just do as I say," Colin ordered.

Dickon pushed Colin along the
paths until Mary, flinging back the
ivy, opened the garden door.

Sunshine lit up sprays of flowers and the air was alive with birdsong.

Colin stared. "I can *feel* things growing," he gasped.

"It's spring," said Dickon. "Makes you feel good. We'll soon have you working in the garden."

"But I can't even stand," Colin faltered, looking at his thin legs.

"Only because you haven't tried," said Mary.

Dickon helped Colin to his feet.

"Try now, Colin. You can walk, you really can," urged Mary.

Unsteadily and clinging to Dickon, Colin forced his weak limbs to move. The others saw his pale face grow rosy in the sunlight.

"Mary! Dickon!" he cried. "I'm going to get well. I can feel it."

Chapter 7

Mr. Craven
comes home

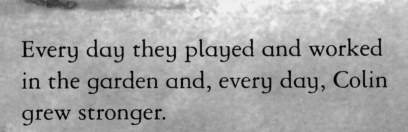

Every day they played and worked
in the garden and, every day, Colin
grew stronger.

57

By the time spring turned into summer, he was completely well. But the three of them pretended he was still ill.

"No one must know," Colin insisted. "I want to surprise my father. If only he'd come home..."

Colin began to wish, "Come home, come home."

One night, Colin's father, far away in Italy, had a strange dream. He heard his dead wife calling his name.

"Where are you?" he pleaded.

"In the garden," came the reply, like the sound from a golden flute.

Mr. Craven woke, determined to return to his manor at once.

"Where's Colin?" he demanded, the minute he arrived home.

Mrs. Medlock gasped, shocked at his sudden appearance.

"He plays in the garden, sir, with Mary and Dickon," she said in a shaky voice. "No one is allowed near them."

"In the garden?" thought Mr. Craven. "My dream..."

As he hurried down the path, he heard children laughing in his wife's old garden.

"The door's locked and the key's
buried," he told himself.
"I must still be dreaming."

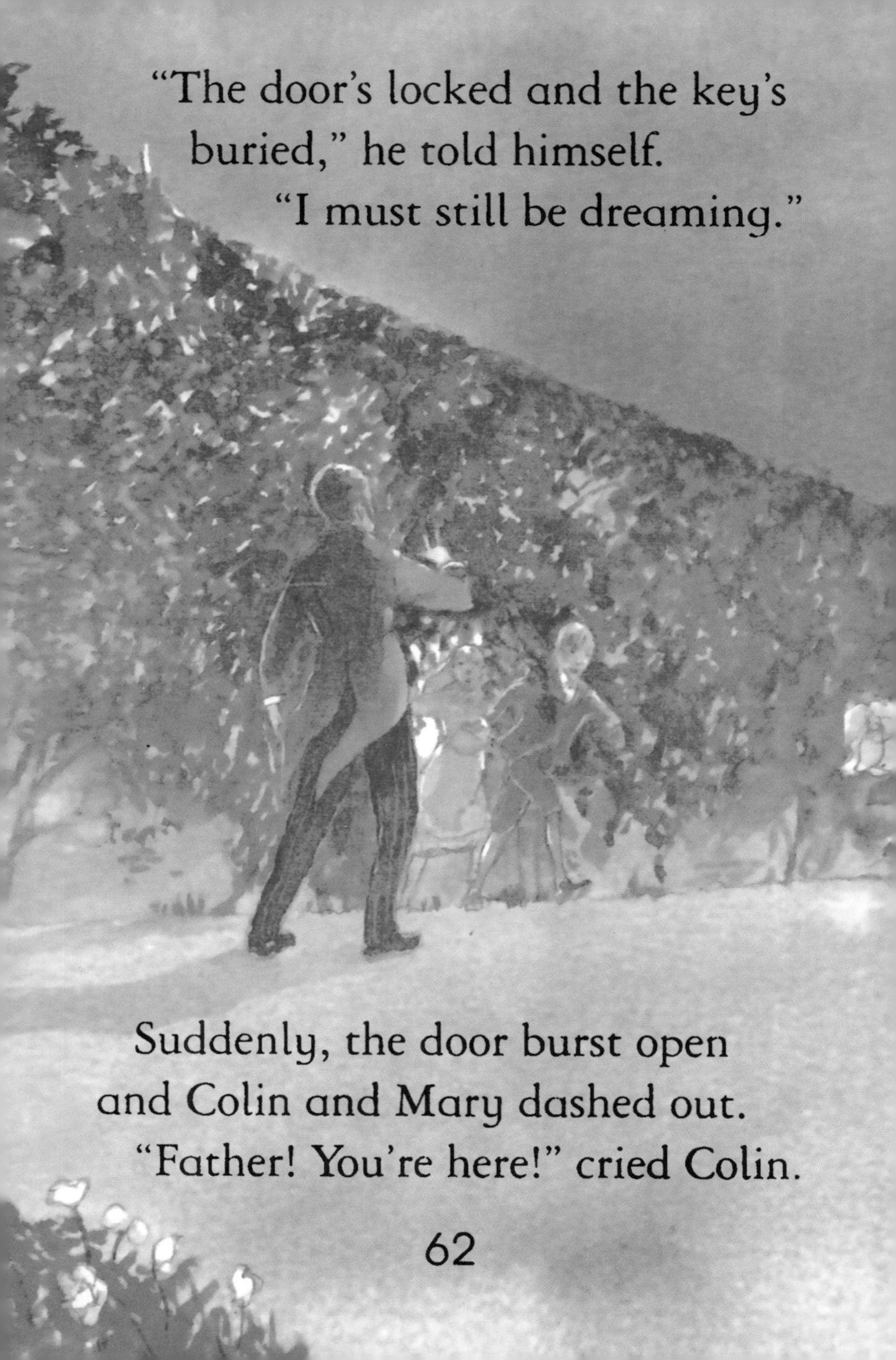

Suddenly, the door burst open
and Colin and Mary dashed out.
"Father! You're here!" cried Colin.

Mr. Craven hugged his son tight. "Is it really you? You're well! However did it happen?"

"It was the garden," said Colin. "And Mary."

"I thought the garden would be dead," murmured his father.

"It came alive," said Mary.

Mr. Craven smiled. "And so has Colin," he said. "Thank you Mary."

Frances Hodgson Burnett

Born in England, in 1849, Frances moved to
America with her family when she was 16.
A year later, Frances sold her first story. She
went on to become one of the most famous
children's writers of all time. Her other
books include *A Little Princess* and
Little Lord Fauntleroy.

Series editor: Lesley Sims
Edited by Susanna Davidson
Designed by Louise Flutter

First published in 2007 by Usborne Publishing Ltd., Usborne House,
83-85 Saffron Hill, London EC1N 8RT, England. www.usborne.com
Copyright © 2007 Usborne Publishing Ltd.

THE
DINOSAURS
NEXT DOOR

Harriet Castor
Adapted by Lesley Sims

Illustrated by Teri Gower

Reading Consultant: Alison Kelly
Roehampton University

Contents

Chapter 1

Mr. Puff

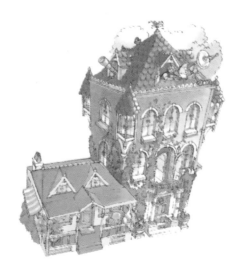

Mr. Puff lived in a tall, blue house. Outside, it looked a little odd. Inside, it was even stranger.

Mr. Puff was an inventor. His whole house was crammed with amazing inventions.

His latest invention moved him from place to place in an instant.

Before that, he invented a robot to clean up spills.

And before that, he invented the Wheelie Cup. (But it spilled most of his tea, which was why he invented the robot.)

His new project wasn't an invention at all. But it was so exciting he had asked Sam, his friend from next door, to see it.

Sam had promised to come over after school.

Chapter 2

The eggs

When Sam arrived, Mr. Puff
was bursting with excitement.

7

He led Sam to his study and
dived under a table.

With a smile, Mr. Puff came
out with a basket.

"Eggs?" said Sam, looking
at the four big eggs.

"These aren't just any old
eggs," said Mr. Puff. "They're...

...dinosaur eggs!"

"What?" cried Sam. "But dinosaurs died out zillions of years ago. How...? Where...?"

Mr. Puff looked mysterious. "Oh, they were to pay me for an invention," he said.

Just then, the blue spotted egg began to jiggle and jump and bump in the basket.

10

A crack appeared, zigzagging along the shell...

...then another...
...and another...

...until finally, a little green head burst out.
"Wow!" said Sam.

11

The creature stared at Sam.
Sam stared back.

"Isn't it wonderful?" said
Mr. Puff.

It's unbelievable!
It's fantastic!

"But is it a dinosaur?" said
Sam. Was it possible? It did
look like a dinosaur.

As they watched, the other eggs began to jiggle and jump and bump in the basket.

Their shells shattered. The eggs had hatched.

The baby dinosaurs were very lively. They looked around, making excited squeaks.

"I expect they're hungry," said Mr. Puff.

"Let me go home for my
dinosaur book!" said Sam and
raced off. Soon, he was back.

"That one looks like ours!"
said Sam. He pointed to a
blue dinosaur with red spikes
on its head.

"That one eats meat then,"
said Mr. Puff. "But some
dinosaurs only eat plants."

They weren't sure what sort
of dinosaurs the others were.

So Sam put out a large plate
of cat food and a large plate
of salad, just in case.

"It's my dinnertime too," said
Sam. "I have to go. But I'll be
back. I must be the only person
with dinosaurs next door!"

Chapter 3

Bigger and bigger

Over the next three days,
Mr. Puff watched the
dinosaurs. He watched
them grow... and grow...

...and grow.

By day four, he had to
invent an extra-long ruler
to measure them all.

19

By the fifth day, he was worried.

20

"They just keep growing!"
he told Sam.

"Can't you invent something
to stop them?" Sam asked.

"That's it!" cried Mr. Puff.
He ran up to his dark, dusty
attic...

...and came back with a silver
box on wheels. A yellow hose
sat coiled like a snake on top.
"What is it?" asked Sam.

"This is my Size-O-Machine,"
Mr. Puff said proudly. "It
makes things shrink or grow."

"Perfect!" said Sam. "Does
it work?"

"Of course it works!" said
Mr. Puff. "Ready, steady, fire!"

23

Chapter 4

KABOOM!

"Oh dear!" said Mr. Puff.
"Something must be wrong."

25

He peered inside the
machine. "Ah!" he said. "I
had my wires crossed. Try
now Sam."

Sam picked up the hose.

"Ready, steady, fire!" said
Mr. Puff.

KABOOM!

The dinosaur vanished.
"Where has it gone?" asked
Mr. Puff. "Did I shrink it
too much?"

Sam looked down the hose.
"Careful!" said Mr. Puff. "I
don't want you shrinking too."

27

They shrank one dinosaur
in the kitchen. Another was
outside, having a snack.

"Ready, steady, fire!" said
Mr. Puff.

But where was the last dinosaur? Just then, they heard a crash from the bathroom.

"Ready, steady, fire!" said
Mr. Puff.

But as Sam took aim, he
slipped. The hose flew from
his hands...

KABOOM!

Chapter 5

Shrunk

Fantastic!
It works on people
too!

Starry smoke filled the room.
When it cleared, Sam was in
shock. He was smaller than
the bottle of bath oil.

31

"It's shrunk us as well as the dinosaur!" began Sam. He heard a roar behind him. "Run!"

Suddenly, the dinosaur
looked at the door. Sam and
Mr. Puff dived for cover.
   The dinosaur should have
hidden too.

Mr. Puff's cat was coming.
She took one look at the
dinosaur and chased it away.

"Quick!" said Mr. Puff.
"We must change to our
normal size before that
dinosaur comes back."

First, they had to move the
dial. Sam pushed. Mr. Puff
pulled. It was hard work.

Then they dragged the hose into place. By now, they were exhausted.

"Everything's hard when you're this small," Sam panted.

"Cheer up!" said Mr. Puff.
"We just have to turn it on."
But they couldn't shift
the lever.

"I hope we don't break it,"
said Sam. Mr. Puff didn't have
any puff to say anything. They
climbed off the machine. What
were they going to do?

Chapter 6

Cat to the rescue

Just then, the cat jumped
up onto the Size-O-Machine.
The lever moved.

KABOOM!

Clouds of smoke filled the
room. Sam and Mr. Puff
started to grow... and grow...
and grow...

They were back to normal
at last.

"Now, what are those
dinosaurs up to?" said
Mr. Puff.

The dinosaurs were running all over the house. Sam tried to help catch them.

The dinosaurs thought it was a game.

"Got you!" cried Mr. Puff
as he scooped up the blue
dinosaur.

"Whew! They're worse than
puppies! What am I going to
do with them?"

Thinking of puppies gave Sam an idea. "If you can train dogs, why not dinosaurs?"

"Brilliant!" said Mr. Puff. "And then maybe you'd like one as a pet. They're very sweet."

"Thank you," Sam said,
"but I'd rather just visit them
sometimes. I think I prefer my
dinosaurs in books!"

Sam never told anyone
about the dinosaurs next door
– or his narrow escape.

But whenever he saw
Mr. Puff's cat, he always
took out a saucer of milk
to thank her.

Try these other books in
Series One:

The Burglar's Breakfast: Alfie
Briggs is a burglar. After a hard
night of thieving, he likes to go home
to a tasty meal. But one day he gets
back to discover someone has
stolen his breakfast!

The Monster Gang: Starting a
gang is a great idea. So is dressing
up like monsters. But if everyone is
in disguise, how do you know
who's who?

Wizards: Here are three magical
tales about three very different
wizards. One is kind, one is clever
and one knows more secret spells
than the other two together.

Designed by
Maria Wheatley and
Katarina Dragoslavić

This edition first published in 2007 by Usborne Publishing Ltd.,
Usborne House, 83-85 Saffron Hill, London, EC1N 8RT, England.
www.usborne.com
Copyright © 2007, 2002, 1995, 1994 Usborne Publishing Ltd.

Stories of
Dinosaurs

Russell Punter

Illustrated by
Cynthia Decker

Reading Consultant: Alison Kelly
Roehampton University

Series editor: Lesley Sims

Contents

Throughout this book you'll see the names of lots of different dinosaurs. Find out how to say them on page 48.

Chapter 1

The wrestling Raptor

The Dinosaur World Wrestling Final was one week away. Kevin 'Crusher' Kritosaurus was fighting Mac, the masked Megalosaurus.

3

Kevin's trainer, Reg Raptor, kept him super fit. Every day, he ran fifty laps around the valley...

rowed sixty lengths of the swamp...

worked out in the gym for three hours...

and did five hundred push-ups.

On Sunday, a huge, horned dinosaur lumbered into Reg's gym. It was Stig Ceratosaurus, Mac's trainer.

"How's training?" sneered Stig. Reg didn't trust his nosy rival. "None of your business," he said.

"Here's some advice, Kev,"
snarled Stig. "Pretend to be
knocked out in the second
round of Saturday's fight."

"That way, Mac and I win
the prize money," he added.
"I won't do it," fumed Kevin.
"That's right," snorted Reg.

6

"Pity," said Stig, as he left. "I only hope you don't have any 'accidents' before the fight."

Kevin and Reg looked worried.

On Monday, Kevin was out on his morning run, when a bridge suddenly collapsed.

On Tuesday,
his rowing
boat sprang
a leak.

Lucky we can
swim.

On Wednesday,
a punchbag filled
with rocks nearly
landed on Kevin's
head.

Look out!

On Thursday, someone put red hot chilli powder in his water bottle.

And on Friday, the ropes around the wrestling ring snapped.

PING!

Whooops.

Kevin and Reg guessed Stig was to blame, but they couldn't prove it. It was too late anyway. The day of the big fight had arrived.

"Ladies and gentle-dinos," bellowed the referee, "please welcome today's wrestlers."
Mac and Kevin bounded up the steps to the ring.

Suddenly, Kevin tripped over
his tail. He crashed down the
steps and
landed in
a heap.

Woah!

"I can't walk," wailed Kevin.
The crowd gasped in shock.
Everyone was disappointed
that Kevin was out of the fight.
Well, almost everyone...

11

Stig smugly waved a piece of paper at Reg. "The rules say that if he can't fight, Mac and I get the money."

We win, losers!

"We won't let you get away with that," said Reg, enraged.
"But what can we do, Reg?" moaned Kevin. "I can't wrestle."

12

"No, but I can," declared Reg.
Stig cried tears of laughter.
"You? Mac would flatten you in
five seconds."

Ha ha!

"Oh yes?" said Reg, storming
up the steps and into the ring.
The startled referee rang the
bell for the fight to begin.

13

Reg shot across the ring and grabbed Mac by the leg. But no matter how hard he tried, Reg couldn't shift the bulky beast.

Grrr! Ngh!

"Give up, shorty!" yelled Stig. "The prize money's ours." But Reg wasn't beaten yet.

He clung on to Mac's tail and tried to swing him around. The mighty dinosaur just swatted Reg like a swamp fly.

Oof!

"Now to finish you off," roared Mac. He lunged at the little Raptor. Reg gulped and ran for his life.

He darted
across the
ring...

scuttled
between
Mac's legs...

leapt over
his tail...

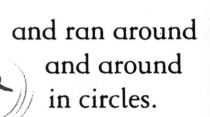

and ran around
and around
in circles.

Mac was strong, but he wasn't fast. The tiny dinosaur ran circles around him. Mac felt dizzier and dizzier, until...

CRASH!

he thudded to the floor in an exhausted daze.

17

The referee dangled Reg by
the arm in front of the crowd.
"The winner!" he declared.

Everyone cheered as Reg and
Kevin collected their prize
money. And Stig had to drag
Mac all the way home.

18

Chapter 2

Dino diner

Tonight, the Raptor brothers, Mike and Albie, were opening their new restaurant. Mike was writing out fancy menus.

19

Raptors' Restaurant

"Meet here for meat"

Your hosts: Michael & Albert Raptor

APPETIZERS

Spinosaurus spikes
with a Tarbosaurus dip

 Pliosaur platter

STARTERS

Allosaurus soup

 Pteranodon Pâté

DISH OF THE DAY

Megalosaurus mixed grill

MAIN COURSES

Baryonyx burger

Cacops chops

Saltopus sausages

Spinosaurus steak

DESSERTS

Pterodactylus pie

Tyrannosaurus tart

Payment: We accept cash
or T-Rex Express Credit Card

Albie polished the knives and forks and ironed the tablecloths. He even folded the napkins into amazing shapes.

Tyrannosaurus.

Allosaurus.

Spinosaurus.

Megalosaurus.

Now all that was left was to cook the food. Mike went to the refrigerator. It was empty – no chops, no steaks, not a sausage...

Where's it all gone?

A tiny dinosaur darted through Albie's legs and out the door. A string of sausages dangled from its mouth.

"Come back, you thieving
Compsognathus!" yelled Mike.
But the rascally reptile was
too fast for them.

"We open in an hour," cried
Albie. "What are we going to
serve to our customers?"

24

The brothers searched every cupboard and drawer. All they were able to find was a stale Megalosaurus meatball.

"We're ruined," wailed Mike.

"We'll have to cancel the opening," sobbed Albie.

Mike checked the restaurant. "Too late," he gulped. "Our first customer is here."

"Oh no," whispered Albie.
"It's Egon Raptor, from the
Good Grub Guide. If he
doesn't like us, we're done for."

"I need to think," said Mike,
scuttling outside. He always
came up with his best menu
ideas in the fresh air.

26

Albie kept Egon busy,
pouring him glass after glass
of sparkling swamp water.

Mike spent twenty minutes
pacing up and down outside.

"What use is a restaurant
without food?" he sighed,
sniffing a flower. Suddenly he
had a wild idea.

Mike ran back into the kitchen clutching a huge bundle of plants. "I've got it!" he cried.

"What *are* you doing?" asked his brother.

"I'm going to cook these," replied Mike, excitedly.

"Yuck!" said Albie. "Are you crazy? No one eats leaves."

Mike chopped
up the ferns...

sprinkled them
with moss...

and drizzled it all
with nettle juice.

Hey presto! One
fern feast.

Albie took the dish to Egon's
table. He whipped off the silver
cover with a flourish. "The chef's
special, sir," he announced.

Egon peered at the green pile
on his plate. He prodded it
with a fork. He stuck his snout
into it and sniffed. Finally, he
took a great big bite...

30

"Yeeuch!" he cried, spitting
a mouthful across the room.
"That's the worst thing I've ever
tasted. You'll get zero out of ten
in my guide book."

Egon ran out, clutching his
tummy. As he left, a strange-
looking dinosaur came in.
"Is there any chance of a
meal?" he asked politely.

31

"Not unless you want this,"
sighed Mike, sliding the plate
of leaves across the table.

The dinosaur licked his lips
and gobbled it all up. "Very
tasty!" he declared.

"You *like* leaves?" said Albie.
"I'm a Stegoceras," replied
the customer. "We never eat
anything else. Could I have a
second helping please?"

The visitor had seven helpings of fern feast. And when he got home, he told all his family and friends about the fantastic food.

From that day on, every meal time was fully booked at the Raptors' new vegetarian restaurant.

Chapter 3

Daisy and the dinosaur

Daisy Dale wasn't enjoying her school trip to the local museum. "Who wants to see a boring old egg exhibition?" she sighed.

On stage stood Professor Hugo Furst, the famous explorer. Next to him were Mr. Bagley, the museum owner, and his wife.

"Good afternoon," boomed the professor. "May I present my latest discovery..."

NATURAL HISTORY MUSEUM

Prof. Hugo Furst's
Egg
Display

GRAND OPENING

TODAY

The professor tugged a sheet to reveal a giant block of ice. Inside was a shiny green egg.

"This is no ordinary egg," he said, proudly. "It was laid sixty million years ago... by a Hadrosaur."

"I discovered it buried in ice at the North Pole," added the professor, waving the sheet around excitedly.

The breeze blew the dust off exhibits nearby... and up Mrs. Bagley's nose.

Mrs. Bagley bumped
into her husband...

who backed into a
microphone stand...

which tripped up a
museum guard...

who fell onto Hugo Furst...

who knocked over the block of ice...

which hit the ground, and smashed into tiny pieces.

Hugo crawled across the floor, searching for his precious find.

"My goodness," said Daisy's teacher. "Let's go somewhere more peaceful and have lunch." She led the class to the cafeteria.

Daisy reached into her bag
for her lunchbox. Instead of
something hard and firm, she
felt something soft and scaly.

A dinosaur!

The creature leaped out in a
spray of eggshell. He looked
around nervously and ran
along the table.

41

Daisy recognized the broken shell. "It's the Hadrosaur egg," she cried. "It must have landed in my bag and hatched."

As the baby dinosaur raced out, Mrs. Bagley strode in.

Aggh!

Daisy raced after the frightened little creature as he crashed through the museum.

He wrecked the rocks...

smashed the bug bottles...

messed up the meteorites...

and sent the stuffed fish flying.

Daisy couldn't catch him.
Luckily, neither could Mrs.
Bagley. "I want it found and
locked up!" she roared.

Catch it now,
professor!

"I can't let them put the
dinosaur in a cage," thought
Daisy. "I must find him first."

"Where would I hide if I were him?" she wondered. "Of course," she cried, rushing to the prehistoric display.

Daisy was right. The baby was snuggled up to a model Hadrosaur.

Honk!

The museum guard appeared,
led by red-faced Mrs. Bagley.

"There it is!" she yelled.

"Honk honk," called the
dinosaur, softly.

The sound was so calming
that everyone stopped.

"Oh. My my," sighed Mrs.
Bagley. "How delightful."

Daisy hugged the Hadrosaur. "Don't lock him up," she begged.

"Of course not," replied Mrs. Bagley gently. "I have a much better idea."

The dinosaur was given a special home at the museum. And every day, people waited for hours to hear the Honking Hadrosaur's calming concerts.

Most of the dinosaur names in this book are the real
ones used by dinosaur experts. Here's how to say them
– the parts of the word in **bold** should be stressed.

	say...
Kritosaurus	Krit-oh-**saw**-rus
Megalosaurus	**Mega**-low-**saw**-rus
Raptor	**Rap**-tor
Ceratosaurus	Ser-at-oh-**saw**-rus
Spinosaurus	**Spine**-oh-**saw**-rus
Tarbosaurus	**Tar**-bo-**saw**-rus
Pliosaur	**Plee**-oh-**saw**
Allosaurus	Al-oh-**saw**-rus
Pteranodon	Ter-**an**-oh-don
Baryonyx	**Bar**-ee-on-iks
Cacops	**Ka**-kops
Saltopus	**Sal**-to-pus
Pterodactylus	**Ter**-oh-**dak**-til-us
Tyrannosaurus	Tie-**ran**-oh-**saw**-rus
Compsognathus	Komp-sog-**nath**-us
Stegoceras	Steg-**oss**-er-ass
Hadrosaur	**Had**-ro-**saw**

This edition first published in 2007 by Usborne Publishing Ltd.,
Usborne House, 83-85 Saffron Hill, London EC1N 8RT, England.
www.usborne.com
Copyright © 2007, 2006 Usborne Publishing Ltd.

Animal Legends

Retold by
Carol Watson

Adapted by Gill Harvey

Illustrated by
Nick Price

Reading Consultant: Alison Kelly
Roehampton University

Contents

Chapter 1

The cat and the rat

You might not believe it now, when cats chase rats and rats hate cats, but long ago, they were best friends.

3

One cat
and rat lived
very happily
together on
an island.

The island
had all they
needed. There were birds for
the cat to chase...

...and plenty of
juicy plants for
the rat to
nibble with
her sharp
front teeth.

4

There was only one problem.
There wasn't much else to do.
Most days they were bored.

Then, one morning, the rat
had an idea.

Why don't we
look for somewhere
else to live?

Purrr-fect! But how
would we get there?

The rat thought about it.
How could they leave the
island? Then she twitched her
whiskers and smiled.

"That's easy," she said.

We'll make
a boat from
the trunk of
a tree!

The rat gnawed at a tree until it toppled over...

Timber!

...and the cat scratched out the inside of the trunk, so they had somewhere to sit.

Finally, the rat nibbled two branches and made them into oars. They were ready to go to sea.

The cat stepped into the boat and took the oars. Then the rat pushed the boat out onto the waves.

"Here goes!" said the cat.

"There's nothing to worry about!" said the rat. "We'll be fine."

They rowed and rowed until
it grew dark.
The cat was
so tired, he
fell asleep.

Oh no!
We forgot to
bring food.

But the rat felt hungry. She

was so
hungry, she
began to
nibble the
side of the
boat.

But she made such a noise,
she woke up the cat.

"Don't worry!" squeaked the
rat. "You're dreaming."
So the cat went back to sleep.

The rat was very greedy
and kept on gnawing at the
boat. Munch... munch...
munch...

Suddenly, she stopped.

Oh no!
What have I
done?

The rat had eaten so much,
she'd made a hole in the boat.

Water started to slosh up through the hole and the boat began to sink.

The cat woke up with a start. "I'm wet!" he squealed.

They had to leap from the boat and swim for their lives.

The cat was very angry. He hated getting wet. "I'm going to eat *you* when we get to shore!" he spluttered.

The rat scrambled up the shore and ran to a sandhill. She dug a hole as fast as she could and dived into it.

Got to dig... got to dig...

The hole was too small for the cat to squeeze into. "I'm safe!" thought the rat.

But the cat didn't give up so easily. He peered into the hole. "I'll wait for you, rat!" he called. "You'll have to come out sometime."

I can wait all week!

So, he sat and he waited... and waited...

16

...and waited. But the rat
never came out.

She dug a tunnel all the way
through the hill and ran out
on the other side.

Whew! I've escaped.

And that is why, today, a
cat will sit for hour upon hour,
waiting to pounce on a rat.

Chapter 2

Why monkeys
live in trees

Many years ago, the king of
the jungle was a gorilla named
Naresh. All the animals wanted
to marry his daughter, but she
didn't know who to choose.

One day, Naresh spotted a big wooden barrel sitting on the grass. "That's new!" he said and looked inside.

Oooh! What's that?

The barrel was full of greasy water. Naresh took a sip. It tasted of fire. "Fire water?" he said. "That might be useful."

19

Naresh took the barrel home and called the other animals

together.

"I have a barrel of fire water!" he said. "And it will help us decide who's to marry my daughter."

Whoever can drink the whole barrel may have my beautiful daughter as his bride.

The animals were very excited. Everyone wanted to try. They pushed and shoved closer to the barrel, but the elephant got there first.

"Just watch. This will be easy!" he boasted.

The elephant dipped his trunk into the barrel. He sucked up some fire water and... sneezed.

Ah-chooooo!

"Oww!" he snorted, spraying water everywhere. "It stings! No one could drink that!" And he rushed off.

The hippopotamus tried
next. "I live in the river and
drink water all the time," he
said. "I'm not scared of a bit
of fire water!"

So he took a big mouthful...

...and almost choked. He spat
out the fire water and ran to
the river to cool his mouth.

Next, the warthog stepped forward.

"I can eat or drink anything," he bragged.

No problem!

He drank from the barrel and coughed. "Ugh! That's horrible!" he shouted.

Yeeeuk!

"What fools you are," cried
a voice. It was the leopard.
"And you're all far too ugly to
marry the king's daughter."

I am handsome,
and I shall drink
the water.

He stepped up to the barrel
and just as quickly stepped
back again. Even the smell of
fire water made him feel sick.

25

The other animals laughed
at the leopard and he crept
away in shame. Then a little
voice piped up.

Please,
Naresh, may I try
the water?

It was a tiny monkey. The
animals stared at him. How
could he drink the water?

Naresh smiled. "You can try if you want," he said. "But you must drink all the water and finish it today."

I don't want a single drop left.

"May I drink a little at a time with rests in between?" asked the monkey.

Naresh was a fair king. "Of course," he said.

So the tiny monkey climbed onto the barrel. The other animals gathered around, grinning. This was going to be funny.

I, Telinga, shall drink the water and marry Naresh's daughter!

RUM

But the monkey seemed very sure of himself.

The monkey gulped a large mouthful of the fire water, then ran off into the bushes.

"Where's he going?" the other animals wondered.

After a few moments, the
monkey was back. He climbed

up the side
of the barrel,
took another
gulp of fire
water...

...and ran
off to the
bushes, just
as he'd done before.

But Telinga, the monkey, had a secret. He wasn't alone. Behind the bushes sat a whole tribe of monkeys, who all looked exactly the same.

Each monkey took turns to drink some of the burning fire water.

By the end of the day, the barrel was empty. The other animals were astonished.

"Now I shall meet my bride," said Telinga proudly.

The monkey stood before the old gorilla. "Well done," said Naresh. "You have completed the task. You may marry my daughter."

But his daughter didn't look too pleased.

Suddenly, the giraffe gave a shout. He had seen something interesting.

"Hey!" he cried. "There's a whole tribe of monkeys hiding in the bushes!"

What are you up to?

"Telinga cheated!" roared the animals. "His friends have helped him!"

The monkeys didn't wait to hear any more. They ran off, leaping into the trees to be out of reach.

Monkeys have lived up in trees ever since. They're much too scared to come down.

Chapter 3

The rabbits and the crocodile

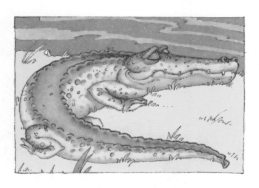

There was once a time when crocodiles lived on land, not in the water. One grumpy old crocodile lived near a river and lazed in the sun all day.

One day, a baby rabbit hopped past, looking for some tasty leaves.

"Hello!" he called and woke up the crocodile. The crocodile was furious.

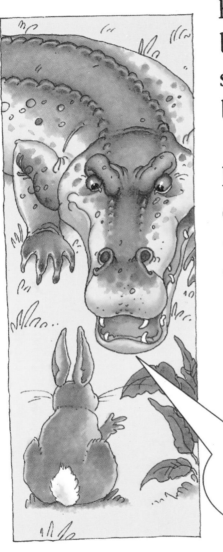

Go away! I'm trying to sleep!

As the crocodile shut his eyes again, the rabbit hopped closer. He had spotted a bunch of fresh green leaves, just by the crocodile's nose.

Mmm... These are yummy!

With loud crunching, he began to gobble them up.

The crocodile's eyes snapped
open.

"Get away from those
leaves!" he roared. And he
snapped at the rabbit with
his enormous jaws.

GO AWAY!

The little rabbit ran and ran. He didn't stop until he reached his burrow.

"The crocodile nearly ate me!" he told his mother. "But I didn't do anything wrong."

His mother was very angry. "It's time that crocodile was taught a lesson," she said firmly. "He's grumpy and lazy and it just won't do."

Is everyone here?

Gathering the other rabbits together, she told them she had a plan.

The next day, the rabbits went into the woods. They collected branches, twigs and leaves and stuffed them into a sack.

"That's enough!" said the rabbit's mother and off they went to find the crocodile.

They didn't have to look far. He was by the riverbank, asleep as usual. The rabbits crept closer.

Sneaking up, they made a big circle of twigs, leaves and branches around the crocodile.

Then the mother rabbit set light to the circle. The fire crackled and spat and smoke billowed up.

The crocodile woke with a jump. When he saw the fire, he bellowed in fear.

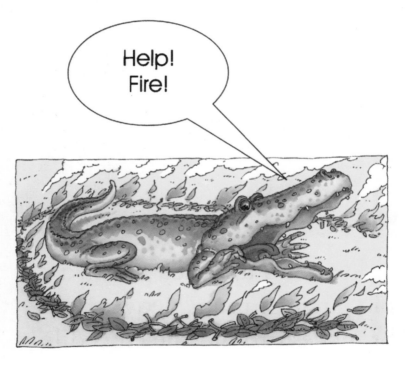

Help!
Fire!

The fire was licking at his  scales. Taking a flying leap, he jumped right over the flames...

Funniest thing I've ever seen!

Ho ho ho!

...and disappeared into the river with a splash.

When the crocodile heard the rabbits laughing, he was very annoyed. He shouted at them from the river.

"Keep off our land then!" cried the rabbits and that's how it's stayed ever since.

Try these other books in
Series One:

Dragons: Stan must outwit a hungry dragon to feed his children. Victor must persuade two dragons not to eat him. Will they do it? Read these tales to find out.

Magical Animals: A horse that can fly? A creature that's half-lion, half-eagle? If you think they sound amazing, wait until you see the other animals in this book.

The Dinosaurs Next Door: Stan loves living next door to Mr. Puff. His house is full of amazing things. Best of all are the dinosaur eggs — until they begin to hatch...

The Monster Gang: Starting a gang is a great idea. So is dressing up like monsters. But if everyone is in disguise, how do you know who's who?

Series editor: Lesley Sims

Designed by
Katarina Dragoslavić

First published in 2007 by Usborne Publishing Ltd., Usborne House,
83-85 Saffron Hill, London EC1N 8RT, England. www.usborne.com
Copyright © 2007, 2003, 1989, 1982 Usborne Publishing Ltd.

48

The Story of
Chocolate

Katie Daynes

Illustrated by
Adam Larkum

Reading Consultant: Alison Kelly
Roehampton University

Contents

Chapter 1

Chocolate drinkers

A thousand years ago, chocolate was a big secret. Only a few people drank it and nobody ate it.

The first chocolate drinkers were farmers who lived by the rainforest in central America.

The rainforest was a jungle full of tropical plants, wild animals and creepy crawlies. It was also home to the small cocoa tree that grew strange, bright pods.

4

Monkeys knew all about the pods. They liked to break them open and suck out the sweet, white pulp. Then they spat out the bitter beans that were in the middle.

If a bean landed on an earthy patch of forest floor, it grew into another cocoa tree.

5

One day, a farmer copied
the monkeys and tasted a pod.
"Yum!" he cried, sucking
the pulp. "Yuck!" he added,
spitting out a bean. Soon
everyone was sucking
pulp and spitting beans.

But then, some villagers
noticed a delicious smell,
drifting up from a pile of
rotting beans.

Over the next few months, the farmers discovered a way to capture this smell by turning the beans into a drink.

They let the beans rot for a few days under banana leaves...

then put them out to dry in the hot sun.

Next, they
roasted the beans
over a fire...

ground them
into a paste...

and stirred in water and
spices. They called their new
drink *chocol haa*. It tasted very
bitter, but they liked it.

To avoid hiking into the jungle for pods, the farmers planted cocoa trees in their own fields.

The farmers were members of a huge group of people called Mayans. Before long, *chocol haa* – or chocolate – was an important part of Mayan life.

Mayan kings and priests began to drink it every day. They liked the froth best.

Pour it from high up to make more froth!

At Mayan weddings, the bride and groom showed their love for each other by exchanging five cocoa beans.

10

In fact, people were so enchanted by the cocoa tree, they painted it on everything – their pots, their mugs and even their walls.

But preparing cocoa beans was hard work and took weeks. Most people were only allowed to drink chocolate as a special treat.

Cocoa beans became so valuable they were used as money. You could buy a rabbit for ten beans and a slave for one hundred.

It's only a small one. I'll give you eight beans.

Chapter 2

Learning the secret

Hundreds of years later, a group of merchants arrived in a Mayan village. They had journeyed for days to find exotic goods for their emperor.

The merchants belonged to a fierce group of people called Aztecs. To avoid trouble, the Mayans offered them some of their precious beans.

When the Aztecs had learned the chocolate secret, they served a cupful to their emperor. He was delighted.

"Perfect!" he cried. "A cool, refreshing drink that doesn't make you drunk." And he ordered all his warriors to drink chocolate before they went into battle.

Where the Aztecs lived it was too cold to grow cocoa. So, they had to buy their beans from the Mayans and carry them all the way home.

15

The Aztec emperor, Montezuma, was crazy about chocolate. He kept the royal warehouses piled high with cocoa beans. Sometimes he ordered 50 cups of chocolate a day, thinking they would make him richer and wiser.

But poorer people could only dream about chocolate.

Over time, a legend grew up about where chocolate first came from.

"Once upon a time, the world had no chocolate," said the storytellers. "Then Quetzalcoatl, the god of farming, appeared from paradise with a cocoa tree."

Quetzalcoatl was the Aztecs' hero. They built him grand temples and left him chocolate drinks as gifts.

But other countries had their eyes on the Aztecs' riches. Chocolate wouldn't stay a central American secret for long...

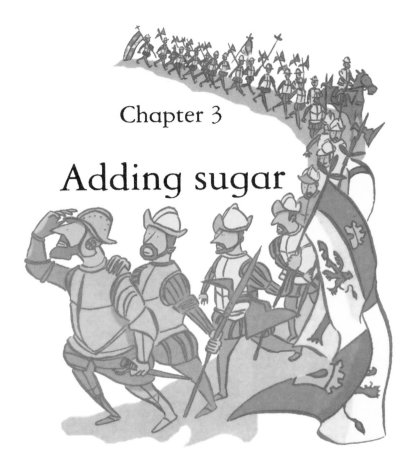

Chapter 3

Adding sugar

In 1519, a Spanish explorer named Hernán Cortés set out with an army to fight the Aztecs.

After many battles, Emperor Montezuma wanted to make peace and he invited Cortés to court. He gave Cortés his first taste of chocolate.

Cortés liked the chocolate but he still conquered the Aztecs. In 1528, when Cortés sailed home, his sacks were bursting with Aztec treasure... including cocoa beans.

Back in Spain, Cortés served the chocolate drink to his friends. They decided it tasted better hot and with lots of sugar. It was so good, they kept it to themselves.

But the Spanish prince,
Philip, soon heard about the
drink. A group of monks took
some visitors from central
America to meet him...
and they brought a tub of
chocolate paste as a gift.

Prince Philip was hooked.
He made sweet, hot chocolate
the drink of the Spanish court.

Chocolate gossip spread fast. People in Europe were talking about it long before they had even seen a potato.

But turning cocoa beans into chocolate paste took a long time and it was very expensive.

Only rich Europeans had enough money to buy the drink. They would sit around in cafés, sipping hot chocolate and talking about the weather.

Chapter 4

Chocolate machines

It wasn't until inventors came up with the steam engine that things changed. Suddenly, lots of goods could be made more easily – including chocolate.

Factories were set up all
over Europe and turning cocoa
beans into chocolate drinks
became big business.

Before long, the drink
had stopped being just a
handmade treat for the rich.

In 1847, an English chocolate maker, Francis Fry, decided there could only be one thing better than drinking chocolate...

and that was eating it. His problem was how to turn chocolate paste into solid bars.

In Holland, Coenraad Van
Houten provided half the
answer. He invented a press
that separated chocolate paste
into brown cocoa powder and
yellow cocoa butter.

Fry noticed that cocoa
butter hardened as it
cooled. "Maybe I can
use that to make
solid chocolate,"
he thought.

28

He stirred warm cocoa butter into his chocolate paste...

added three scoops of sugar...

poured the mixture into square tubs...

and waited. Slowly, it went hard. Fry had invented the world's first chocolate bar!

In no time, factories were making bars of rich, dark chocolate. They called it *delicious chocolate to eat.*

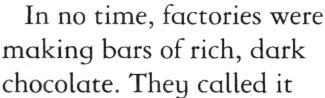

Meanwhile, in Switzerland, there lived a candlemaker named Daniel Peter. But candles were going out of fashion and he was losing money.

When he fell in love with a
chocolate maker's daughter, he
had a brilliant idea.

"I'll make chocolate instead!"

By now, there was lots of
competition in the chocolate
business. Peter needed to make
his bar special.

He tried adding milk, but that made the chocolate too runny. Peter was stuck. Luckily, Henri Nestlé lived next door and he knew a lot about food.

Are you sure about this?

Nestlé earned his living
making baby food. He soon
found a way to thicken Peter's
chocolate mix.

In 1883, Peter won a
gold medal for his new,
creamy chocolate recipe.
Milk chocolate was a hit.

33

Chapter 5

Tasty inventions

By the 20th century, people had learned how to make milk chocolate smoother, creamier and even more tasty. We still use the same methods today.

First, the chocolate mixture is put through heavy rollers, to squeeze out every lump.

Then an enormous vat, invented by Rodolphe Lindt, is used to blend the mixture into a smooth, velvety paste.

The chocolate is cooled and warmed and cooled and warmed until it has a glossy shine. Finally, it is poured into trays to set.

For years, eating-chocolate was only made in solid bars. But Milton Hershey, an American chocolate maker, thought bars were boring.

In 1907, he tried squirting glossy chocolate into little peaks. When the peaks hardened, he wrapped each one in foil to make them look more exciting.

I'll call them "kisses". Then everyone will want one!

It wasn't long before factories were making chocolates in all shapes and sizes.

37

The next challenge was to mix chocolate with other scrumptious ingredients.

In 1912, an American candy maker called Howell Campbell was feeling adventurous. He stirred peanuts, caramel and marshmallows into glossy, melted chocolate.

Then, he spooned gooey blobs of the mixture onto a tray. As the chocolate set, the blobs hardened and Campbell took his first bite.

It's deliciously gooey!

He called his invention the Goo Goo Cluster. It was one of the first mixed chocolate snacks, and an instant success.

That same year, a Belgian chocolate maker, Jean Neuhaus, made another leap in chocolate history. He invented hard chocolate shells that could hold soft fillings.

After stuffing them with a creamy, nutty mix, he sealed them up with more chocolate.

From then on, there was no stopping the chocolate makers. Silky caramel, chewy toffee, nutty almonds, creamy vanilla – you name it, they added it.

Factories churned out hundreds of different chocolate snacks, while smaller companies made amazing chocolates by hand.

Chapter 6

Chocolate families

Some of today's chocolate companies are gigantic. But most of them began as small family businesses.

In 1824, John Cadbury opened a shop in England. Along with tea and coffee, he sold his own drinking chocolate.

It was so popular, Cadbury set up a cocoa and chocolate factory. Now Cadbury's drinks and chocolate bars are sold across the globe.

In 1911, Frank and Ethel Mars set up a business in America, selling homemade butter-cream candies. Their big break came in 1923 when Frank invented a malted milk chocolate bar.

He made a fluffy, malty nougat...

topped it with caramel...

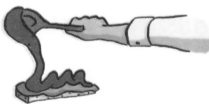

and coated it in milk chocolate.

Then, in 1941, their son Forrest developed another sweet idea: sugar-coated chocolate drops that wouldn't melt in your hand.

An American, named Bruce Murrie, gave Mars some money for the project. So they called their new chocolates M&M's.

Here's to Mars and Murrie!

Today, you can buy the Mars family's chocolates almost anywhere in the world and they're nothing like the Mayans' bitter drink.

When the Mayans first caught a whiff of rotting cocoa beans, they knew they had found something exciting. But they had no idea how popular chocolate would become.

A chocolate recipe

Glossy chocolate sauce

Ingredients:
100g (½ cup) dark (semi-sweet) chocolate chips
2 tablespoons golden syrup (corn syrup)
15g (1 tablespoon) butter
2 tablespoons water

What to do:
Put all the ingredients
in a small saucepan and
heat them gently. Keep
stirring until they mix into
a smooth, glossy sauce.

Be careful!
The saucepan
and sauce will
be hot.

Eat the sauce poured over slices
of banana or scoops of ice
cream. You could sprinkle
it with marshmallows or
nuts if you like.

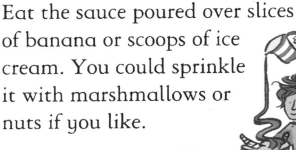

47

With thanks to Catherine Atkinson for the recipe
and John Davidson-Kelly for helpful advice

Series editor: Lesley Sims
Designed by Russell Punter
and Katarina Dragoslavic

This edition first published in 2006 by Usborne Publishing Ltd.,
Usborne House, 83-85 Saffron Hill, London EC1N 8RT, England,
www.usborne.com
Copyright © 2006, 2004 Usborne Publishing Ltd.

The story of
Heidi

Johanna Spyri

Retold by
Mary Sebag-Montefiore

Illustrated by Alan Marks

Reading Consultant: Alison Kelly
Roehampton University

Contents

Chapter 1
Meeting Grandfather

Heidi felt cross and tired as Aunt Dete pulled her up the steep slope. "I'd go faster if I wasn't wearing *all* my clothes," said Heidi.

3

"You'll need them at your grandfather's and I don't want to carry them," said her aunt, angrily.

"Do you think Grandfather will want me?" Heidi asked nervously.

Aunt Dete shook her head. "I don't know. He's a miserable old man and he hasn't seen you since you were a baby. But I've taken care of you for long enough. Now it's his turn."

At last they reached
Grandfather's hut, at the
very top of the mountain.
Dete rapped sharply on
the door. It creaked
open and an old
man peered out.

"What do you want?"
he asked, gruffly.

"This is your granddaughter, Heidi," Dete explained. "Your dead son's child. I've brought her to live with you."

"I don't want her," said the old man, trying to shut the door.

"I don't care," Dete snapped. "You have to take her. Both her parents are dead. I've found a good job in Frankfurt and she can't come with me."

With that,
Heidi's aunt turned
and ran down the mountain.

7

Grandfather stared silently at Heidi. Heidi stared back.

"He doesn't want me," she thought, sadly, "but where else can I go?"

"Well... you'd better come in," said Grandfather, with a scowl.

Heidi stepped into the hut and
looked around. There didn't seem
to be room for her anywhere.

"Where shall I sleep?" she asked.
Grandfather shrugged. He didn't
even look at her. "You'll have to
find your own bed," he growled.

9

Heidi looked again and saw a ladder in the corner. Feeling curious, she climbed up into a hayloft. From the window, she could see a green valley far below and hear pine trees whooshing in the wind.

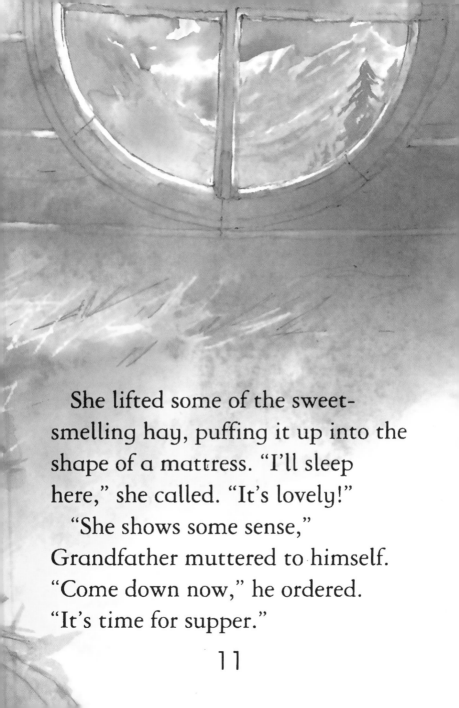

She lifted some of the sweet-smelling hay, puffing it up into the shape of a mattress. "I'll sleep here," she called. "It's lovely!"

"She shows some sense," Grandfather muttered to himself. "Come down now," he ordered. "It's time for supper."

11

Heidi watched Grandfather blow
onto the embers of the fire, making
the flames blaze. Fetching a bowl,
he filled it to the brim with rich,
creamy milk.

"Here you are," he said.
Then he toasted bread and cheese
over the fire until they were a
glorious golden brown.

Delicious smells filled the hut and Heidi realized how hungry she was. She licked up oozing drips of cheese, crunched the toast and drank the milk to the last drop.

Through the open door, she saw the sky and mountainside glow in the setting sun. "I like it here, Grandfather," she said.

13

That night, Heidi snuggled down
in the hayloft. As she fell asleep she
wondered why Grandfather lived
all alone, high on the mountain.
What had happened to make him
so sad and unfriendly?

Chapter 2

The goat boy

What's that?

Early next morning, Heidi woke to
the sound of bells. She sat up.
Sunshine poured through the
hayloft window, turning her straw
bed into shimmering gold.

Quickly, she dressed and shot
down the ladder. A boy was
standing at the door, whistling.

"This is Peter, the goat boy,"
Grandfather told her. "He's come
for Little Swan and Little Bear."

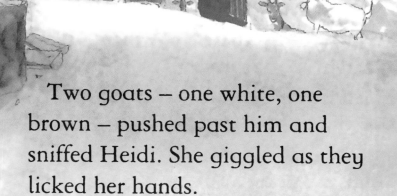

Two goats – one white, one
brown – pushed past him and
sniffed Heidi. She giggled as they
licked her hands.

"Their tongues tickle!" she said.

16

"Do you want to come with me?" Peter shouted over the bleats and bells. "I'm going up the mountain to find fresh grass for them."

"Can I?" Heidi asked Grandfather.

"I suppose," he replied. "But have your breakfast first." He sat on a stool and milked Little Bear, then handed Heidi a bowl of fresh milk.

17

"Come on!" said Peter, as soon as she'd finished. "You can stay at the back and make sure none of the goats get lost."

As they ran over rocks to the mountain pastures, Peter showed Heidi the mountain's secrets.

18

He pointed to an eagle's nest
hidden in the craggy peaks and the
spots where wild flowers grew. The
mountain looked as if a giant had
scattered handfuls of jewels over it.

Heidi had never seen so many
flowers. She picked great blue and
yellow bunches for Grandfather.

Every day, Heidi went out with
Peter and the goats. And every
day, her cheeks grew rosier and her
eyes more sparkly. Grandfather fed
her crusty bread, tasty cheese and
Little Swan's milk. At night, he
told her stories by the fire.

Heidi had never been happier...
until one morning, when the door
flew open and there stood Aunt
Dete in a brand new dress.

"I've come for Heidi," she
announced. "I should never have
left her with you in the first place."

"No," cried Heidi, suddenly
afraid. "I like it here. I want to
stay with Grandfather."

Dete ignored her. "I've found a place for Heidi in Frankfurt," she told Grandfather. "Clara Sesemann, a little girl who's always ill, wants a friend to keep her company."

"If Heidi behaves," her aunt went on, "Mr. Sesemann will pay her and buy her some fine new clothes. It's a great chance for her."

Grandfather had been looking crosser and crosser during this speech. "Take her and spoil her then!" he bellowed at Dete. "But don't bother coming back. Ever!"

Just go!

Ignoring Heidi's protests, Dete gripped her arm and dragged her outside. As they left, Heidi saw Grandfather sitting alone, his head in his hands.

"Poor Grandfather!" cried Heidi, tears trickling down her face.

"Come *on*, Heidi," said Dete, pushing her down the mountain. "I'm sorry I ever left you with that sad old man."

"Why is he so sad?" asked Heidi.

"He thinks the world is a bad place," her aunt replied. "First, his wife died. Then your father, his only child, wasted all his money and died too. But your grandfather's just made things worse for himself."

"He said there was only misery in the world and shut himself away up here. Forget him Heidi. Think about Frankfurt."

"I'll never forget him!" cried Heidi.

"It's for your own good," Dete declared, striding off.

Heidi was quiet, but secretly she made a promise. "One day I'll come back to him."

Chapter 3

Heidi and Clara

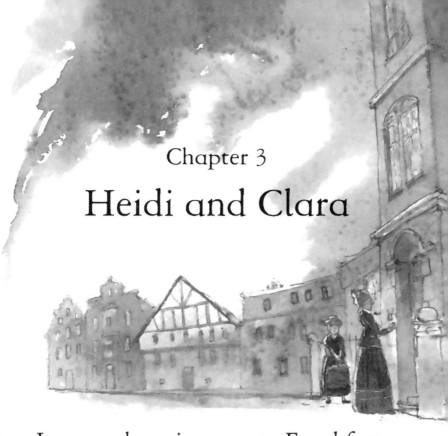

It was a long journey to Frankfurt. The sun was beginning to set when they stopped before a grand house in a cobbled street. Dete pulled the bell. "This is it," she muttered.

A well-dressed servant opened the door and led them into a vast hall.

Heidi felt very small and shabby.
She felt even worse when the
housekeeper, Mrs. Rotenmeyer,
saw her.

"You look most unsuitable,"
she said to Heidi with a sigh.
"I suppose you'd better
meet Clara."

Clara lay on a heap of pillows in
a frilly four-poster bed. Her face
was pale and the room was hot.

28

"Thank you for coming, Heidi,"
she said, quietly. "I'll like having
company. I can't get out of bed."

"Why not?" asked Heidi.

"I've been sick and I'm still
weak," Clara explained. "I don't
think I'll ever get better."

"No one could get better in this
hot, stuffy room," Heidi thought.
She ran over to a window and
flung it wide open.

The street below jostled with people, horses and carriages. Heidi could hear strange music mixed in with the clattering hooves and footsteps.

Leaning out, she saw a ragged boy with a street organ. A pair of kittens peeked out of his pockets.

30

Heidi rushed downstairs and onto the street. "Can you come here?" she called, beckoning him over. "There's someone I want you to play for."

Moments later, they were both bounding up the stairs.

"Surprise!" shouted Heidi, throwing open Clara's door and letting in the ragged boy.

31

Downstairs, Mrs. Rotenmeyer the housekeeper was puzzled. She could hear singing, laughing, music, even kittens — and all coming from Clara's bedroom.

"What's going on in here?" she shrieked, as she stormed into Clara's room.

"How did this dreadful boy get in?" she demanded. "I blame you," she said, glaring at Heidi. "I knew you were trouble from the moment I saw you. Go to your room at once."

"No," pleaded Clara. "Heidi was only trying to cheer me up." She held Heidi's hand. "Please don't send Heidi to her room. We want to have our supper together."

There was nothing Mrs.
Rotenmeyer could do. She had to
obey Clara. "All right," she said
crossly, turning to go, "but get
that dirty boy out of here now!"

Mrs. Rotenmeyer returned
carrying a tray loaded with rich
food. Greasy chunks of meat swam
in a cream sauce. Clara pushed it
around her plate and hardly ate
anything. Heidi didn't like it either.

"I don't get hungry lying in bed," Clara murmured.

"You'd soon get hungry running up the mountain to Grandfather's hut," Heidi told her.

Clara looked sad. "But since I've been ill, I can't walk."

"That's terrible," said Heidi.

The warm room and heavy meal were making her feel sleepy. She had to go outside to breathe some fresh air. Stale smells hung over the noisy street.

NO DOGS

NO BALL GAMES

Heidi longed for the cool clear air of the mountain and the soft breeze that made the pine trees rustle.

Some time after Heidi's arrival, the servants started claiming the house was haunted by a ghost.

"A white figure floats down the stairs at night," said a maid.

The servants were so upset, Mrs. Rotenmeyer grew worried. "I must tell Clara's father," she decided.

Mr. Sesemann only laughed
when he heard the news. "There's
no such thing as ghosts," he said.
"I'll catch your ghost to prove it."

The next night he waited in the
hall at the bottom of the stairs.
Heidi came down, wearing a
white nightgown. She tried
to open the locked front
door, then sobbed.

Mr. Sesemann went over to her
and saw she was still fast asleep.

"Heidi has been sleepwalking," Mr. Sesemann explained to Clara and Mrs. Rotenmeyer, the next morning. "The poor child is so homesick, her dreams felt real. I think she'd better go home."

Thank goodness she's going.

I'm going back to Grandfather!

I'll miss you.

Chapter 4

Heidi goes home

The following week, Grandfather looked out of the window and could hardly believe his eyes. A peculiar procession was stumbling up the mountain slope.

Two men were struggling with suitcases. A third hauled a wheelchair and a fourth carried a child bundled up in a shawl. The men puffed and panted, their shirts drenched in sweat.

This is steep!

I need a drink.

Ahead of them all danced Heidi.

She raced up the slope and threw herself into Grandfather's arms.

"Heidi!" he cried. "You've come back to me."

"I missed you," Heidi said. "Look, Mr. Sesemann has written you a letter to explain."

Dear Sir,

Heidi was too homesick to stay with us but Clara could not bear to say goodbye. I hope you will forgive me for sending her with Heidi to stay for a month.

Clara, alas, is still very weak after a long illness. She has no appetite and cannot walk. I hope her visit to you on the mountain will give her new strength.

With all my thanks and best wishes,

Yours sincerely,

Hans Sesemann

Grandfather turned to Clara.
"I'm very pleased to meet you," he
said. "And thank you for bringing
Heidi back to me. You'll soon feel
better breathing our mountain air."

Grandfather put Clara's
wheelchair in the sunshine, so she
could see the wonderful view, and
gave her a bowl of fresh milk.

"Guess who really gave you the milk?" Heidi teased, bringing Little Swan over. The goat butted Clara gently, until she realized Little Swan wanted to be stroked.

Clara drank thirstily. "This tastes much nicer than Frankfurt milk," she said.

"Heidi?" came a shout. Peter ran up the path to them. "I heard you were back," he said to Heidi.

"Come out with me tomorrow," he urged her.

"Peter, I can't," said Heidi. "I have to stay with Clara."

Peter gave Clara a jealous look.

"You go Heidi," Clara insisted.

I'll be fine.

I'll pick you some flowers.

All the same, when they set off next morning, Clara looked sad.

"I'll be quick," Heidi promised. "I just want to climb the ridge where the biggest, bluest flowers grow."

Clara watched them go longingly. She would have given anything to be running with them, with strong legs that could skip and jump.

"I wish you'd come," Heidi told Clara when she returned. "We watched an eagle soar above our heads and did somersaults down the mountain."

Clara sighed.

"Cheer up," Grandfather said, trying to comfort her. "The sun has already brought roses to your cheeks. I'm sure you'll soon feel stronger."

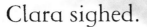

I won't leave you again.

Oh, I wish I could walk...

From where he stood, high on the mountain, Peter could see Heidi and Clara talking together. His heart burned with jealousy.

"I wish that girl hadn't come," he thought. "Heidi's *my* friend. I'll *make* Clara go home." And a plan began to form in his mind.

50

Chapter 5
Peter's plan

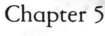

Before sunrise next morning, Peter
crept to Grandfather's hut. All was
quiet and still.

Just as Peter hoped, Clara's
wheelchair stood by the door.
Noiselessly, he pushed it to the
edge of the mountain and
rolled it over a steep,
stony cliff.

The chair hit the rocks with a
terrible clatter. An endless echo
followed its fall, BANG...
CLANG... again and again.

Peering over the cliff, Peter saw
the jagged rocks had smashed the
wheelchair into a thousand pieces.
Peter looked at what he had done...
and fled.

When he arrived at the hut for the goats, Heidi told Peter about Clara's chair. "The wind must have caught it," she said. "Grandfather has to carry Clara everywhere."

"Then Clara will have to go home, won't she?" Peter demanded.

"Aha," murmured Grandfather. "I think I know who blew that puff of wind."

54

Heidi was shocked. "Did you do it, Peter?" she asked, sharply.

Peter went red. "I'm... I'm sorry," he stammered. "I wanted her to go. You don't have time for me now."

"Peter, you must hate me," said Clara. "You think I've taken Heidi away from you."

"Never mind," Heidi interrupted. "We can all still be friends."

But Grandfather shook his head.

"Mr. Sesemann may not be so forgiving," he said. "Clara's chair is still broken."

"If only Clara could walk..." said Heidi.

"I do feel stronger," Clara whispered. "Perhaps I could try."

She edged herself forward and put her slender feet on the ground. Grandfather gently took hold of her hands and helped her to stand.

"My legs feel so weak," said Clara, trembling.

"Be brave," said Grandfather.

Slowly, Clara put one foot in front of the other.

Clara wobbled, but Grandfather supported her.

"Rest now," he ordered. "You can try again tomorrow."

Every day, Clara walked a little more. Hungry from the exercise and fresh mountain air, she wolfed down huge meals. Strength flowed into her and she tingled with energy. "Won't Father be amazed?" she thought.

Chapter 6

A surprise for Mr. Sesemann

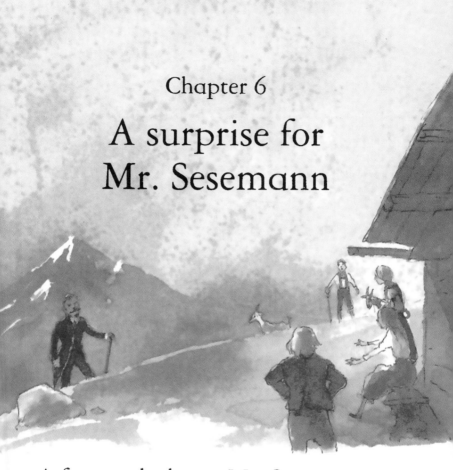

A few weeks later, Mr. Sesemann arrived for Clara. He hardly recognized his daughter with her glowing face, bright eyes and thick, shiny hair.

59

When Clara stood up, he was astonished and when she walked up to him, he had to sit down.

"Is it really you?" he said. "I can't believe it. You're walking!"

"Isn't it wonderful," laughed Clara. "Grandfather and Heidi made it happen."

"And Peter," Grandfather put in, his eyes twinkling.

"You did it, Clara," said Heidi.
"It was your hard work."

"It's a miracle," Mr. Sesemann
beamed. "Clara, I'm proud of you.
Thank you, thank you everyone."

"You must come back to the
mountain whenever you want,"
Heidi told Clara.

"And you must come to Frankfurt
— Peter too," said Clara. "We'll find
the ragged boy again and dance."

When Clara and her father had gone, Heidi and Grandfather went outside to watch the sunset. The sky and mountains shone red-gold, just like Heidi's first evening.

"It's beautiful," said Grandfather.

"Once I was sad and lonely," he told Heidi, "but you've made me a happy man."

Johanna Spyri (1827-1901),
a doctor's daughter,
was born in the
Swiss countryside
and grew up loving
the mountains.
Heidi was first
published over a
hundred years
ago, in 1881, and
is still a much loved
children's book today.

Series editor: Lesley Sims
Designed by Russell Punter

First published in 2006 by Usborne Publishing Ltd., Usborne House,
83-85 Saffron Hill, London EC1N 8RT, England. www.usborne.com
Copyright © 2006 Usborne Publishing Ltd.

Beauty
& the Beast

Retold by Louie Stowell

Illustrated by Victor Tavares

Reading consultant: Alison Kelly
Roehampton University

Contents

Chapter 1

Beauty

There was once a very rich man, named Pierre, who gave his three daughters *everything* they wanted.

"Bring us rubies and silks from the market!" demanded Sophie and Marie, his eldest daughters.

Oh, and a satin dress!

And pearls.

Pierre turned to his youngest daughter. "Don't you want anything, Beauty?" he asked.

4

"May I have a rose?" asked Beauty. "They always seem to die in our garden."

"I wonder why?" said Marie.

"It's a mystery," added Sophie. "And *such* a shame when you love them so."

Pierre waved goodbye to his daughters and galloped away on his sleek white horse.

As he rode, a thick fog filled the air. Pierre couldn't see the path ahead, or even his horse below him.

He went on blindly,
until suddenly...

...the fog rolled back to reveal
a towering castle.
Pierre gasped. "Where am I?"

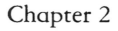

Chapter 2

The Beast

The horse's hooves
clattered up to
the castle gates.
They opened before
him with a
ghostly creak.

Pierre rode into a courtyard. As he raised his hand to knock on the castle door, it swung open.

"Hello?" he called. No one answered. He tried again. "Hello?" But Pierre only heard his own voice, echoing off the stone walls.

Is anybody here?

"What's going on?" he
murmured, his heart beating faster.
Then a mouth-watering smell
made him forget his fear.

Pierre followed his nose to an
enormous feast. He sat down,
nervously. "Where are the guests?"
he said to himself.

A full plate floated over to him
and he cried out in surprise. But he
was cold and starving and the food
smelled so good.

"I hope no one minds," he
thought, picking up a silver fork.

Invisible hands poured him rich,
sweet wine.

Feeling full and tired, Pierre rose from the table. Instantly, a bed appeared before him. Pierre was too exhausted to question it. He just lay down... and fell fast asleep.

He woke in a beautiful bedroom. A pile of clean clothes sat on a seat by the bed. They were just his size.

"I must find the owners and thank them," Pierre thought, and set out to search the castle corridors. Invisible hands opened all the doors, but he couldn't find a single living person anywhere.

"Perhaps everyone's outside?" Pierre wondered.

In the garden, he found a beautiful rosebush. As he sniffed the blooms, he remembered his promise to Beauty.

14

The instant Pierre plucked a
flower, a huge shadow fell over the
rosebushes. He spun around,
clutching the bloom to his chest...

15

...to see a hideous creature before
him. Its eyes glittered fiercely.
Before Pierre could cry out, it
grabbed him and pulled him close
to its angry face.

Chapter 3

Prepare to die!

"How dare you steal from the Beast?" demanded the terrifying creature. "I gave you food and shelter, and this is how you repay me? Thief!"

"I'm s-s-sorry," said Pierre, trembling all over.

The Beast glared at him and gave a low growl.

"I'll pay for the flower!" cried Pierre, desperately.

"Yes, you'll pay," said the Beast. "You'll pay with your life!"

"Please don't harm me," begged Pierre. "I just wanted a rose for Beauty – for my daughter."

The Beast fixed his burning eyes on Pierre. "I'll let you live if you send Beauty to me. If she refuses, you must return in a week to meet your fate," he declared. "Or I'll come after you!"

"I can't risk Beauty's life," Pierre thought. With a heavy heart, he told the Beast he would return.

Before Pierre left, the Beast put a ruby bridle on the horse's muzzle. "He'll be able to find his way to your home and back," said the Beast. "The bridle will guide him."

"I'm home!"
called Pierre, as
he came down the
path. Beauty ran
to him, smiling.
"How was the trip?"
"Fine," said Pierre.
He couldn't bear
to tell her the truth.

As the week passed,
Pierre grew thin and pale.
"What's wrong, Father?"
Beauty asked.
"Nothing," he replied.
"Please don't worry
about me."

That night, Beauty
thought she heard
him crying.

She found him asleep at his desk the next morning, with a letter in front of him. She picked it up and started to read.

Dearest daughters,

When you read this letter I will have left you forever. I took a rose from the garden of a monstrous beast and he has sworn to kill me unless I bring him my youngest daughter. I could never do that to you, Beauty, so I have gone in your place.

Farewell,

Your loving Father x x

"Oh no!" cried Beauty. "This is all my fault."

Looking out
of the window,
Beauty saw her
father's horse saddled
up, ready to go. She knew what
she had to do. Quickly and quietly,
she scribbled a note for him.

Dear Father,
I have gone to the Beast's
castle instead of you.
All my love,
Beauty

Her father's horse seemed
to know the way. He galloped
down the twisting paths as if
guided by a magic force.

As the Beast's
castle came into view, Beauty
gripped the reins in fear.

Chapter 4

Beauty and the Beast

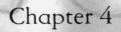

First, the castle gates creaked
open before her, then the door to
the castle itself. "This place must
be enchanted," Beauty realized.
She took a deep breath and
stepped inside.

27

Beauty tiptoed down a long
and dusty corridor until she
found an open door. It led into
a sweet-smelling garden. But as
soon as Beauty stepped into
the sunlight...

...she heard a
terrible growl. "What are
you doing here?" roared the Beast.

28

"I'm B-b-beauty, Pierre's daughter," she stammered.

"He sent you to die, did he?" the Beast growled. "Coward!"

"Don't say that!" said Beauty. She was so angry she forgot her fear and glared at the Beast.

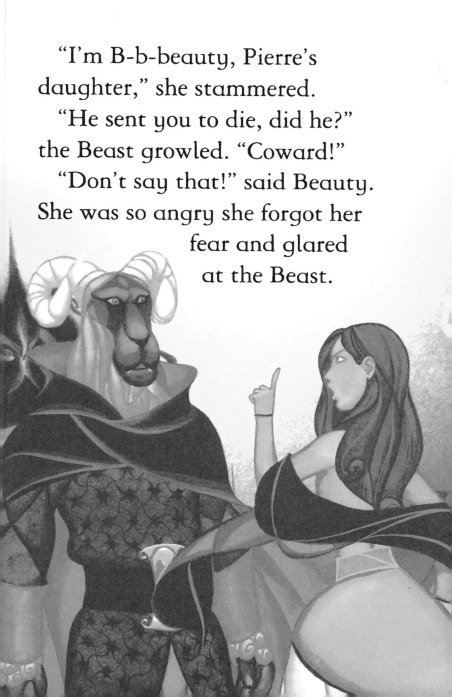

"You have courage," said the Beast, gazing back at her. As he spoke, Beauty was shocked to see great tears forming in his eyes.

"What's wrong?" she asked.

"Having you here makes me realize – I've been alone for so long," sniffed the Beast.

"Poor Beast," said Beauty, her heart filling with pity. "I'll stay with you, if you like."

The Beast grasped her hand, his eyes shining with hope. "Thank you," he said gruffly.

But you must let my father know I'm safe.

The Beast strode out to the courtyard and tied a note to Pierre's horse, then sent it on its way.

That evening, Beauty and the Beast dined together. The Beast told Beauty a story about a princess who turned a frog into a prince with a kiss.

In return, Beauty told the Beast
all about her family and her life.
"You're a very good listener," she
said. "My sisters always interrupt."

The Beast looked at Beauty very
seriously, then knelt before her.

"I know this is sudden," he said
in a low voice, "and I know I'm
ugly, but... will you marry me?"

"I can't," gasped Beauty. "I don't even know you."

"Very well," said the Beast, bowing his head. "Goodnight, Beauty. Your room is next door," he added, and left her alone.

Chapter 5

Beauty explores

Beauty dreamed of home and woke wishing she was there. Then, as she dressed, she saw a mirror by her bed. Peering into it, she was amazed to see her father, eating breakfast back at home.

A magic mirror!

Seeing him safe and well lifted her spirits. "It's time to explore," she decided, and set off down the shadowy corridors.

In one room she saw fairies performing a play on an enchanted stage.

In another, she
found a library with shelves
that seemed to stretch to the sky.
"Here you will find every book in
the world," boomed a voice. "Books
from both the past and the future."

When Beauty went out into the garden, she saw exotic flowers and magical animals.

But she didn't see the Beast all day.

At eight o'clock, a gong rang for dinner. The Beast was waiting for Beauty in the dining room. "Did you find the mirror?" he asked, eagerly. "I loved it. Thank you," Beauty replied. After dinner, the Beast went down on one knee again.

Marry me, Beauty.

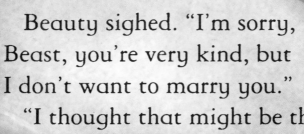

Beauty sighed. "I'm sorry,
Beast, you're very kind, but
I don't want to marry you."
"I thought that might be the
answer," said the Beast, sadly,
and left her alone.
That night, Beauty had
a strange dream.

She was dining with a handsome prince.

"How can you bear to look at that ugly Beast?" he asked.

"He's not ugly inside," said Beauty.

"But he's a monster," said the Prince.

How could anyone love a beast?

Beauty woke to the sound of birds singing. The Prince from her dream had vanished. "Is that all he was... a dream?" Beauty wondered. She spent the day wandering from room to room. The castle seemed empty without the Beast beside her.

Beauty was trying
to choose a book
from the library,
when she noticed
a portrait.

She couldn't
believe her eyes.
It was the Prince
from her dream.

At dinner that evening, she asked the Beast about him. "I dreamed of a prince last night," she said, "and then I saw a painting of him in the library. Do you know who he is?"

"I know him," said the Beast. "But I haven't seen him for years."

For the rest of the meal the Beast refused to talk more about the Prince. After they finished, he asked her to marry him again.

"I like you, but I don't love you," Beauty said softly. "I'm sorry, but I won't marry you."

The Beast sighed and said goodnight.

The next morning,
Beauty watched her family
in her mirror. She missed
them more than ever.
At dinner that
evening, she hardly
ate a thing.

"What's the matter?" the Beast asked her, with a worried frown.

"I'm homesick," said Beauty.

The Beast pulled a ring from his pocket.

"Oh Beast, I still won't marry you," she said quickly.

The Beast shook his head. "This isn't a wedding ring. It's magic. It will take you back to your father."

"But you must promise me you'll
return in two weeks," he went on.

"I promise," said Beauty.
"Oh thank you, Beast!"

"Keep it safe in your pocket.
When you're ready to return,
put the ring on your bedside
table," he told her.

Beauty nodded. She put
on the ring and the room
melted away. She felt
herself falling... falling...
until suddenly she was
standing on solid ground
again. She was back at
home and her father
was staring at her,
open-mouthed.

"Oh Father!" she cried, throwing
her arms around him.

Chapter 6

Tricked

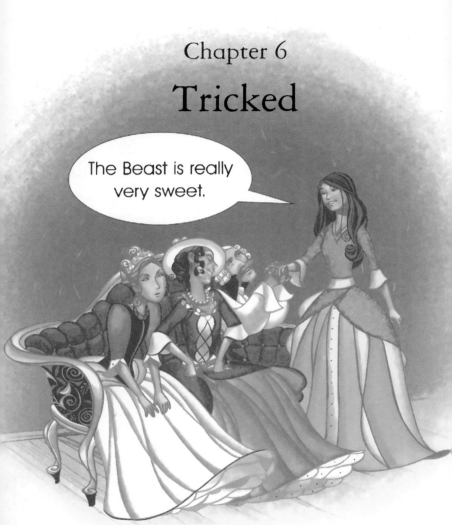

The Beast is really very sweet.

Beauty's father was overjoyed to see her... unlike her sisters.

When they heard she had to return in two weeks, they hatched a secret plan.

"If we make her stay longer, the Beast will be angry. With any luck, he might even eat her," said Marie, with a sly smile.

"With little Beauty gone, we'll have Father and his fortune all to ourselves," added Sophie.

So the sisters started being very
sweet and loving to Beauty.

Beauty was surprised at the
change in them. "They must have
really missed me," she thought.

The two weeks flew
by, but Beauty kept
thinking of the Beast.
Was he lonely
without her?

When the time
came for her to
return, her sisters
burst into noisy sobs.

"We can't live without you!"
they howled. "If you loved us,
you'd stay!" said
Sophie, clutching
Beauty's hands.

Reluctantly, Beauty stayed...
until one night, she dreamed she
saw the Beast lying in his garden,
under a rose bush.

Beauty woke with a start.
"Something's wrong," she realized.
"I must go to him."

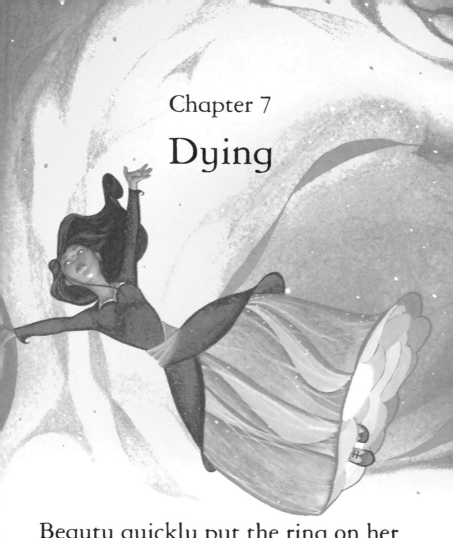

Chapter 7

Dying

Beauty quickly put the ring on her bedside table. A cloud of swirling smoke surrounded her. The next instant, she vanished.

55

Beauty was back in the garden. The Beast was lying under the rose bush, just as in her dream.

"Beast?" whispered Beauty, kneeling down beside him.

The Beast struggled to open his eyes. "Is that you Beauty?" he asked. "I'm dying."

"No!" cried Beauty, horrified. "Why? What happened?" She stroked his velvety face and kissed him. "You can't die! Please, Beast. I love you. Don't die."

There was a blinding flash and
a deafening bang.

The Beast disappeared. A second
later, there was another, brighter
flash and an even louder bang.

Kneeling before her was a
handsome prince.

"You were in my dream... and in
the painting!" cried Beauty.

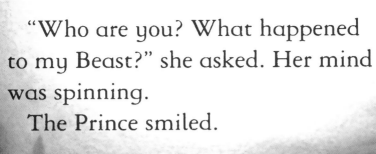

"Who are you? What happened to my Beast?" she asked. Her mind was spinning.

The Prince smiled.

I am your Beast.

"Many years ago," he explained, "an angry fairy turned me into a Beast because I refused to marry her. Only the love of a beautiful girl could make me human again."

"But why were you dying?" asked Beauty.

"The fairy said if I loved
a girl who did not love me,
I would die of a broken heart,"
the Prince replied.

"You don't need to be afraid,"
said Beauty. "I do love you."

Beauty and the Prince were married the next day, in a church filled with roses.

Beauty's sisters left early in bad tempers. "Why does she get to marry a prince? It's not fair!"

"Life isn't fair," said a tiny voice. It was the fairy who had cursed the prince.

"Your sister broke my spell," she said, "but at least I can give you exactly what you deserve."

"What?" yelped the sisters.

"As you have hearts of stone," the fairy declared, waving her wand, "that's what you'll be... forever!"

Then, feeling much better, she flew off to steal some wedding cake.

Beauty and the Beast was first written
down in 1740 by a French woman named
Gabrielle de Villeneuve. There have been many
different versions since, including a Disney
cartoon and a number of novels. This version
is based on Villeneuve's story and a retelling
from 1756 by another French writer,
Marie Le Prince de Beaumont.

Edited by Susanna Davidson
Series editor: Lesley Sims
Designed by Natacha Goransky

First published in 2006 by Usborne Publishing Ltd.,
Usborne House, 83-85 Saffron Hill, London EC1N 8RT, England. www.usborne.com
Copyright © 2006 Usborne Publishing Ltd.

STORIES OF
HAUNTED
HOUSES

Russell Punter

Illustrated by
Mike Phillips

Reading Consultant: Alison Kelly
Roehampton University

Contents

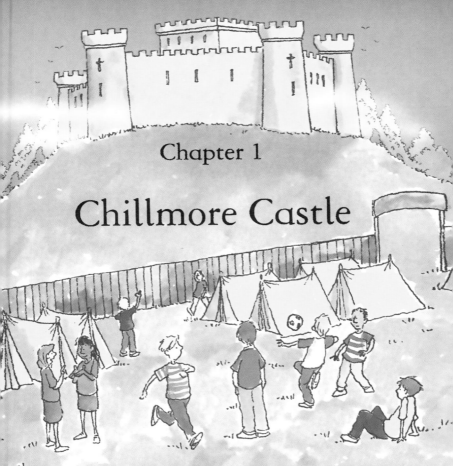

Chapter 1

Chillmore Castle

Max Moon was on a school field trip to Chillmore Castle. Everyone was looking forward to the guided tour. Everyone except Max, that is.

3

He was in a group with Nat and Norm Nuckle. The bullies were always picking on him. As they waited to go in, the brothers marched up to Max.

"You're not brave enough for this, Moon face," sneered Nat.

"Why not?" asked Max.

"Didn't you know, dimbo?" said Norm. "The castle is haunted by a terrifying ghost."

Scaredy cat!

Tremble puss!

"I don't believe you," said Max, trying to sound brave. "This way!" called the guide, and the castle tour began.

They climbed to the top of the tallest tower...

and peered into the murky moat.

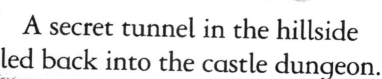

Yuck!

A secret tunnel in the hillside led back into the castle dungeon.

"This is the very spot where people have seen Sir Hal the Horrible," said the guide.

"Wh-who?" asked Max.

"A fierce knight who lived here long ago," she replied. "He's supposed to haunt the castle at midnight."

"Whooah!" yelled Max as a
ghostly chill shot down his back.
Everyone laughed. Then Max
saw why. Norm had put ice
cubes down his shirt.

Max didn't dry out until that
evening. As the others told ghost
stories around the campfire,
Nat and Norm grabbed Max.

The twins dragged Max back to the castle and down the secret tunnel to the dungeon.

"Let's see how brave you are now," sneered Norm.

"We dare you to spend the night here alone," said Nat.

"Okay," said Max. The bullies scared him more than a ghost.

"You'll never last the night," said the brothers as they left.

Max soon discovered that the gloomy dungeon was even creepier at night. "There's no such things as ghosts," he told himself.

Just then, Max heard a clanking sound echoing behind him. He turned... to see a ghostly, floating figure.

"Woo, um, I am Sir Hal the Horrible," said the ghost, faintly. "Please beware," he added, in a whisper.

Max couldn't help smiling.

"Kindly leave the castle at once," Hal asked softly. "And do not return... if you don't mind."

Max burst out laughing.

"Don't laugh," begged the ghost. "I'm supposed to be scary."

"I'm sorry," said Max. "You're too friendly to be frightening."

"That's what my boss, King Hugo says," moaned Hal. "I'm not even a real knight. The king says I'm too feeble."

Max felt sorry for the ghost. "Perhaps I can help," he said.

Max spent the night giving the ghost tips on being scary. He told him to...

bellow and boom...

swoop and sway...

and lurch and loom.

13

"Whew! Where did you learn these scaring skills?" asked the breathless spirit.

"The Nuckle twins scare me all the time," said Max sadly, telling Hal about the bullies.

Max glanced nervously at his watch. "It's time I went out and faced them," he said.

Quietly, Max crept back to
his tent – to find Nat and
Norm waiting for him.

"I did it," declared Max.
"Don't believe you," said
Norm, with a snort.
"You're too much of a wimp,"
added Nat, shoving Max.

There was a swirl of smoke
and Hal towered over the boys.
"Who dares to shove loyal
Max?" he roared.

The two bullies went as white
as their T-shirts.
"Call him off!" screamed Nat.
"Take him away!" yelled Norm.

"We'll never bully again,"
they promised, terrified.

Suddenly, the ghost of King
Hugo appeared in front of Hal.

"You are now a true knight,"
he declared, placing his sword
on Hal's shoulder.

And, with a wave to Max,
the proud knight and his king
faded away.

Chapter 2

Highwayman's Halt

Polly Small helped her father
run The Highwayman's Halt.
The creaky wooden inn was
over three hundred years old.

18

But it looked like the Smalls wouldn't be living there for long. They had so few customers they were losing money.

"What will we do?" groaned Polly's dad, as he served lunch to Mr. Trix, the only guest.

"There's always Flintlock's treasure," suggested Polly.

19

"What's that?" asked Mr. Trix. "Percy Flintlock was a highwayman who lived at the inn, long ago..." Polly began.

"One night, he robbed a coach and soldiers chased him here."

"Before he was caught, he hid the money somewhere in the building."

"But his bag of gold coins was never found."

"I'm not surprised," Mr. Small said, with a shiver. "They say Percy's ghost will appear if anyone tries to steal his money."

"Ghosts don't scare me," said Polly. "I'll find the treasure."

Mr. Trix smiled sneakily. "Not if I can find it first," he thought.

21

Polly spent the day searching the inn from chimney to cellar.

All the time, she had the feeling that someone was watching her every move.

Polly couldn't find a thing, not even in the garden. "Percy certainly hid his treasure well," she said.

The ghwayman's Halt

As Polly looked back at the inn she spotted something.

"The sign!" she cried. She fetched her dad's ladder from the shed. Then she climbed up to the carved wooden board.

23

She forced open the lid of the highwayman's chest. Inside was a leather bag.

Flintlock's treasure!

As Polly climbed down, a ghostly figure appeared.

"Hand back my money!" he boomed.

"P...p...please Mr. Flintlock," said Polly, "We really need it."

Percy listened to Polly's tale. "Hmph!" he said, "I suppose I could spare you a coin or two."

"Not so fast, Flintlock!" said a grizzly voice behind them.

"I'll take that!" snapped Mr. Trix. He grabbed the bag from Polly and ran to his car.

"Come back here, you
bounder!" barked Percy.
"No way, spooky," shouted
Trix as he sped away.

We'll never
catch him.

I wouldn't
bet on it.

Percy gave a sharp whistle
and Polly heard an eerie clip-
clopping sound coming closer...
and closer...

Suddenly, a ghostly horse galloped around the corner.

"Meet Jess," said Percy. "She's faster than a pistol shot."

"Grab hold of my cloak!" he added. Polly clung on as Percy leapt into the saddle.

"Tally-ho!" cried the highwayman, and they were off.

"He's heading for the port,"
called Polly.

"I know a shortcut!" cried
Percy, steering Jess down a
back road.

"I'll be on the first boat out of here," laughed Trix as he reached the dockside.

With a bound, Jess leapt out of a side street to block his way.

Stand and deliver!

"I'll push that meddling spook into the sea," thought Trix, driving straight at Jess.

But as Trix zoomed forward, Percy tugged on the reins. Jess floated over the car as it flew off the dock into the sea.

The police dragged Trix from the water, but the gold was lost forever.

Polly didn't mind. Everyone wanted to stay at the inn — and meet the famous ghosts.

Chapter 3

Grimly Grange

Grimly Grange was a crumbling old house full of spiders and spooks. Tourists who popped in got the fright of their lives.

But recently the Grange
hadn't had a single visitor.

"I'm bored," said Sir Sidney
Snuff one day. "I haven't
scared a living soul in weeks."

"Nor me," sighed Miss Lacey.
"This is no life for a dead lady."

"Nothing exciting has
happened in ages," moaned
Darcy Buckle.

Suddenly, Lord Digby Ruff
floated in. "Look in the
courtyard!" he shouted.

"Who are they?" asked Sir
Sidney.

"Who cares?" replied Darcy
eagerly. "As long as they're
scared of ghosts."

As the visitors explored, the ghosts spied on them from the Grand Gallery.

"It's the Spook Spotters," gasped Miss Lacey.

"Who?" asked Sir Sidney.

"They have a splendid show on the television box," said Miss Lacey excitedly. "They hunt for ghosts. We shall be famous."

"I'll look *so* handsome on the TV screen," boasted Digby.

"Riches!" said Darcy.

"Stardom!" sighed Sir Sidney.

"I can see it now," he added dreamily, "The Sir Sidney Snuff Show..."

"Come my dears, let us get ready," said Miss Lacey.

The ghosts spent the rest of the day preparing for the TV cameras.

They picked out their fanciest outfits...

powdered their biggest wigs...

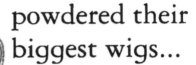

and polished their best buckles.

Finally they were ready for the show.

With a bong, the clock in the hall chimed midnight. Sue Snoop, the presenter, stood in front of the camera. "Hello viewers," she whispered.

Tonight we're reporting live!

Or should that be *dead* ?

Beside Sue stood Claude Aura, world famous ghost expert.

"Are you sensing any spirits, Claude?" asked Sue.

"Not yet," he replied. "Perhaps this place isn't haunted after all."

At the top of the stairs, Sir Sidney was about to make his entrance. "Not haunted, eh?" he muttered. "Prepare yourself for a shock, sir!"

40

Sir Sidney jumped on the
banister and slid down
at top speed.

He slid so fast, he flew off
the end, across the hall and
out of the window.

"Do you feel anything,
Claude?" asked Sue.

"Only the breeze from this
open window," replied Claude
and slammed it shut.

Sir Sidney tried to untangle
himself from the bushes.

The disappointed TV crew
went into the Great Hall.

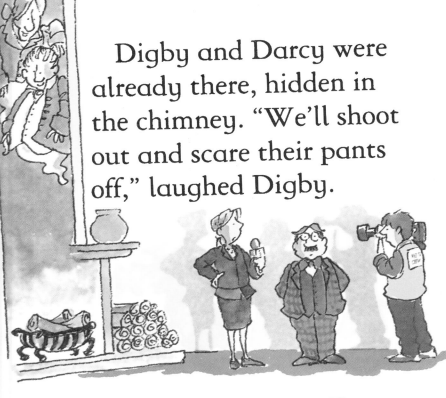

Digby and Darcy were already there, hidden in the chimney. "We'll shoot out and scare their pants off," laughed Digby.

His giggling brought down a thick pile of soot. Suddenly, the ghosts were buried up to their wigs.

"What's that?" asked Sue.
"Just a chimney that needs sweeping," Claude said sadly.
"This is a spook-free zone."

The TV crew moved on to the ballroom...

...where Miss Lacey was waiting behind a curtain. With a last look in a mirror, she floated out to greet them.

Eek!

But her wig caught on a light. "I'll die of embarrassment if they see me like this," she thought. "And I've already died once."

Miss Lacey ducked back
behind the curtain.

"No ghosts here," sighed
Claude. "Just a rather silly wig.
Let's try elsewhere."

Moments later, the ghosts
met in the Hall of Mirrors.

"What a mess we all look,"
wailed Sir Sidney.

"Oh, the shame," sniffed Miss Lacey, clutching her bald head. "No one must see us like this." Suddenly, the TV crew burst in.

"Ghosts!" yelled Claude.

"Oh yes!" cried Sue.

"Oh no!" screamed the ghosts, and they ran off into the night.

Series editor:
Lesley Sims

This edition first published in 2007 by Usborne Publishing Ltd.,
Usborne House, 83-85 Saffron Hill, London EC1N 8RT, England.
www.usborne.com
Copyright © 2007, 2005 Usborne Publishing Ltd.

48

STORIES OF
ROBOTS

Russell Punter

Illustrated by
Andrew Hamilton

Reading Consultant: Alison Kelly
Roehampton University

Contents

Chapter 1

The terrible Tidybot

"Luke, you're the laziest boy in the world!" cried Mrs. Lively. His room was so untidy, she could hardly get in.

3

"Look at all this mess!"
sighed Luke's mother as she
clambered over a pile of books,
clothes and toys.

Um, uh-huh,
yeah.

"All you do all day is play
on that beeping computer,"
said Mrs. Lively, crossly.

Luke wasn't listening. He had just reached level twelve on *Android Attack.* Now he needed to concentrate.

"You have one week to clean up this room or the computer goes," threatened Mrs. Lively. "I mean it!"

Luke heard *that* loud and clear. He couldn't possibly live without his computer. But cleaning his room would take forever.

What I need is someone to clean up for me.

He spent the next two hours searching the Internet for cleaning companies. They were all too expensive.

Luke had almost given up hope, when an advertisement popped up on the screen.

"That's just what I need," cried Luke. "It can clean my room, then I'll send it back."

7

Just under a week later, the Tidybot arrived at Luke's house. He managed to sneak the box up to his room, before his mother dashed past on her way out.

"I want that room clean by the time I come back!" she shouted.

The front door slammed behind her. Luke had just two hours.

8

He ran to his room and
excitedly tore open the box.

First, he read the instruction
booklet. Then he aimed the
remote control. The Tidybot
was ready for action.

Luke pressed a red button twice and the robot jerked to life.

ALLOW ME TO PUT AWAY YOUR CLOTHES, SIR.

In minutes, all Luke's pants, shirts and socks were off the floor and neatly put away. Luke was impressed.

He pressed button after button. The robot whizzed around the room, obeying every command.

11

In no time at all, the
bedroom was cleaner than it
had ever been. Luke couldn't
wait to see his mother's face
when she returned.

He took a step back to
admire the Tidybot's work. As
he did, he heard a loud crack.

The remote control was bent
and broken.

How can I return
this now?

But Luke had more important
things to worry about. Breaking
the control unit had made the
Tidybot go crazy.

ALLOW ME TO PUT
AWAY YOUR
BOOKS, SIR.

It hurtled around the room
until it was messier than ever.

ALLOW ME TO PUT
AWAY YOUR
CLOTHES, SIR.

Before Luke could stop it, the
rampaging robot zoomed out
of his
bedroom
and down
the stairs.

It went through every room in the house, leaving a messy trail behind.

Finally, the robot's battery went flat and it ground to a halt. Luke stared at the house in horror. What would his mother say?

He spent the next hour sweeping, mopping and polishing. Then he repacked the robot and hid it in the shed.

When he'd finished, he was
so tired that he went to his
bedroom to lie down. He was
in for a shock.

As he slumped onto his bed in
despair, his mother returned.

"Look at this room!" she cried. But Luke was so exhausted, he didn't hear.

Mrs. Lively shook her head as she carried off Luke's computer. "You really *are* the laziest boy in the world!" she said.

Chapter 2

Robot robbery

Jay C. B. was the hardest-working robot on the building site. He had ten different tools, so he was always digging and drilling.

19

But Jay liked the end of each day best. Only then could he switch off and recharge his battery.

Ahh. Time for a rest.

One night, as Jay was recharging, someone broke in and carried him off.

When Jay was fully
charged, he awoke to find
himself in a strange workshop.
   A wild-haired man was
fiddling with Jay's control
panel.

"Who are you?" cried Jay,
"and what do you want?"
   "The name's Filch," snapped
the man. "The rest you'll find
out soon enough."

21

"But I should be digging back at the site," cried Jay.

"I have a much better job for you," said Filch. "I want you to dig for me... into Bullion's Bank!"

I'm not taking orders from you!

"When I've reprogramed you, you'll do whatever I want," snarled the crook.

Later that day, Filch ordered
Jay to follow him to the bank.
"No!" said Jay.

Filch pushed a button on a
remote control. Jay followed.

Okay, metal muscles – start digging!

But Jay refused to dig. Filch
angrily flicked two switches on
his remote control.

"I obey!" said Jay, and
began burrowing into the
ground at top speed.

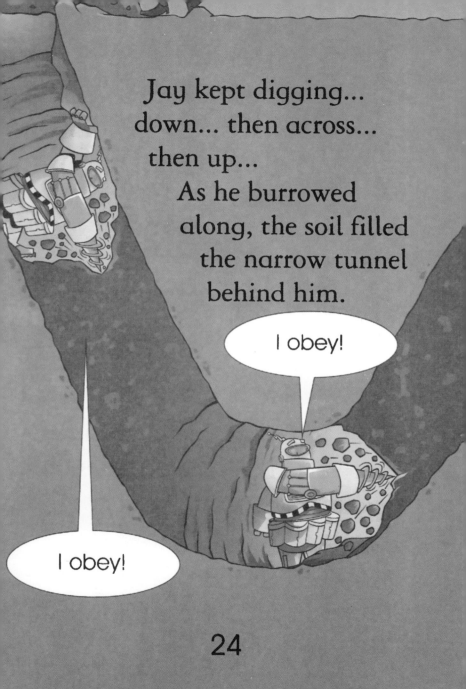

Soon Jay emerged in Bullion's Bank. Outside, Filch watched Jay's progress on a tiny screen. He twisted a dial and Jay drilled through a thick metal door.

Filch was delighted.

"Only the electric inner door left to go," he said with a grin. "Then all the bank's gold will be mine!"

Ha ha!

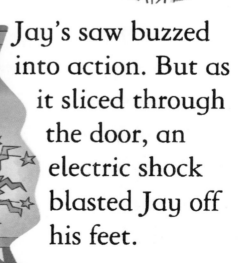

FIZZZWW!

Jay's saw buzzed into action. But as it sliced through the door, an electric shock blasted Jay off his feet.

26

Suddenly, Jay felt different.
He could switch off his saw.
"I'm free!" he cried. "That
electric shock must have
stopped Filch's program."

"Now I'll fix
that no-good
crook,"
thought Jay.

27

Minutes later, Jay popped
out of the tunnel and handed
Filch two big sacks.

"Run!" he cried. "The guards
saw me stealing the gold."

Filch ran home as fast as
he could. But he was in for
a surprise.

The greedy crook excitedly tipped out the contents of the sacks, only to to find...

Jay had filled the sacks with rubble from the tunnel.

Filch spat out a mouthful of dirt. "That's the last time I trust a robot!" he shouted.

29

Chapter 3

Robot racers

Squeaky the cleaning robot hated his job. He was out in all weather, sweeping streets. What he really wanted was to win the Botsville road race.

The winning robot would
get a new memory chip and a
head-to-wheel polish.

But Squeaky didn't dare
enter. He was so rusty and
clanky, he wasn't sure he could
even finish the race.

He was feeling sorry for himself when a noisy robot zoomed past.

Out of the way, rust bucket!

Hey!

Tanktop was the biggest, meanest robot in town. Everyone was certain he would win tomorrow's big race.

Tanktop wasn't taking any chances. He had a plan to make sure none of the other racers even started.

That night, as the Botsville robots recharged themselves, Tanktop visited each of his rivals in secret.

He gave
Tina Turbo a
puncture...

stole Cyber
Sid's memory
chip...

undid Andi
Droid's battery
pack...

and reset
Betty Byte's
built-in
alarm clock.

She'll sleep right
through the race!

The next morning, Tanktop
was the only robot at the
starting line. It looked as if his
plan had worked. The judge
was puzzled.

It seems you're the only contestant!

I'll take my prize now!

"There must be someone else
willing to race," cried the
judge desperately. Tanktop
was making him look stupid.

Just then a tinny voice piped up. "I will!"

Everyone in the crowd turned. "Is that Squeaky?" said someone in amazement.

You? What chance have you got?

I'd still like to try.

Squeaky's joints were feeling especially stiff today, but he couldn't miss this chance.

"Very well," said the judge, with a sigh of relief. "Robots, on your marks!"

Tanktop hadn't bothered to charge up his battery that morning. But he was confident he could still beat Squeaky.

The robots set off on their lap of the town. Tanktop raced off with a roar and Squeaky clattered off in hot pursuit.

As soon as he was out of sight of the crowd, Tanktop opened a flap in his back.

Ha ha! These nails will slow down that robo wreck.

By the time Squeaky spotted the spiky trap, it was too late.

Luckily, Squeaky was so old that his wheels were made of solid rubber. They didn't burst and he was still in the race.

"I'll show that cheat!" thought Squeaky. He put on a burst of speed. Soon, he'd caught up with Tanktop.

"Let's see you get out of this!" boomed Tanktop, as he opened another compartment.

Oil!

Squeaky shut his eyes and hoped for the best, as he slithered and slid all over the road.

Woooaah!

40

Squeaky was left battered and dented, but at least he was still in one piece. He tried to get up and found he couldn't move. His joints were too stiff.

As he sat there, Squeaky realized what he needed was all around him. Unwinding his hose, he guzzled up every last drop of oil.

Ahh! That feels good.

SLURP!

Soon, Squeaky was back on his rival's tail. Tanktop was running out of power fast.

But Tanktop still had one trick up his sleeve – his telescopic arms. He reached out to Squeaky's front wheel and undid the screw.

Sparks flew through the air as Squeaky's wheel bounced past Tanktop. In seconds, Squeaky had ground to a halt.

As the crowd came back into view, Tanktop used the last of his power to roar across the finishing line.

FLASH!

I've won! Ha ha!

Tanktop was already boasting to the crowds as poor old Squeaky was carried across the line.

"Congratulations!" cried the judge as he shook Squeaky by the hand.

"Well, I suppose I almost won," Squeaky sniffed, sadly.

"Not almost," said the judge. "You *did* win. Look!"

He showed Squeaky and Tanktop the photograph taken at the finishing line.

"Your wheel crossed the line a second before Tanktop. That makes you the winner!"

Squeaky clunked with delight, the crowd cheered and Tanktop blew a fuse.

Series editor:
Lesley Sims

This edition first published in 2006 by Usborne Publishing Ltd., Usborne House, 83-85 Saffron Hill, London EC1N 8RT, England. www.usborne.com
Copyright © 2006, 2004 Usborne Publishing Ltd.

48

The
Billy Goats
Gruff

Retold by Jane Bingham

Illustrated by
Daniel Postgate

Reading Consultant: Alison Kelly
Roehampton University

Contents

Chapter 1

On the farm

We're the Gruff brothers.

Once upon a time, three billy goats lived on a farm, in the shadow of a mountain. They were brothers and their last name was Gruff.

Beanie was the youngest. He was small and skinny, always hungry...

and always in trouble.

Bertie was the middle brother.

He was crazy about sports.

Biffer was the oldest. He was big and strong and looked after his brothers.

6

Chapter 2

Time to go

One winter, there was very little food on the farm.

7

"I'm so hungry," moaned
Beanie, "I've only eaten a
piece of hay today."

"Fibber," said Bertie, "I saw
you at the clothesline earlier.
You ate two socks and a shirt."

Biffer was worried. "I think it's time we made a move," he said. "We'll starve if we stay here."

"Where will we go?" asked Beanie.

"To the Juicy Fields beyond the hills," Biffer replied. "No one lives there, so we'll have plenty of food. We just have to cross the Rushing River."

Bertie looked terrified. "We can't go over the river!" he cried. "That's where the Terrible Troll lives."

"He's huge and green," said Beanie. "He'll gobble us up."

"Don't be silly," Biffer said. "There's no such thing as trolls. That's farmyard talk."

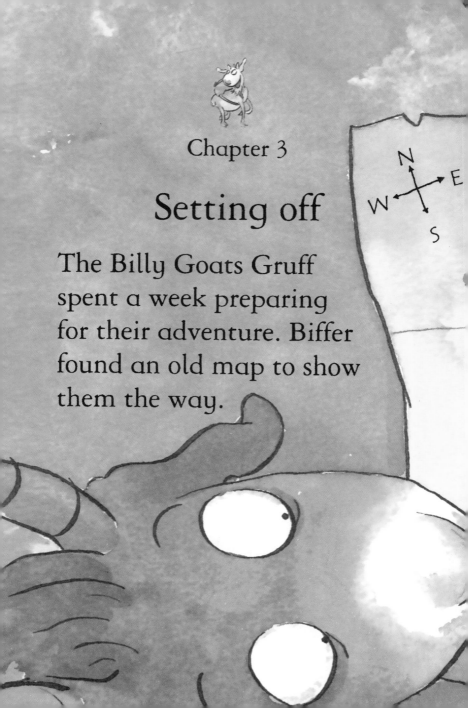

Chapter 3

Setting off

The Billy Goats Gruff
spent a week preparing
for their adventure. Biffer
found an old map to show
them the way.

Then Beanie and Bertie
had to learn to climb
up hills.

Oof!

Beanie was better
at coming down.

After a few days, they were both excellent climbers.

Finally, the brothers had to pack for their journey.

At last, the Billy Goats Gruff were ready to set off. All the other farm animals came to say goodbye.

The younger animals wanted to go too. But the older ones shook their heads. "Let's hope they make it past the bridge," they muttered.

17

Chapter 4

Into the forest

Bertie and Beanie were still dreaming of the Juicy Fields as they left the farm.

18

Ahead of them loomed the Dark Forest.

"I'm not sure I want to go in there," said Beanie.

"We'll be fine," said Biffer, "as long as we stick together."

The billy goats trotted along
the path. The only sound was
the tap-tap-tapping of their
hooves on the forest floor.

Suddenly, a thick mist
swirled around them.

Beanie shivered. "I don't
like this forest. It's spooky," he
said. "Do you think there
might be ghosts here?"

"Yes," said Bertie, with a grin. "Lots of ghosts. And more than anything, ghosts like scaring little billy goats."

"Shut up, Bertie," said Biffer sternly. "Stop scaring Beanie."

21

The billy goats walked on in silence.

"Um, Biffer?" Beanie said after a while.

"Yes, Beanie?"

"I think someone's following us."

Listen!

The billy goats stopped and listened. They strained their ears... and heard a thumping sound. It grew louder with every second.

"Oh no," shrieked Beanie.
"Look behind us!" A strange
shape was coming down the
path – and it was heading
straight for them.

It's a ghost!

"Run!" cried Bertie. "Run for
your lives."

Before Biffer could stop
them, Beanie and Bertie had
raced off down the path.

"It's not a ghost. It's a..."

Biffer waited, as the shape slowly appeared out of the mist. "It's only a rabbit," he said.

"I'm not *only* a rabbit," said the rabbit. "I'm a rare breed of tall, lop-eared rabbit and my name is Buffy."

"I'm Biffer. Nice to meet you," said Biffer quickly, "but I must find my brothers before they get lost."

Sorry, no time to chat.

"Where are you going?" Buffy asked.

"To the Juicy Fields by the mountains," Biffer called, running after his brothers.

"Watch out for the troll," Buffy shouted after him. Biffer didn't hear. He had already headed deeper into the forest.

Oh dear. No one's ever made it past the troll.

Chapter 5

Tricking the troll

Hello? Anyone there?

Meanwhile, Bertie was
wandering alone through the
forest. He had lost Beanie in
the mist and he didn't know
which way to go.

28

Beanie had been luckier. He had found the path that ran straight through the forest.

Whew! That was close.

"I can't wait to get to the Juicy Fields," Beanie thought, as he headed to the river.

The only way to cross the
Rushing River was over a little
wooden bridge. Next to the
bridge was a big wooden sign.

WARNING
Goats
beware!

"I wish I could read,"
thought Beanie.

30

His hooves went clippety-clop, clippety-clop over the bridge. But as he reached the middle of the river...

Help!

...a large, green hand smashed through the wooden planks and grabbed Beanie's leg.

Beanie screamed.

"Who's that going over my bridge?" roared a terrible voice. "I'm coming to gobble you up!"

Let go!

Beanie's eyes bulged with terror. There, crouched under the bridge, was a fat and warty troll.

"Please don't eat me," cried
Beanie. "I'm only a little goat.
My big brother is coming
behind me. He'll be much
tastier than me."

I'm sure
you'd rather
eat him.

"I think I can wait a little
longer for my dinner," said the
troll. "Now get off my bridge."

Shaking with fear, Beanie
wobbled off the bridge and
went to hide in some bushes.
"I hope Bertie can save
himself," he thought.

Chapter 6

Bertie on the bridge

Bertie arrived soon after
and trotted onto the bridge –
clappety-clop-bonk, clappety-
clop-bonk. (He was bouncing
his ball.)

"Who's that bouncing over my bridge?" bellowed the troll.

Oh no!

Bertie peered over the bridge, and gulped. "I didn't think trolls were real," he said.

"I'm real and I'm hungry," said the troll, "and I'm coming to gobble you up!"

I don't want to be dinner.

"You'll make a very tasty meal," the troll went on. "Nice fresh billy goat. Yum, yum."

"Stop!" cried Bertie, thinking quickly. "You can't eat me. I'm only a medium-sized billy goat. My big brother is coming behind me. He's much fatter."

What big teeth he has...

"Humph," said the troll, rubbing his stomach. "I'll wait for the fattest one then. He had better be juicy."

Chapter 7

Brave Biffer

At last, Biffer came out of the
forest. When he spotted his
brothers on the other side of
the river, he raced to the bank.

Beanie and Bertie leaped
out of the bushes, waving their
hooves wildly.

"Stop Biffer!" they cried.
"STOP! There's a troll under
the bridge."

It was too late. Biffer was already crossing. His heavy hooves went clunkety-clop, clunkety-clop and the bridge strained under his weight.

By this time, the troll was starving.

"Who's that stomping over my bridge?" he roared.

But Biffer stood his ground. "I'm an enormous billy goat," Biffer said, "and I'm ready for a fight."

Biffer lowered his head and caught the troll on his horns.

He bounced the troll into the air. Then, with a toss of his head, Biffer whacked him into the Rushing River.

The troll landed with an enormous SPLASH. He sank under the water and was never seen again.

45

Beanie and Bertie couldn't believe it.

"You're the best, Biffer!" they cried.

Just then, a stream of animals came out of the forest – deer, squirrels, rabbits and foxes. In a large crowd, they skipped across the bridge.

"Where are you going?" Biffer asked a rabbit.

"We're off to the Juicy Fields," she replied. "We've been trapped in the forest for years, because of the troll. Now, at last, we're free."

This retelling of *The Billy Goats Gruff* is
based on the folktale from Norway.

Edited by Susanna Davidson

Designed by Russell Punter
and Natacha Goransky

Series editor: Lesley Sims

First published in 2004 by Usborne Publishing Ltd., Usborne House,
83-85 Saffron Hill, London EC1N 8RT, England. www.usborne.com
Copyright © 2004 Usborne Publishing Ltd.

The Railway Children

E. Nesbit

Adapted by
Mary Sebag-Montefiore

Illustrated by Alan Marks

Reading Consultant: Alison Kelly
Roehampton University

Contents

Chapter 1
Change

It all began at Peter's birthday party. The servants were just bringing out the birthday cake, when the doorbell clanged sharply.

"Bother!" exclaimed Father.
"Who can that be? Start without me
everyone. I'll be back in a minute."

Peering into the hallway, Peter
saw Father leading two men into
his study.

"Who are they, Mother?" asked
his sister, Phyllis.

"I don't know," said
Mother, frowning.
"Stay here. I'm going
to find out."

Mother disappeared into the
study for ages.

"What's going on?" asked Phyllis.

"We'll just have to wait and see,"
replied Bobbie, the eldest.

Mother emerged just as the front door slammed shut. Bobbie saw a carriage and horses driving rapidly away into the night. Mother's face was icy white and her eyes glittered with tears.

"Where's Father?" demanded Peter, running into the empty study.

"He's gone away." Mother was shaking now. Bobbie reached for her hand and held it tight.

"But he hasn't even packed his clothes," said Phyllis.

"He had to go quickly – on business," Mother replied.

"Was it to do with the Government?" asked Peter. Father worked in a Government office.

"Yes. Don't ask me questions, darlings. I can't tell you anything. Please just go to bed."

Upstairs, the children tried endlessly to work out where Father had gone. The next few days were just as strange.

All the maids left. Then a
FOR SALE sign went up outside
the house. The beautiful furniture
was sold and meals now consisted
of plain, cheap food. Mother was
hardly ever at home.

"What's happening?" asked Peter, finally. "Please tell us."

"We've got to play at being poor for a bit," Mother replied. "We're going to leave London, and live far away in the countryside."

"Father is going to be away for some time," she went on. "But everything will come right in the end, I promise."

Chapter 2

A coal thief

After a long, long journey, they arrived at the new house, late at night. Mother rushed around, digging sheets out of suitcases.

The next day Bobbie, Peter and Phyllis woke early to explore. They raced outside until they came to a red-brick bridge.

Suddenly there was a shriek and a snort and a train shot out from under the bridge.

"It's exactly like a dragon," Peter shouted above the noise. "Did you feel the hot air from its breath?"

"Perhaps it's going to London," Phyllis yelled.

"Father might still be there," shrieked Bobbie. "If it's a magic dragon, it'll send our love to Father. Let's wave."

They pulled out their handkerchiefs and waved them in the breeze. Out of a first class carriage window a hand waved back. It was an old gentleman's hand, holding a newspaper.

After that, the children waved every day, rain or shine, at the old gentleman on the 9:15 train to London.

The weather grew colder. Mother sat in her icy bedroom wrapped in shawls, writing stories to earn money for them all.

Bobbie, Peter and Phyllis didn't notice the cold much. They were too busy playing. But one morning, it snowed so much they had to stay inside.

"Please let me light a fire, Mother," begged Bobbie. "We're all freezing."

"Not until tonight, I'm afraid. We can't afford to burn coal all day. Put on more clothes if you're chilly."

Peter was furious. "I'm the man in this family now," he stormed. "And I think we ought to be warm."

Over the next few days Peter began to disappear without saying where he was going.

"I can't understand it," Mother said soon after. "The coal never seems to run out."

"Let's follow Pete," Bobbie whispered to Phyllis. "I'm sure he's up to something."

They trailed him all the way to the station, and watched him pile a cart with coal from a huge heap. Then suddenly, Peter screamed.

A hand had shot out of the
darkness and grabbed him by
the shoulder.

It was Mr. Perks, the station master. "Don't you know stealing is wrong?" he shouted.

"Wasn't stealing. I was mining for treasure," sulked Peter.

"That treasure belongs to the railway, young man, not you."

"He shouldn't have done it, Mr. Perks," said Bobbie, shocked. "But he was only trying to help Mother. He's really sorry, aren't you, Pete?" She gave him a kick and Peter muttered an apology.

"Accepted," said Perks. "But don't do it again."

"I hate being poor," grumbled
Peter, kicking the cobbles on their
way home. "And Mother deserves
better than this."

Soon after, Mother got very sick.
Bobbie didn't know how they were
going to pay for her medicines, until
she had a brilliant idea.

She wrote a letter to the old gentleman on the 9:15 train to London and asked Mr. Perks to give it to him.

Dear Mr. (we don't know your name),

Mother is sick and we can't afford the things the doctor says she needs. This is the list:

Medicine   Port Wine

Fruit   Soda water

I don't know who else to ask. Father will pay you back when he comes home, or I will when I grow up.

Bobbie

P.S. Please give them to Mr. Perks, the station master, and Pete will fetch them.

The very next day, a huge
hamper appeared, filled with
medicines, as well as red roses,
chocolates and lavender perfume.

A week later, Bobbie, Peter and
Phyllis made a banner and waved
it at the 9:15 train. It said:

THANK YOU!
SHE IS MUCH BETTER!

But Mother was furious when she
found out. "You must never ask
strangers for things," she raged.

Bobbie was nearly in tears.
"I didn't mean to be naughty."

"I know, my darling,"
said Mother. "But you mustn't
tell everyone we're poor.
We have enough to
live on – just.
Now we won't
say any more
about it."

Chapter 3

Red for danger

They all felt miserable for upsetting Mother. "I know what will cheer us up!" said Bobbie. "We can ask Mr. Perks for the magazines people leave on trains. They'd be fun to read."

"Let's climb down the cliff and walk along the track to the station," suggested Peter. "We've never gone that way before."

"I don't want to. It doesn't look safe." Phyllis sounded frightened.

"Baby! Scaredy-cat!" teased Peter.

"It's all right, Phil," Bobbie comforted her. "The cliff isn't that steep."

"Two against one," crowed Peter. "Come on, Phil, you'll enjoy it."

Slowly Phyllis followed her brother and sister, muttering, "I still don't want to..."

They scrambled down the cliff.
Phyllis tumbled down the last bit
where the steps had crumbled
away, and tore her dress.

Now her red petticoat flapped
through the tear as she walked.

"There!" she announced. "I told
you this would be horrible, and
it is!"

"No, it isn't," disagreed Peter.

"What's that noise?" asked
Bobbie suddenly.

A strange sound, like far off
thunder, began and stopped. Then
it started again, getting louder
and more rumbling.

30

"Look at that tree!" cried Peter.
The tree was moving, not like a
normal tree when the wind blows,
but all in one piece.

All the trees on the bank seemed
to be slowly sliding downhill, like
a marching army.

31

Suddenly, rocks, trees, grasses,
bushes and earth gathered speed
in a deafening roar and collapsed
in a heap on the railway track.

"I don't like it!" shrieked Phyllis.
"It's much too magic for me!"

"It's all coming down," said
Peter in a shaky voice. Then he
cried out, "Oh!"

The others looked at him.

"The 11:29 train! It'll be along any minute. There'll be a terrible accident."

"Can we run to the station and tell them?" Bobbie began.

"No time. We need to warn the driver somehow. What can we do?"

"Our red petticoats!" Bobbie exclaimed. "Red for danger! We'll tear them up and use them as flags."

"We can't rip our clothes!" Phyllis objected. "What will Mother say?"

"She won't mind." Bobbie was undoing her petticoat as she spoke. "Don't you see, Phil, if we don't stop the train in time, people might be killed?"

34

They quickly snapped thin
branches off the nearby trees, tore
up the petticoats and made them
into flags.

"Two each. Wave one in each
hand, and stand on the track so
the train can see us," Peter directed.
"Then jump out of the way."

Phyllis was gasping with fright. "It's dangerous! I don't like it!"

"Think of saving the train," Bobbie implored. "That's what matters most!"

"It's coming," called Peter, though his voice was instantly wiped out in a whirlwind of sound.

36

As the roaring train thundered nearer and nearer, Bobbie waved her flags furiously. She was sure it was no good, that the train would never see them in time...

"MOVE!" shouted Peter, as the train's steam surrounded them in a cloud of white. But Bobbie couldn't. She had to make it stop.

With a judder and squeal of
brakes the train shuddered to a
halt and the driver jumped out.
"What's going on?"

Peter and Phyllis showed him the
landslide. But not Bobbie. She had
fainted and lay on the track, white
and quiet as a fallen statue, still
gripping her petticoat flags.

The driver picked her up and put her in one of the first class carriages. Peter and Phyllis were worried, until finally Bobbie began to cry.

"You kids saved lives today," said the driver. "I expect the Railway Company will give you a reward."

"Just like real heroes and heroines," breathed Phyllis.

Chapter 4

The terrible secret

The Railway Company did want to reward the children. There was a ceremony at the station, with a brass band, bunting and cake.

All the passengers who had been on the train were there, as well as the Railway Director, the train driver, Mr. Perks, and best of all, their own old gentleman.

The Railway Director made a speech praising the children, which they found very embarrassing, and gave them each a gold watch.

When it was all over, the old gentleman shook their hands.

"Oh do come back for tea," said Phyllis.

They climbed up the hill together. Bobbie carried the magazines Mr. Perks had collected for her. He'd made a parcel of them, wrapped in an old sheet of newspaper.

Back home, Mother, Phyllis and Peter chatted with the old gentleman.

Bobbie went into her room, to sort through the magazines. She undid the newspaper wrapping and idly looked at the print. Then she stared.

Her feet went icy cold and her face burned. When she had read it all, she drew a long, uneven breath.

"So now I know," she thought.

It was a report of a spy trial, with a photograph of the accused. It was a photograph of Father. Underneath it said: GUILTY. And then: FIVE YEARS IN JAIL.

Bobbie scrunched up the paper. "Oh Daddy," she whispered. "You never did it."

Time passed. The old gentleman left and it grew dark outside. Supper was ready, but Bobbie couldn't join the others.

Mother came to find her. "What's the matter?" she asked.

Bobbie held out the paper. "Tell me about it," she begged.

Mother told her how Father had been arrested for being a spy. Papers had been found in his desk that proved he had sold his country's secrets to enemies.

"Didn't they know he'd never do such a thing?" Bobbie asked.

"There was a man in his office he never quite trusted," Mother replied. "I think he planted those papers on Father."

"Why didn't you tell the lawyers that?" Bobbie wanted to know.

"Do you think I didn't try everything?" Mother demanded. "We just have to be patient and wait for him to come back to us."

"Why didn't you tell us?"

"Are you going to tell the others now you know?"

"No," said Bobbie.

"Why?"

Bobbie thought hard. "Because...
it would only upset them."

"Exactly," said her mother. "But
now you've found out, we must
help each other to be brave."

They went in to supper together,
and though Bobbie's eyes were still
red with tears, Peter and Phyllis
never guessed why.

Chapter 5

The man in the train

The long, cold winter blossomed
into spring, and then summer.
Bobbie couldn't bear the way time
passed with nothing happening.

Mother was unhappy, Father was in prison, and she couldn't do anything to help. So she wrote a letter. And once more it was to the old gentleman.

Dear Friend,

Mother says we are not to ask for things for ourselves, but this isn't just for me.

You see what it says in this paper.

It isn't true. Father is not a spy.

Could you find out who did it, and then they would let Father out of prison.

Think if it was your Daddy, what would you feel? Please help me.

Love from your good friend,

Bobbie

Soon after she sent the letter, Bobbie had her twelfth birthday. Mother gave a bracelet she no longer wore, Peter and Phyllis made a cake, and Mr. Perks brought a bunch of flowers from his garden.

It was very different from her last
birthday when she'd had a huge
party and lots of presents. This one
was happy enough. But Bobbie
missed Father so badly, her mind
was filled with wanting him.

Then, one late summer's day,
when the roses were out and the
corn was ripening to gold, Bobbie
found it impossible to concentrate
on her lessons.

"Please, Mother," she begged.
"Can I go outside?"

"Do you have a headache?"
asked Mother.

Bobbie thought. "Not really,"
she replied. "I just feel in a daze.
I'd be more alive in the fresh
air, I think."

Mother let her go and Bobbie
found herself walking down to
the station. She felt as if she were
in a dream.

At the station, everyone smiled
at her and Mr. Perks shook her
hand up and down.

"I saw it in the papers," he
grinned. "I'm so pleased. And here
comes the 11:54 London train,
bang on time."

"Saw what in the papers?" Bobbie asked, puzzled, but Mr. Perks had turned away, blowing his whistle.

As the train drew into the station, Bobbie was astonished to see handkerchiefs fluttering from every window.

Only three people got out. An old woman with a basket of squawking hens, the grocer's wife with some brown-paper packages, and the third...

"Oh! My Daddy, my Daddy!" Bobbie's cry pierced the air.

People looked out of the windows to see a tall thin man and a little girl rush up to each other with open arms.

"I felt something strange was going to happen today," said Bobbie as they walked up the hill, "but I never guessed what."

"Didn't Mother get my letter?" Father asked.

"There weren't any letters this morning," Bobbie replied.

"Mother wrote to tell me you'd found out," he said. "You've been wonderful. The old gentleman has too. He helped them catch the real spy. Now, Bobbie, run ahead and tell Mother and Peter and Phyllis I'm home."

He paused in the garden,
looking around at the rich
summer countryside with the
hungry eyes of someone who has
seen too little of flowers and trees
and the wide blue sky.

Mother, Bobbie, Peter and Phyllis stood in the doorway. Father went down the path to join them.

We won't follow him. In that happy moment, in that happy family, no one else is wanted just now.

E. Nesbit (1858-1924)

Edith Nesbit wrote her
books a hundred years ago,
when most people rode by
horse, not car, and television
hadn't been invented. Her
stories are full of excitement,
adventure and magic.
The original versions are
much longer than Young
Reading books, and they
may seem a little old-fashioned,
but they're well worth reading.
The Railway Children, first published
in 1906, is one of her most famous books.
It has been adapted for the television four
times and has twice been made into a film.

Edited by Susanna Davidson
Series editor: Lesley Sims
Designed by Natacha Goransky

First published in 2007 by Usborne Publishing Ltd.,
Usborne House, 83-85 Saffron Hill, London EC1N 8RT, England.
www.usborne.com Copyright © 2007 Usborne Publishing Ltd.

Alice in Wonderland

Lewis Carroll
Adapted by Lesley Sims

Illustrated by
Mauro Evangelista

Reading Consultant: Alison Kelly
Roehampton University

Contents

Chapter 1

Down the rabbit hole

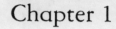

Alice was getting tired of sitting
with her sister. She had tried
reading her sister's book, but as it
didn't have any pictures or people
talking, it was very dull indeed.

She was just wondering whether to pick some daisies for a daisy-chain when a White Rabbit ran past. Now, seeing a rabbit isn't so very remarkable.

Alice wasn't even surprised when the Rabbit cried, "Oh dear! Oh dear! I shall be too late." But when it took a watch out of its pocket, she jumped up. For whoever saw a rabbit with a pocket — or a watch?

4

She chased after it and was
just in time to see the Rabbit
pop down a large hole. In a
flash, Alice followed.

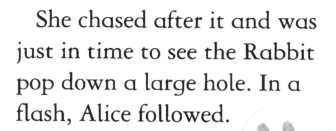

At first, the hole
went on like a
tunnel. Suddenly,
it dipped and
Alice found herself
falling down a deep well.

The well was lined with shelves full of interesting things – and either it was very deep, or Alice fell slowly, for she had plenty of time to look around.

"I must be near the middle of the earth," she thought, after a while. "What if I fall right through? I might end up in New Zealand!"

Down,
    down,
        down...
Alice began to think the fall
would never end. She was
daydreaming about
her cat, Dinah,
when *thump!* she
landed on a
heap of dry
leaves.

Not in the least hurt, Alice stood up and looked around. A long passage stretched ahead of her and the White Rabbit was hurrying down it. Alice went after him like the wind.

Oh my ears and whiskers, how late it's getting!

She had almost caught up with him when he turned a corner... and vanished.

Alice was in a long hall, with doors down both sides. Excitedly, she tried each one. But every single door was locked.

Just as she thought she might never get out, she saw a glass table with a golden key on top.

Alice walked down the hall once more, but the key was too small for the doors. Then she spotted a tiny door, half-hidden by a curtain. Holding her breath, she tried the golden key in the lock. It worked!

Beyond the door was the most beautiful garden Alice had ever seen, with bright flowers and cool, sparkling fountains. Alice tried to squeeze through the door, but not even her head would fit.

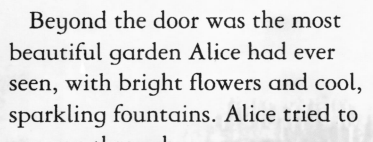

If only I could shrink...

"I'll go back to the table," she decided. "Perhaps it has another key to a bigger door."

But instead of a key, she found a bottle with a label saying *Drink me.* "That wasn't here before," thought Alice, checking it carefully. Since it wasn't marked *Poison*, she took a sip.

It tasted so delicious (a mix of cherry-tart, custard, toffee, pineapple and hot buttered toast), that she had very soon finished it.

"What a curious feeling," Alice said next. "I think I'm shrinking!" And she was. Soon, she was small enough to go into the garden.

I hope I don't shrink away to nothing...

To her huge disappointment, the garden door had closed — and she'd left the golden key on the table. She could see it glittering through the glass, a long way out of reach.

12

Alice tried to climb a table leg, but it was too slippery. After three tries, she fell to the floor and began to cry. "That won't help," she told herself sharply. As she wiped her eyes, she noticed a glass box under the table.

The box held a cake. "I'll eat it," thought Alice. "If I grow larger, I can reach the key. If I grow smaller, I can creep under the door. Either way, I'll get into the garden."

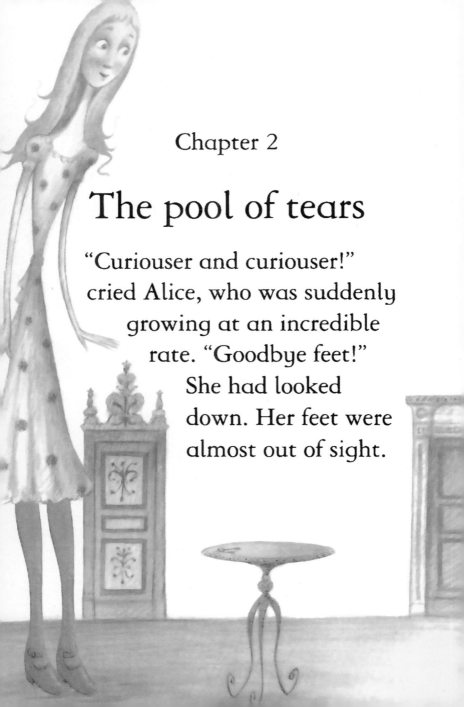

Chapter 2

The pool of tears

"Curiouser and curiouser!"
cried Alice, who was suddenly
growing at an incredible
rate. "Goodbye feet!"
She had looked
down. Her feet were
almost out of sight.

She only stopped growing when her head hit the ceiling. Quickly, she grabbed the key and hurried to the door. Now she was far too big.

Alice began to cry again, sobbing and sobbing until a pool of tears spread around her.

After a while, she heard pattering feet and dried her eyes. It was the White Rabbit, trotting along in a great hurry, and carrying a pair of gloves and a fan.

15

"If you please, Sir," Alice began. The Rabbit jumped in the air and scurried away, dropping the gloves and fan as he went.

Alice picked them up and began to fan herself. "How very strange everything is today!" she thought.

Alice was wondering just what could happen next, when she began to shrink again.

16

Moments before she shrank away altogether, she realized the fan was to blame and dropped it.

"That was a narrow escape," she sighed. "Now for the garden!" But the tiny door had closed and the golden key was back on the table.

Things were worse than ever. Just then, her foot slipped and *splash!* she was up to her chin in salty water.

She'd fallen into her pool of tears.
Something else was splashing
around too. At first, Alice thought
it was a walrus or a hippo. Then
she remembered how small she was
and saw it was only a mouse.

I wish I hadn't
cried so much!

The pool was soon crowded with
creatures that had fallen in. Alice
led the way and the whole group
swam to shore.

Chapter 3

A caucus race

It was a very odd party that gathered on the bank, and all of them were dripping wet, cross and uncomfortable. The first question, of course, was how to get dry.

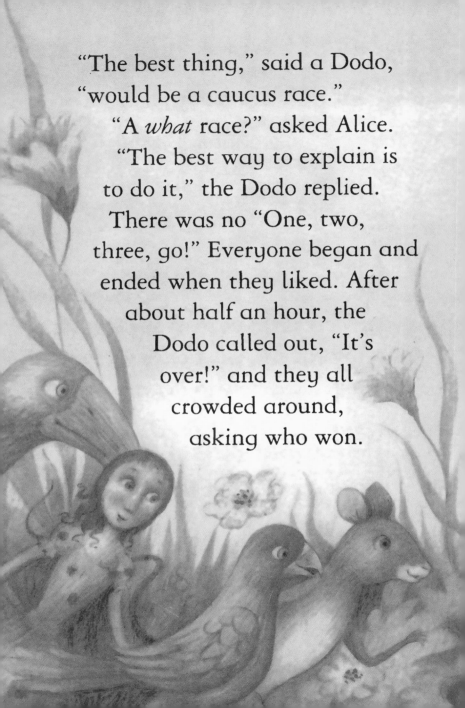

"The best thing," said a Dodo,
"would be a caucus race."

"A *what* race?" asked Alice.

"The best way to explain is
to do it," the Dodo replied.
There was no "One, two,
three, go!" Everyone began and
ended when they liked. After
about half an hour, the
Dodo called out, "It's
over!" and they all
crowded around,
asking who won.

They surrounded Alice, demanding prizes. In despair, she felt in her pocket and pulled out a tin of peppermints. There were enough for exactly one each.

"But she must have a prize too," said the Mouse.

"Of course," said the Dodo. "What else is in your pocket?"

Alice took out a thimble and the Dodo solemnly presented it to her.

Then they sat down in a circle. The Mouse started to tell them a story, but he left in a huff when he thought Alice wasn't listening.

"I wish Dinah was here," said Alice. "She'd soon bring him back.'

"Who's Dinah?" asked a bird.

"Our cat," Alice said eagerly and, in no time at all, the creatures had gone.

Chapter 4

The White Rabbit's house

As the creatures left, the long hall vanished and the White Rabbit appeared. "Mary Ann!" he snapped, when he saw Alice. "Run home and fetch me some gloves and a fan."

"He thinks I'm his maid!" Alice thought, but she ran off in the direction he pointed. Soon, she came to a small house with *W. Rabbit* on a brass plate outside.

Racing in, she found a fan and some gloves on a table.

Alice was about to leave, when she saw a bottle. This one had no label but she drank it anyway. *Something* interesting was bound to happen...

And it did. She had barely drunk half, before she grew as big as the room. She went on growing... and growing... until one arm was out of the window and her foot was stuck up the chimney.

"Mary Ann!" called the Rabbit, crossly. "Where are my gloves?"

Alice trembled, quite forgetting she was now a thousand times larger than him and had no reason to be scared.

When he couldn't open the door – because Alice's elbow was against it – he tried the window. Alice waved her hand and heard a shriek.

"Pat! Where
are you?"
the Rabbit
shouted and
Alice heard a
new voice reply,
"Over here sir."
"Well, tell me," asked
the Rabbit, "what's
in this window?"
"An arm, sir,"
said the voice.

"An arm, you goose!" said
the Rabbit. "Whoever saw
one that size? Take it away!"

The next thing Alice knew, the
Rabbit had yelled, "Bill! Go down
the chimney."

Alice waited until she
heard a little animal
scrabbling inside the
chimney and gave
a sharp kick.

We must burn the
house down.

Don't you
dare!

There goes Bill.

There was silence for a moment,
then a shower of pebbles came
rattling through the window.
To Alice's surprise, they turned
into cakes.

"If I eat them," she thought,
"they're bound to change my size.
And as I can't grow any larger, I
expect I'll grow smaller."

Alice shrank at once. As soon as she could squeeze through the door, she fled. And she didn't stop running until she reached a forest.

"The first thing I have to do," she decided when she had caught her breath, "is to grow to my right size. Then I must find a way into that lovely garden."

It was an excellent plan. The only problem was how to do it. "I suppose I should eat or drink something," she said. "But what?"

Alice looked around and saw a mushroom. Standing on tiptoe, she peered over the edge to see a large caterpillar, quietly minding its own business.

Chapter 5

The Caterpillar's advice

The Caterpillar and Alice looked at each other for a while.

"Who are *you*?" the Caterpillar asked finally, in a sleepy voice.

"I- I hardly know, sir," said Alice.

"What do you mean?" demanded the Caterpillar. "Explain yourself!"

"Try reciting a poem," ordered the Caterpillar. Clearing her throat, Alice began.

'You are old, Father William,'
the young man said,
'And your hair has become very white,
And yet you incessantly stand on your head
Do you think, at your age, it is right?'
'In my youth,' Father William replied to his son,
'I feared it might injure the brain,
But, now that I'm perfectly sure I have none,
Why, I do it again and again.'

"Wrong from beginning to end!"
said the Caterpillar. He paused.
"What size do you want to be?"
"Larger than this," said Alice.

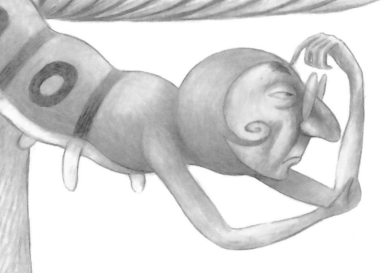

"It's such a wretched height."
  "It's a very good height indeed,"
said the Caterpillar (who was
exactly as tall as Alice). He slid
off the mushroom angrily.

"One side makes you taller, the other makes you shorter," he remarked, as he crawled away.

"One side of *what?*" wondered Alice. "Oh, the mushroom!" She broke off two pieces and nibbled first one, then the other, until she was back to her right size.

Alice continued through the forest until she came to a little house. "I don't want to scare anyone," she thought and ate some more mushroom to shrink herself.

Chapter 6

Pig and pepper

As Alice looked at the house, a fish dressed as a footman ran up and rapped wetly on the door. It was opened by a frog. Alice crept closer.

They bowed low and their wigs got tangled. Alice laughed so loudly, she had to run back into the trees. When she came out, the fish had gone.

I shall sit here till tomorrow... or the next day.

Timidly, Alice went up to the door and knocked. "There's no use knocking," said the Frog. "I'm on the same side as you. Besides, they're making too much noise to hear."

"How will I get in?" asked Alice.

"Are you to get in at all?" said the Frog. "That's the question."

"Hopeless!" thought Alice and marched straight into a large kitchen. A grumpy Duchess sat in the middle holding a baby, a cat at her feet. Pepper filled the air.

Alice sneezed. "Why is your cat grinning?" she asked the Duchess.

"It's a Cheshire cat," the Duchess replied briskly.

"I didn't know cats *could* grin," Alice said.

"They all can," said the Duchess, "and most of 'em do."

"I don't know any that do," said Alice.

"You don't know much and that's a fact."

All of a sudden, the Cook began throwing pans at the Duchess, who simply ignored her and sang a lullaby to the howling baby.

Speak roughly
to your little boy
And beat him
when he sneezes
He only does it to annoy
Because he knows
it teases.

"Here!" she finished suddenly, flinging the baby at Alice. "You look after it. I must get ready for the Queen."

41

Alice caught the baby and left before they were hit by a flying frying-pan. The baby grunted and Alice glanced down. To her surprise, it was turning into a pig.

"Oh!" she cried and let it go. Alice was thinking it was more handsome as a pig, when she saw the Cheshire Cat grinning at her.

"Cheshire Cat," she said, shyly, "where should I go now?"

"Well, that way is a Hatter," said the Cat, waving a paw, "and *that* way is a March Hare. Both mad."

"But I don't want to visit mad people," Alice said.

"We're all mad here," said the Cat, fading away.

Chapter 7

A mad tea party

"As it's May, the March Hare might not be quite so mad," Alice thought and decided to visit him. The March Hare was sitting in front of his house having tea with the Hatter.

"No room! No room!" they cried
when they saw Alice.

"There's plenty of room!" she
said indignantly, sitting down.

The Hatter stared at Alice.
"Why is a raven like a writing
desk?" he demanded.

Then he took out his watch and
shook it. "Two days wrong," he
complained.

He sighed and turned to Alice.
"Have you guessed the riddle yet?"
"I give up," she said. "What is it?"
The Hatter shrugged. "No idea."
"You shouldn't waste time asking
riddles with no answer," she snapped.

"Oh, time and I aren't speaking," said the Hatter. "We argued at a concert given by the Queen of Hearts. I sang a song, you know."

Twinkle, twinkle, little bat!
How I wonder what you're at!
Up above the world you fly
Like a tea-tray in the sky...

"I'd hardly finished the first verse," he went on, "when the Queen shouted I was murdering time. It's been tea time ever since."

47

"I'm bored," the March Hare interrupted. "I want a story." And he pinched a large Dormouse, who was dozing beside them.

Once upon a time, three girls lived down a treacle well...

"This is the stupidest tea party ever!" thought Alice and walked off.

Back in the forest, she noticed a
tree with a door in the trunk.
Curious, she stepped inside...

The tree led her back to the long
hall and, this time, the door behind
the curtain was open. At last, she
could enter the beautiful garden.

49

Chapter 8

Meeting the Queen

At the garden's entrance was a tree covered with white roses, which three gardeners were busily painting red.

Before Alice could ask what they were doing, one of them called out, "The Queen!" and all three threw themselves flat on their faces. Alice looked around, eager to see her.

"Who are *these*?" the Queen
barked, spotting the gardeners.
"How should *I* know?" said Alice.
"Off with her head!" screamed
the Queen.
"Nonsense!" Alice said, firmly.
The Queen looked at the rose tree
and turned to the gardeners.
"Off with *their* heads!"
Quickly, Alice threw
the gardeners
into a pot.

"Come and play croquet," the
Queen shouted at Alice next.

Alice had never played such a
strange game.

Everyone played at once and the
Queen stomped about shouting,
"Off with their heads!"

Alice was wondering if she could
escape when she saw a grin.

"How are you getting along?" asked the Cheshire Cat, as soon as its mouth was all there.

Alice waited for its ears before replying. "They don't follow any rules," she complained, "and as for the Queen..."

"...she's too good," Alice finished quickly, as the Queen walked by.

"Off with his head," the Queen snapped at the Cat.

Instantly, the Cat's body vanished.

"I can't cut off a head if there's no body to cut it from," declared the executioner.

"Anything with a head can be beheaded," the King argued.

"Everyone will lose their heads in a minute," said the Queen and sent for the Duchess to sort out her Cat.

The game went on until the Queen's soldiers had arrested almost everyone. While the King was letting them go again, someone suddenly shouted.

"Time for the trial!"

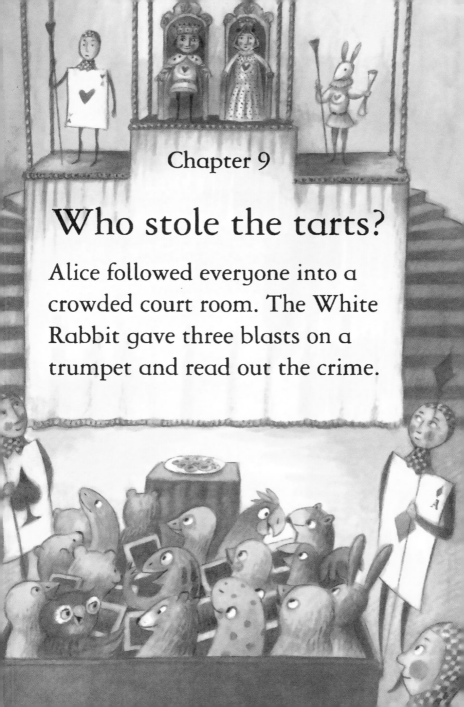

Chapter 9

Who stole the tarts?

Alice followed everyone into a crowded court room. The White Rabbit gave three blasts on a trumpet and read out the crime.

The Queen of Hearts, she made some tarts
All on a summer day
The Knave of Hearts, he stole those tarts
And took them quite away!

"Consider your verdict," the King ordered the jury.

"Not yet!" cried the Rabbit.

"Call the first witness!"

This was the Hatter, who walked in trembling. He was shaking so much, both his shoes fell off.

As Alice watched, she felt an odd sensation. She was growing larger.

"He's useless!" said the King and sent the Hatter away. "Next!"

The Duchess's Cook came in.

The Cook annoyed the King even more. "Who's next?" he shouted.

Alice wanted to know too. The witnesses so far had been terrible. Imagine her surprise when the White Rabbit called out, "Alice!"

Chapter 10

Alice's evidence

"Here!" Alice cried, jumping up. But she'd grown so big, she sent the jury box flying and everyone fell out.

"What do you know about all this?" demanded the King.

"Nothing," said Alice.

"Let the jury consider their verdict," the King announced.

"Sentence first, verdict later," insisted the Queen.

Nonsense!

Off with her head!

By now, Alice had grown to her
full size. "You're nothing but a
pack of cards!" she scoffed. At this,
the whole pack rose into the air
and came flying down upon her.

Alice screamed... and woke up to find her sister gently brushing dead leaves from her face. "Oh, I've had such a wonderful dream," she said and told her all about it, before running off for tea.

Lewis Carroll (1832-1898)

Lewis Carroll was the made-up name of Charles Lutwidge Dodgson, a vicar and teacher. He first told the story *Alice's Adventures Underground* to amuse his young friend, Alice Liddell, during a boat trip. She asked him to write it down and in 1865 it was published with the title *Alice's Adventures in Wonderland*. A sequel, *Through the Looking-Glass, and What Alice Found There*, was published six years later.

Designed by Katarina Dragoslavic

Cover design by Russell Punter

First published in 2006 by Usborne Publishing Ltd.,
Usborne House, 83-85 Saffron Hill, London EC1N 8RT, England.
www.usborne.com
Copyright © 2006 Usborne Publishing Ltd.

The Story of
Toilets,
Telephones
& other useful inventions

Katie Daynes

Illustrated by
Adam Larkum

Reading Consultant: Alison Kelly
Roehampton University

Contents

Chapter 1

The story of toilets

Long ago, people didn't even have houses, so building a toilet was the last thing on their minds.

3

Then they learned to farm the land and made themselves homes to live in.

Some built a toilet in the yard, but it was only a hole in the ground. When the hole filled up, they simply covered it with mud and dug another. This worked fine... until they ran out of space.

The ancient Romans had a much better idea – public toilets. They placed a long, stone slab with holes over a deep trench. Then they decorated the toilet room with marble and mosaics.

Going to the toilet became
a great way to meet people.
Romans sat in a row, chatting
about politics and plays.
Below them, water flowed
through the trench and
washed everything away.

At Roman banquets, rich guests didn't even have to leave the room. They simply asked a slave to bring in a silver pot and filled it there and then.

In later times, people were more shy about these things. Lords and ladies preferred to go alone, using fancy, cushioned toilet boxes, often hidden behind a curtain.

These were a lot more comfortable – though someone then had to empty them.

Castles and fortresses had
basic toilets built into their
design. Some jutted out from
the main building,
emptying onto
the moat below.

Yuck!

Stinky moats were great
protection. No enemy wanted
to wade through them.

10

But the smells were about
to get worse. Medieval towns
were being built and everyone
had forgotten the Roman
public toilets. Luckily, they
still had pots.

These allowed people to go
in the comfort of their own
bedroom. They were known as
chamber pots.

But the pots had to be emptied and the easiest way was out of a window.

Unlucky passers-by got a yucky surprise. With nowhere for the waste to drain away, the smell on the streets was disgusting. It's a wonder anyone ever went shopping.

Kings and queens had to introduce toilet laws.

"I forbid you from dumping filth in rivers or on streets," Edward III announced to the people of London.

Where else can it go?

The problem was finally solved by laying pipes and drains underground. Toilet filth could now glide away *under* the street, not over it.

Of course, when something got stuck, the mess was awful.

In 1596, Sir John Harington, godson of Queen Elizabeth I, had a brainwave. "I'll invent a toilet that flushes!"

A royal flush!

Making the flush work properly took ages. In fact, most people didn't have a flush for another 200 years.

Many plumbers worked hard to improve toilet designs, including a man named Thomas Crapper. He set up his own Crapper plumbing shops in London and took charge of the royal toilets.

By 1880, the toilet had really arrived. Since then, only the shapes and decorations have changed.

Some are fitted into the wall...

...others are made to look like thrones.

Space toilets even have bars to stop you from floating away.

16

Today, we take toilets for granted. But spend a day in the woods and you'll soon learn how things were for our ancestors.

Telephones

Alexander Graham Bell was a boy with a mission. While his father taught deaf people how to talk, Alexander wanted to find out how words travel.

His mother was deaf, but
young Alexander found a way
to make her hear. If he talked
with his lips pressed against
her forehead, she could feel
his words and understand him.

When Bell grew up, he got a job teaching deaf people to speak. In his spare time, he loved to experiment with sound.

One day, he played a chord on a piano and heard the exact notes echo on a piano next door.

"The notes can travel through air," he realized. His mind buzzed with ideas. If all sounds could travel, perhaps he could send speech from one place to another.

21

In those days, 150 years ago, the quickest way to send messages over long distances was by telegraph. A message was tapped at one end of an electric wire...

dot dot dash dot dash dash dot dot dot dot dash dash dot dot

...and finally received at the other.

The tapping code had been invented by an American professor, Samuel Morse. But changing messages in and out of code took forever.

Bell thought long and hard about telegraph wires and speech. One day, he jumped up in excitement.

"I'll turn speech into an electric current," he thought. "Then it can travel down the telegraph wires."

In 1876, with the help of Thomas Watson, an electrical engineer, he invented a mouthpiece and an earpiece. They looked exactly the same and were joined together by an electric wire.

"When I speak into the mouthpiece, a metal flap will move," said Bell, "and my words will travel down the wire as an electric current."

"Then the flap on the
earpiece will move," added
Watson, "and I'll be able to
hear you!"

They quickly put their
theory to the test. Watson sat
alone, holding the earpiece...
Suddenly, Bell's voice
boomed out.

26

And so the life of the phone began. In 1877, Bell set off through North America and Europe to promote his new invention.

"How modern!" thought Queen Victoria, immediately ordering one for her palace.

Tell John Brown to saddle up the horses.

The first phones needed
operators to connect people.
    "Number please," said an
operator, when someone lifted
a receiver. Once the operator
had linked two telephone lines
together, a conversation
could begin.

By the late 1890s, automatic switchboards had been invented and lots of operators were out of a job. Within ten years, everyone wanted a phone.

Early phones had a handle you turned as you listened.

Then there were boxes that people spoke into...

a speaker shaped like a candlestick...

and the cradle phone.

Today, millions of people own mobiles. A phone with no wire would have really impressed Alexander Bell – especially one that can send pictures too.

Chapter 3

Frozen food

It was 1913 and an American
named Clarence Birdseye was
trading fur in northern Canada.
"How can anyone live in this
icy place?" he wondered.

A local man offered to show him around. Dressed in a thick fur coat, Birdseye joined a huddle of fishermen around three holes in the ice. Everyone was dangling a line into the chilly water.

With a sudden tug, one of the men yanked out a fish. It flipped in the air and froze, before landing on the ice with a clunk.

"Is that tonight's supper?" asked Birdseye.

"No way," replied the fisherman. "We've already got enough fish to last a month!"

34

Birdseye was amazed. Where he came from, fish went rotten and smelly within a day. Did frozen fish really keep fresh? That evening at supper he tasted the answer.

Birdseye's brain started working overtime. "At home, people would pay good money for frozen food!" he thought.

Back in America, he invented a quick freeze machine and started the world's first frozen food company – Birds Eye.

Chapter 4

Soccer nets

John Brodie was crazy about
soccer. Every Saturday he sat
in the stadium cheering as his
team won, lost or drew.

At one match, Brodie and
his friends watched their top
striker kick the ball between
the goal posts.

"Hooray!" they cheered,
but the referee shook his head.
He didn't think a goal had
been scored.

For the rest of the match, Brodie sat sulking. Then he had an idea. "I'll design a net to go behind the posts," he thought. "It will trap the ball and prove there's been a goal."

39

Chapter 5

Safety razors

King Camp Gillette was
trying to shave on a steam
train. Despite his grand name,
he was only a salesman going
to a meeting.

As the train jerked forward, he cut his chin.

"Ow!" he cried, looking at a drop of blood on his cut-throat razor. "There must be a safer way to shave..."

At the meeting, Gillette sat dabbing his chin with a blood-spotted handkerchief.

The company president was making a long, boring speech.

"Toothbrushes are big business because they always need replacing," he said. "We must sell more products that wear out quickly."

How about toothpicks?

Or toilet paper?

Years later, Gillette stood
in front of his mirror, making
a face. He'd bought a new
kind of razor, but already the
blade was blunt.

"I spend my life sharpening
blades," he thought.

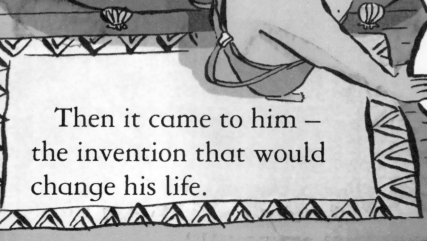

Then it came to him —
the invention that would
change his life.

"I'll make a razor with a safe, removable blade!" he cried. "When it goes blunt, you can throw it away and buy another. No one will bother sharpening any more — they'll just keep coming back for new blades!"

This is the future of shaving.

And they did.

45

Other useful inventions

Before the **wheel** was invented, 5,500 years ago, carrying things and going places took ages.

If it wasn't for Stanislau Baudry, we'd still be waiting for the bus. He started the first **bus service** in 1827 to take people to his baths outside Paris.

Until 1850, no one had a **refrigerator**. Without fridges today, the food we keep would smell awful.

In 1938, Ladislao Biro was fed up with ink pens that smudged. So, he invented a pen with quick drying ink and called it a...

46 *Biro*

When people started exploring space, it led to even more exciting inventions.

Have you noticed **bar codes** at supermarkets? They were first used to label the millions of parts that make up a spacecraft.

The material used in **firefighters' suits** and the flexible folds on **ski boots** were originally designed for astronauts.

The first **smoke detector** was made for a space station. Now most homes have one too.

Series editor: Lesley Sims

Designed by
Russell Punter and Natacha Goransky

Goal net advice:
National Museum of Football

This edition first published in 2007 by Usborne Publishing Ltd.,
Usborne House, 83-85 Saffron Hill, London EC1N 8RT, England.
www.usborne.com Copyright © 2007, 2004 Usborne Publishing Ltd.

The
Minotaur

Retold by
Russell Punter

Illustrated by Linda Cavallini

Reading consultant: Alison Kelly
Roehampton University

Contents

Some pages show you how to say unusual names.
The parts of the word in bold should be stressed.

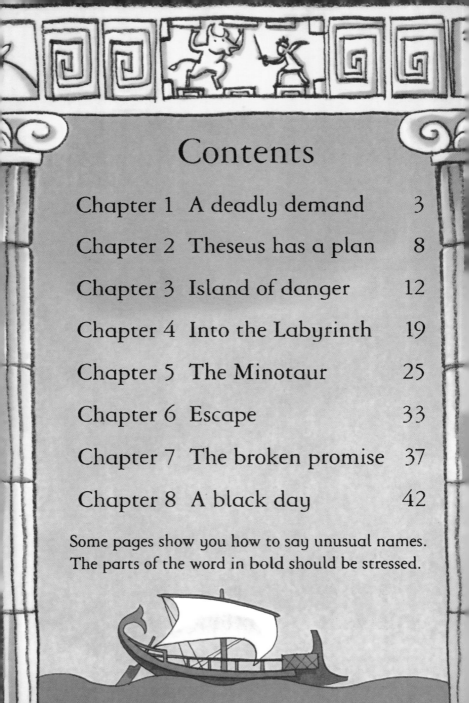

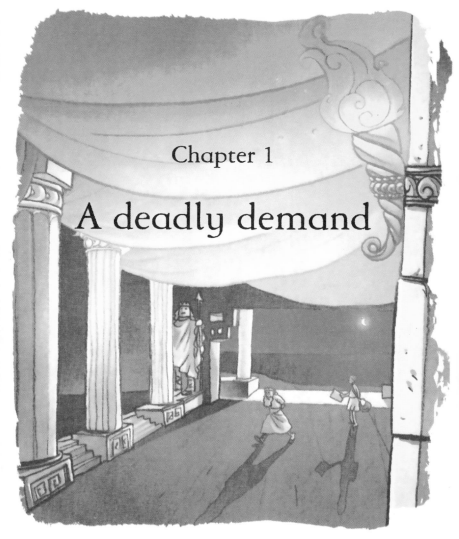

Chapter 1

A deadly demand

Long ago, a king ruled the city of Athens. One day, he received a terrible letter.

"Oh no," he sighed. "Not again. What shall I do?"

"What's wrong?" asked his son, Theseus.

King Aegeus* waved the letter under Theseus's nose. "Read this," he moaned.

*say ee-jee-oos

To: King Aegeus of Athens

Send fourteen of your people to me by the end of the month.

signed
King Minos of Crete

P.S. I want 7 men and 7 women
P.P.S. If you don't do as I ask, there will be <u>trouble!</u>

I don't understand.

"Every nine years, King Minos demands fourteen people from Athens," said Aegeus.

"He sends them into a giant maze called the Labyrinth."

"Sounds fun," said Theseus.
"Fun?" spluttered his father.
"At the heart of the Labyrinth
is a Minotaur*."

"It's a terrible creature."
Aegeus shivered. "It's half man,
half bull... and it eats people!"

7

*say **my**-n -tore

Chapter 2

Theseus has a plan

"I have an idea," said Theseus.
"I'll be one of the seven men."

"Are you crazy?" said his
father. "The Minotaur will eat
you alive."

"Don't worry, Dad," said
Theseus. "I'm the best sword
fighter in Athens."

Aegeus sighed. "Even if you kill the monster, no one has ever escaped the Labyrinth."

"I'll find a way out somehow," said Theseus confidently.

King Aegeus begged his son not to go. But it was no use.

10

Theseus boarded a
ship with the others.
Aegeus was still very
worried.

"If Theseus survives," he said
to the sailors, "fly white sails
on the ship when you return."

Chapter 3

Island of danger

Wind filled the ship's sails.
Theseus and the others were
on their way.

Before they arrived at Crete, Theseus hid his sword under his clothes. Soldiers were waiting for them as they docked.

"Welcome!" roared King Minos. "Enjoy your last meal. At dawn you enter the Labyrinth."

Guards took the prisoners away. They locked them in a dark, dank dungeon.

That night, Ariadne*, the king's daughter, took them bread and water.

As soon as she saw Theseus, Ariadne fell madly in love.

15

"I can't let you spend the rest of your life in the Labyrinth," she whispered.

"Then help me to kill the Minotaur and escape," said Theseus.

Ariadne thought for a
moment. "Very well," she said.
"If you promise to marry me."

"Er, all right," Theseus
agreed nervously.

"Take this ball of magic string," said Ariadne.

String?

"Tie it to the entrance of the Labyrinth, as you go in."
"Then what?" asked Theseus.
"You'll see," smiled Ariadne.

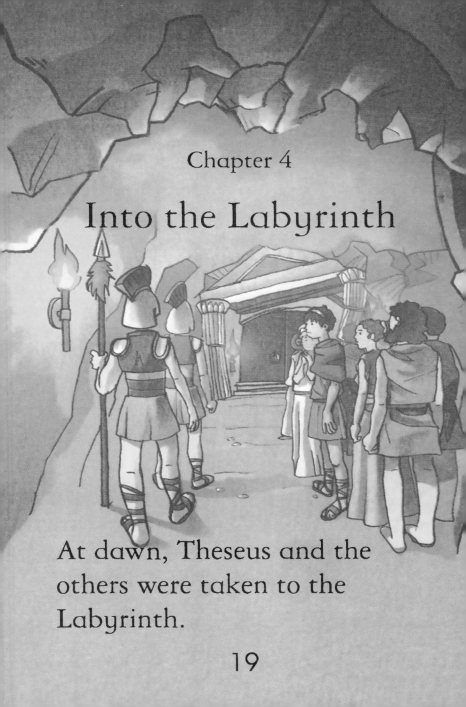

Chapter 4

Into the Labyrinth

At dawn, Theseus and the others were taken to the Labyrinth.

When the guards weren't looking, Theseus tied one end of his string to a rock.

"Get inside, all of you!" shouted a guard. One by one, they entered the Labyrinth.

As Theseus went in, the ball
of string jumped from his hand.

Theseus couldn't believe his
eyes. The string rolled along
the ground by itself.

21

"Which way shall we go?"
said the others.

"Follow me!" said Theseus.

The magical string wound this way and that. Soon they were deep inside the Labyrinth.

The ball of string stopped in a cave.

"Now what?" asked one of the women. **Raaaggghh!**

A terrifying roar echoed around them.

"It's the Minotaur," cried Theseus, "coming this way!"

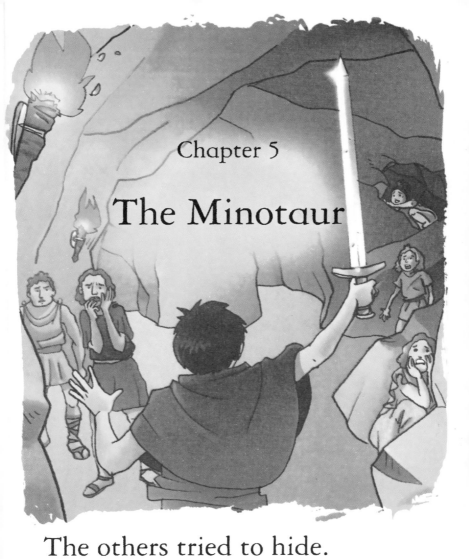

Chapter 5

The Minotaur

The others tried to hide.
"Don't worry," said Theseus,
pulling out his sword.

The ground shook. Heavy footsteps came nearer... and nearer. The mighty Minotaur stormed into the cave.

Raaaggghh!

The Minotaur gave a loud
snort. Clouds of smelly breath
shot from its nostrils.

With an ear-splitting roar,
it charged. The young prince
swung his sword at the
terrifying monster.

The Minotaur was wounded,
but it didn't give up. It chased
Theseus around the cave.

"Come on, Theseus!" shouted
the others. "Don't let it get us."

Theseus tried to fight back, but the monster dodged every blow. Then Theseus tripped.

He looked up to see the Minotaur looming overhead. The hungry creature reached out to grab him.

With one last thrust,
Theseus plunged his sword
into the monster's chest.

The Minotaur gave a
blood-chilling cry, and fell
to the ground with a thud.

31

"Well done, Theseus!" cried
the others. "You've saved us."

"It's not over yet," puffed
Theseus. "We still have to find
a way out."

Chapter 6

Escape

Theseus noticed the magic string lying on the ground. "Perhaps this will help us."

Following the trail of string,
Theseus led the others out of
the Labyrinth.

Theseus crept up behind the guards at the entrance. Swiftly, he tied them up with the string.

Theseus found Ariadne
waiting at the dock. He
climbed aboard his ship.

I knew you'd
escape.

"Don't forget your promise to
marry me," said Ariadne.
"Promise?" said Theseus.
"Oh, er, yes. Come with us."

Chapter 7

The broken promise

On the voyage home, the ship
stopped at the island of Naxos.
"We'll spend the night here,"
said Theseus.

But Theseus couldn't sleep.
He didn't want to marry King
Minos's daughter.

So while Ariadne was asleep,
he woke the others. He ordered
them back to the ship, and
they sailed away.

38

When Ariadne woke the next morning, she was heartbroken. She cried to the gods for revenge.

A god called Dionysus*
appeared and Ariadne told
him her tale.

Dionysus felt sorry for
Ariadne. "I will punish Theseus
for breaking his promise to
you," he declared.

40

Dionysus cast a spell across the sea. "Forget, sailors!" he boomed. "Forget, forget, forget!"

Chapter 8

A black day

Theseus was nearly home.
"I can't wait to be back in
Athens," he told a sailor.

"Um, me too," said the man,
looking up at the black sails.
"What's the matter?"
asked Theseus.

"I think I was supposed to do
something," replied the sailor.
"But I can't remember what."

"That's funny," said another
sailor. "I had the same feeling."
"And me," cried a third.

"Oh well," said Theseus, "I'm
sure it was nothing important."

Up on the cliffs, King Aegeus looked out to sea. "My son's ship has returned," he cried.

"Oh no, black sails!" he sobbed. "Theseus must be dead."

Aegeus felt terrible. He jumped into the sea and was never seen again.

When Theseus landed, he heard the dreadful news about his father.

Theseus had beaten the Minotaur and escaped from the Labyrinth...

but his father never knew.

About the Minotaur legend

The story of the Minotaur was first told about 3,000 years ago in ancient Greece. Some people think that the noisy Minotaur was invented to explain earthquakes. In 1900, archeologists discovered underground storage passages on Crete. Perhaps they were the inspiration for the Labyrinth?

Usborne Quicklinks
To find out more about ancient Greece, go to the Usborne Quicklinks Website at
www.usborne-quicklinks.com
Read the internet safety guidelines, and then type the keywords "The Minotaur".

Series editor: Lesley Sims

First published in 2009 by Usborne Publishing Ltd., Usborne House, 83-85 Saffron Hill, London EC1N 8RT, England. www.usborne.com
Copyright © 2009 Usborne Publishing Ltd.

The Wizard of Oz

L. Frank Baum

Retold by Rosie Dickins

Illustrated by Mauro Evangelista

Reading consultant: Alison Kelly
Roehampton University

Contents

Chapter 1

The cyclone

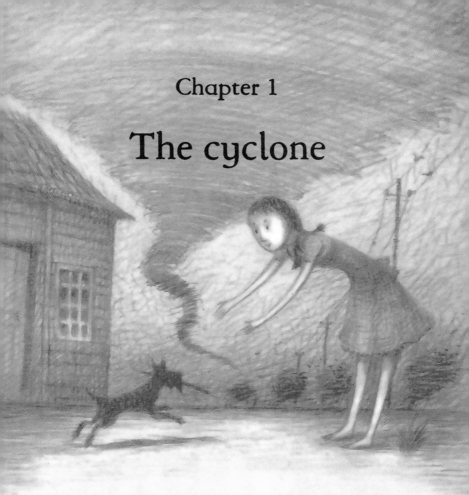

Dorothy lived on a lonely farm in Kansas, with only her Uncle Henry, her Aunt Em and her little dog Toto for company. One day, as they played outside, the sky grew dark...

Then the wind whipped up, with a chilling moan.

"There's a cyclone coming," called her Uncle Henry. "Quick, into the cellar!"

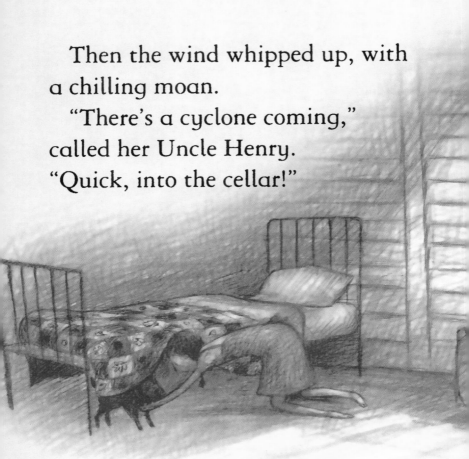

In a panic, Toto ran to hide under her bed. Dorothy dashed after him, as the wind shrieked and the whole house shook.

With a mighty wrench, the
cyclone whirled the house into the
sky. Dorothy shivered with terror.
"What will happen to us Toto?"
she whispered.

The house sailed through the sky for hours... Suddenly, with a sickening jolt, they landed.

"Welcome to Oz," cried a man in a pointed hat, "and thank you! You've just killed the Wicked Witch of the East and set us free."

"Who? What?" asked Dorothy, horrified. "I haven't killed anyone."

"Well, your house did," a woman told her. "Look!" Two scrawny legs stuck out from under a wall.

As Dorothy looked,
the legs vanished, leaving only a
pair of silvery shoes behind. The
woman handed them to Dorothy.

"These are yours now," she said.

Dorothy took the shoes in a daze. "Do you know the way to Kansas?" she asked. "I have to go home."

The strangers shook their heads.

"Maybe the Great Wizard can help," suggested the woman. "He lives in Emerald City, at the end of the yellow brick road..."

Chapter 2

A scarecrow, a tinman and a lion

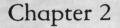

Emerald City

Dorothy packed some food and set out for the city at once. She walked briskly along the yellow road, her silver shoes tinkling on the bricks.

9

As she passed a field, a scarecrow winked at her. Dorothy jumped in surprise.

"How do you do?" he asked.

"He talks too!" thought Dorothy. "H-hello," she said, shyly. "How are you?"

"Not so good," the scarecrow said. "It's very boring stuck up here..."

"Where are you off to?" he asked, a moment later.

"To see the wizard," Dorothy replied. "I need help to get home."

"Wizard? What wizard?" said the scarecrow. "I don't know anything," he added sadly. "I have no brains."

"Oh dear," said Dorothy. "Well, why don't you come with me?"

Maybe the wizard could give you some brains.

So they went on together. The land grew wilder until, by evening, they were walking through a thick forest. That night, they sheltered in a log cabin.

Dorothy woke to hear strange groans. A man made of tin was standing, as still as a statue, by a pile of logs.

"Are you alright?" she asked.

"No!" the tinman grunted. "I can't move. I was caught in the rain and I've rusted."

Dorothy spotted an oil can and swiftly oiled the tinman's joints.

"Thank you," he sighed. "I might have stood there forever. What brings you here?"

"The scarecrow and I are going to see the Great Wizard," Dorothy told him. "I want to go home and the scarecrow wants a brain."

The tinman thought for a second. "Do you think the wizard could give me a heart?" he asked.

"I expect so," said Dorothy.

"Then I'll come too," he decided.

The new companions had just set
off when a lion leaped onto the
road. Opening his slobbery jaws,
he gave a terrible roar.

As the lion towered over Toto, Dorothy smacked him on the nose.

"Stop it!" she cried. "You must be a coward to pick on a little dog."

The lion looked ashamed. "You're right," he mumbled. "I only roar to make people run away."

"You should ask the wizard for courage," said Dorothy and told him where they were going.

The lion nodded eagerly. "I'll come with you!" he growled.

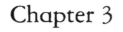

Chapter 3

A dangerous journey

The companions strolled on to the edge of the forest, where a deep ditch barred their way.

"We're stuck," sighed the lion.

But the scarecrow had an idea. "If the tinman chops down this tree, we could use it to cross the ditch."

The tree made a perfect bridge. They were almost across when they heard fierce growls from behind.

"A tiger monster!" whimpered the lion. "We're all doomed..."

"Quick tinman!" ordered the scarecrow. "Chop away the tree."

The tree bridge fell with a
crash and the monster plummeted
into the ditch. Dorothy and her
friends hurried on. Soon, they
arrived at a broad river.

"We need a raft," declared the
scarecrow and the tinman set to
work once again.

19

The raft bobbed along happily until they reached the middle of the river. Here, the current was so strong, it swept them away.

The lion dived in, took hold of the raft and swam as hard as he could. Slowly, he pulled them ashore.

Safely over the river, they went on, through a field bursting with poppies. A spicy scent filled the air and Dorothy felt drowsy. She sank into the flowers and wouldn't wake.

"It's the poppies..." yawned the lion. "They've sent... her... to sleep."

Luckily, the tinman and the scarecrow – who weren't made of flesh – stayed wide awake.

"Run!" the scarecrow ordered the lion. "We'll bring Dorothy."

The lion bounded ahead, leaving the scarecrow and tinman to carry Dorothy and Toto from the field.

On and on the pair staggered.
Almost at the end of the poppies
they passed the lion – fast asleep.
Quickly, they laid Dorothy in
the open air to recover and went
back. With much pushing and
pulling, grunting and groaning,
they dragged the lion to safety.

Chapter 4

Emerald City

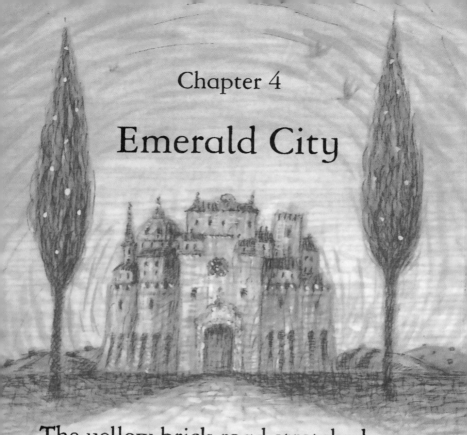

The yellow brick road stretched off into the distance, but on the horizon, something sparkled. Soon, a vast green city loomed ahead.

"We've made it!" said Dorothy.

"Look," added the lion, pointing to a gate studded with emeralds.

Dorothy knocked on the gate and
a man in a green uniform appeared.
"Yes?" he said.
"Please may we see the Great
Wizard?" asked Dorothy.

"I can take you to his palace,"
said the man, "but you must wear
glasses. Our city is dazzling." And
he pulled out a pair of green glasses
for each of them, including Toto.

Inside, the city was an incredible
sight. The streets and houses were
built of shining green marble and
all the people wore green. The
shops sold green popcorn, green
hats and green shoes. Everything
was green – even the sky.

The gatekeeper led them to a grand palace.

"We'd like to see the wizard," Dorothy told the soldier on guard.

"Enter one at a time," he barked. "You first."

Nervously, Dorothy went inside.
"I am the wizard," boomed a
giant head. "Why do you seek me?"
Dorothy took a deep breath. "Can
you send me home to Kansas?"
The head frowned. "Only if you
do something for me first," it
snapped. "Kill the Wicked Witch
of the West. Now go!"

Then the scarecrow stepped in.
A lady with green wings was
sitting on the throne. "I am the
wizard," she said gently. "What
do you seek?"

"I am only a scarecrow, stuffed
with straw. I ask you for brains."

First, kill the Wicked Witch of the West. Now go!

Whatever you want, you must first kill the Wicked Witch of the West!

The tinman saw a terrible beast with five eyes and five limbs.

"I am the wizard," roared the beast. "Why do you seek me?"

"I am made of tin and have no heart. Please give me a heart, so I can love and be happy," he begged. But he too was turned away.

30

The lion went last. Now, above the throne, blazed a ball of fire.

"I am the wizard," hissed the ball. "Why do you seek me?"

"I am a c-c-coward," stammered the lion. "I want c-c-courage, so I may truly be King of the Beasts."

First, kill the Wicked Witch of the West. Now go!

Outside the palace, the friends were glum. "We can't defeat a witch," moaned the scarecrow.

"But we can try," said the lion. So they walked back to the gate.

"Good luck," said the gatekeeper, pointing out the path to the witch's castle. "You'll need it!"

Chapter 5

The Wicked Witch

The Wicked Witch of the West had only one eye, but it saw a long way. She spotted the friends as they left the city. "Strangers coming here?" she screeched. She blew a whistle and a pack of wolves ran up. "Tear the strangers to shreds," she said.

33

The wolves bared their teeth and dashed away. Luckily, the tinman heard them coming.

As the first
wolf reached them,
he chopped off its head. Again and
again he swung his hatchet, until
all the wolves lay dead.

The witch scowled. She blew her whistle twice and a flock of crows flew down. "Peck the strangers to pieces," she snapped.

This time, the scarecrow saw them coming. As the first crow flew at him, the scarecrow grabbed him and wrung his neck. One by one, he wrung the neck of every single crow.

Now the witch was furious. She blew three times on her whistle to fetch a swarm of bees. "Sting the strangers to death!" she screamed.

Quickly, the scarecrow scattered straw over Dorothy, Toto and the lion to hide them. The bees tried to attack the tinman instead, but they snapped their stingers on his hard, tin body and died.

The witch gnashed her teeth, but she had one last trick up her sleeve – a cap which gave its owner three wishes. The witch had one wish left.

As she put on the cap, a crowd of magic monkeys appeared in a rush of wings. "Kill the strangers!" she howled. "Except the lion. I want him as my slave."

The monkeys flew off and seized the friends. They pulled out the scarecrow's stuffing and dropped him in the trees. They threw the tinman onto a rocky plain, smashing him to pieces. And they tied up the lion to carry him to the castle.

But at Dorothy, they stopped. "We can't hurt her," they said. "Let's take her to the witch."

Dorothy didn't know it, but the silver shoes gave her great power. The witch gulped when she saw them... until she noticed how frightened Dorothy was.

"She doesn't know about the shoes!" the witch thought gleefully, and set Dorothy to work.

The lion was tied up outside. Dorothy couldn't see how they would ever escape. Every way out was guarded by the witch's slaves.

But the witch had lost much of her power. "My wolves, my crows, my bees... all dead," she thought angrily. "Even my cap has no more wishes left. Well, I must steal those silver shoes."

Silently, the witch put an invisible
iron bar on the ground. Dorothy
tripped over it and one of her shoes
flew off. The witch pounced on it.

"Give me back my shoe," said
Dorothy crossly.

"Never," cackled the witch. "And
I shall steal the other one too!"

Dorothy was so angry she threw
a pail of water over the witch. At
once, the witch began to shrink.

"Agh! I'm melting..." she wailed.

Soon, all that was left of the witch
was a brown puddle and one silver
shoe. Dorothy hastily put her shoe
back on and raced out to the lion.

"The witch is dead!" she shouted.

Chapter 6

The wizard's trick

The witch's slaves danced with joy and helped Dorothy and the lion look for their friends. It didn't take long to find the battered remains of the scarecrow and the tinman.

We're free!

The tinman was soon put back together and after the scarecrow had been stuffed with fresh straw, he felt as good as new.

"Now," said Dorothy, "let's go and claim our rewards!" So they packed her basket with food from the witch's kitchen, covered it with a cloth cap and set off.

After several hours, they stopped for lunch. "I can't wait to see the wizard," said Dorothy, as she unpacked the basket.

I wish we were in Emerald City!

There was a fluttering of wings and, to everyone's surprise, the magic monkeys appeared.

All at once, the friends were
flying through the air. Before long,
they could see the shining roofs of
Emerald City. The monkeys set
them down, bowed and flew away.

The wizard kept them waiting
for ages. Finally, a soldier with a
green beard ushered them in.

This time, the room was empty,
but a voice echoed, "I am the
wizard. Why do you seek me?"

"To claim our rewards," said the
friends. "The Wicked Witch is dead."

"But..." began the voice.

"We want our rewards!" roared
the lion. Toto jumped in fright and
knocked over a screen in the corner...

...to reveal a little old man, with fuzzy hair and glasses.

"Who are you?" demanded the tinman, waving his hatchet.

"I'm the wizard," croaked the man. "But you can call me Oz."

"What about the head — the lady — the beast — the ball of fire?" cried the friends.

"Um, they were tricks," Oz said, sheepishly. "I'm not a real wizard. I'm not even from here. I was in a hot-air balloon that blew off-course. Since I appeared from the sky, the people thought I was a wizard."

"They asked me to rule them and I built Emerald City. Isn't it green?" Oz asked proudly. "Of course, you have to wear green-tinted glasses for the full effect," he admitted.

"The witches were my only fear. I was so glad when your house killed the first one. I would have said anything to get rid of the other."

"But what about our rewards?" asked the friends together.

"You don't need them," Oz replied. "Scarecrow, you're full of ideas. Lion, you're brave, you just lack confidence. And tinman, hearts make most people unhappy."

"But you promised!" they said.

Oz sighed. "I'll do my best."

Can you send me home to Kansas?

I'll try.

Chapter 7

Oz's rewards

Oz summoned everyone the very next day. "Scarecrow first," he said.

He took the scarecrow's head and tipped in a handful of pins. "This will make you as sharp as a pin!"

And the scarecrow felt very wise.

Next came the tinman. "Here's your heart," Oz said, giving him a heart-shaped cushion. "It's a very kind one." The tinman beamed.

Then Oz produced a green bottle. "This is courage," he told the lion.

The lion gulped it down. "Now I feel brave!" he roared.

Finally, Oz led
Dorothy to a basket.
"I mended my
balloon," he said.

We'll fly
home!

He lit a fire and hot air swelled
the balloon. The basket began to
lift. "Hurry!" Oz cried to Dorothy –
but she was looking for Toto. She
swept him up and ran to the basket.

55

Just as she reached it, a rope
snapped and the balloon took off.
"Come back!" she called.

It was too late. "Now I'll never
get home," she wept. Her friends
hated to see her so unhappy. The
scarecrow racked his new brains.

"I know," he said. "Wish for the magic monkeys to take you!"

But they couldn't help. "We can't leave this land," they explained.

Then a soldier spoke up. "Why not ask the Good Witch Glinda?"

So Dorothy and her friends set off once more.

Chapter 8

Home again

Glinda lived far in the south. It would have been a difficult journey without the cap's third wish.

"Please take us to Glinda," said Dorothy and the monkeys carried them to a beautiful castle.

"What can I do for you?" Glinda asked her visitors kindly.

Dorothy told her the whole story. "And now I just want to go home," she finished.

"Bless you," said Glinda, smiling. "I'm sure I can get you all home. But I'll need the wishing cap."

She turned to the others. "What will you do when Dorothy leaves?"

"I'll live in Emerald City," the scarecrow told her.

"I'll go back to my cabin," said the tinman.

"And I'll go home to the forest," added the lion.

"I'll ask the monkeys to take you all where you wish," said Glinda. "Then I'll set them free."

"You're very kind," said Dorothy,
"but please, how can I get home?"

"Your silver shoes will take you,"
replied Glinda. "Just knock the
heels together three times and say
where you want to go."

With glistening eyes,
Dorothy said goodbye to
her friends. Then she hugged
Toto tightly and clicked her heels
together. "Take me home!"
she cried.

At once, she was whirling
through the air... and rolling on
the soft grass of a familiar field.

Aunt Em dropped her watering can and rushed over. "My darling child!" she said, covering Dorothy with kisses. "Wherever did you come from?"

"From Oz," said Dorothy. "And oh, Aunt Em, I'm so glad to be home!"

L. Frank Baum grew up in a wealthy American family. He had several jobs before becoming a writer, including running a store and breeding chickens. But he always loved telling stories – and people loved reading them. "The Wizard of Oz" was an instant hit when it was published, sparking off a whole series of books set in Oz, as well as a famous film.

Series editor: Lesley Sims
Designed by Katarina Dragoslavic

First published in 2006 by Usborne Publishing Ltd.,
Usborne House, 83-85 Saffron Hill, London EC1N 8RT, England.
www.usborne.com

Stories of
GHOSTS

Russell Punter

Illustrated by
Mike Phillips

Reading Consultant: Alison Kelly
Roehampton University

Contents

Chapter 1

The story of Shiverham Hall

Have a frightful stay, madam.

Shiverham Hall was a hotel with a difference. All the guests were dead.

3

Ghosts came from the spirit world to be greeted by Shiverham's spooky staff.

There were twenty-two ice-cold bedrooms...

Aahh, I..I..lovely.

a poltergeist-powered jacuzzi...

and a string quartet playing haunting tunes.

No living soul dared visit the
hotel. It was far too creepy. The
ghosts were left in peace.

Then, one afternoon, the
hotel's deathly hush was
shattered.

SLAM!

Most of the ghosts were
napping. Mr. Quiver, the hotel
manager, had come down for
a glass of water.

Suddenly, a round-faced man flung open the front door and strode up to the reception desk.

"This is just what I've been looking for," he boomed.

A tall, thin man scuttled in after him.

"Um, are you sure, Mr. Slate?" he asked nervously.

"Of course I'm sure, Simkins," barked Slate. "This will make the perfect site for my new hotel. I've had it all designed."

Slate proudly spread out a large plan in front of his assistant. Behind them, Mr. Quiver sneaked up to get a better look.

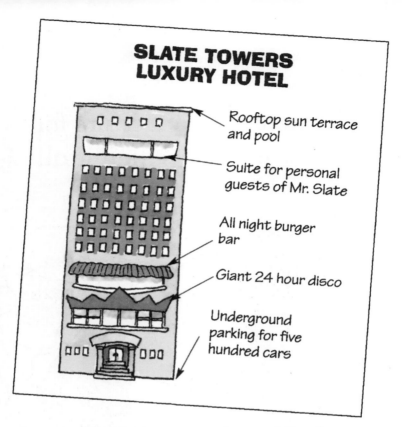

SLATE TOWERS LUXURY HOTEL

Rooftop sun terrace and pool

Suite for personal guests of Mr. Slate

All night burger bar

Giant 24 hour disco

Underground parking for five hundred cars

Mr. Quiver was horrified. "I'll have this place demolished in no time," Slate went on. "But perhaps I'll look around and see if there's anything worth saving first."

8

"Don't be too long," gulped Simkins. "They say the place is haunted."

"Ridiculous!" cried Slate. "Ghosts don't exist. And I'll stay the night to prove it."

"We don't exist, eh?" thought Mr. Quiver, as he floated upstairs.

Minutes later, he gathered the hotel staff together. No one was happy about Slate's plans.

"We'll never get any peace in his noisy new hotel," wailed Charlie the waiter.

"And where will our ghostly guests go?" asked Elsie the maid.

"Slate will have to be frightened off," said Mr. Quiver. "As soon as it gets dark, we'll start haunting."

10

Slate was climbing the
rickety stairs to bed, when
Mr. Quiver appeared in front
of him.

Slate looked a little surprised.
But then he shrugged.

"Out of my way, potato
head!" he shouted.

11

Mr. Quiver had never been so insulted in his life. Or his death.

But the ghosts weren't finished yet. As Slate brushed his teeth, Igor the porter popped up through the plughole.

The staff didn't give up.
That night, Slate was visited
by a stream of ghosts...

Elsie brought the
bed sheets to life.

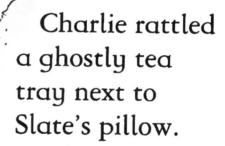

Charlie rattled
a ghostly tea
tray next to
Slate's pillow.

Cora the cook
sent possessed
pots flying
through the air.

Even the hotel guests tried to put the shivers up the unwelcome visitor.

Sir Gauntlet showed off his battle scars.

Lord Doublet lost his head.

And Miss Gauntly, the wailing lady, moaned the entire night.

But none of them could raise a single goosebump.

Next morning, Mr. Quiver listened in on Slate's meeting with Simkins.

"You were right," said Slate. "This place *is* full of ghosts."

"R..r..really?" stuttered Simkins, nervously. "So you'll forget your plans?"

"No way!" said Slate. "People will pay even more to

stay in a luxury *haunted* hotel. I'll soon have those spooks hard at work."

I'll make a fortune!

Within minutes, the ghosts' tragic tale appeared on the Spirit World Wide Web.

Ghosts' Online Gazette

SO LONG SHIVERHAM!

HISTORIC HOTEL TO BE FLATTENED - STAFF FACE SLAVERY TO SLATE

The staff of Shiverham Hall are to become a 'tourist attraction' in a new hotel built by Percival Slate.

Percival Slate

It looked as if the ghosts' peaceful life was coming to an end. Next day, the staff watched from the shadows as Slate dreamed of what was to come.

Suddenly, a spooky figure appeared from nowhere. "Yoo hoo!" she cried.

"Aha!" said Slate. "Another spook, and a very ugly one."

"Don't you recognize me Percy?" said the ghost. "It's me, your Great Aunt Mabel!"

Slate's ghostly aunt planted a slobbery wet kiss on his cheek. Slate's face turned bright red.

"I read all about you on The Ghosts' Gazette website," said Mabel. "So I've decided to come and live in your lovely new hotel."

Live here? B..b..but...

"I'll look after you, Percy," cried Mabel. "I'll feed you up on my special cabbage soup and I'll make sure you get a bath and a big kiss every bedtime!"

Slate had been terrified of his aunt when she was alive. Now she was even scarier.

"I've ch..changed my mind," he stammered, tore up his plans, and ran.

All the ghosts cheered. Mr. Quiver approached Great Aunt Mabel and bowed.

"Thank you, madam," he said. "Please stay as our guest for as long as you want – for free."

Chapter 2

School for spooks

Tammy Tremble was learning how to be a ghost. But her first week at Creepy College had been a disaster.

Things began badly on Monday. Miss Hover, the poltergeist, had shown the class how to make objects float in mid-air...

...but Tammy couldn't seem to get anything off the ground.

On Tuesday, Tammy took a
fright class with Miss Screech.
But no one was remotely
scared by her efforts — not
even Marley, the school cat.

On Wednesday came Miss Faintly's lesson on how to walk through walls. The rest of the class slid through with ease and received gold stars.

The only stars Tammy saw were the ones spinning around her swollen head.

By the end of the week, Tammy was the unhappiest pupil in the school.

I'm never going to make the ghostly grade.

While the rest of the college went on a haunting field trip, Tammy had to stay behind and study her spookery.

Slowly, Tammy's skills improved – but could she keep them up?

She was taking a well-earned rest, when a cloud of smoke wafted by.

Marley the cat had knocked over one of Miss Screech's torches. The school was on fire! Tammy had to call for help.

The only phone in the school was in Miss Creepy's study. When Tammy got there, she found the door locked.

There was only one thing to do. Thinking back to Miss Faintly's lesson, Tammy crossed her fingers and charged at the door.

To her amazement, Tammy
found herself on the other side.
She'd done it at last!

Tammy quickly called the
firefighters, but they couldn't
get there for fifteen minutes.

She had to find a way to put
out the fire – and fast. Tammy
opened a window and floated
out of the school in search of
help.

She was hovering over a nearby construction site, when she saw just what she needed.

Can I borrow your truck, please?

Get back to school, kid.

Getting through the study wall had given Tammy new confidence. Now she was ready to try her scaring skills.

Woooooooo!

Help!

The driver leapt out of his cab in terror.

Now came Tammy's biggest test. She concentrated on the truck. It was a lot heavier than a toad.

Using all her energy, Tammy lifted the truck into the air. Moments later, it was hovering above the blaze.

Tammy made one last effort
and flipped the truck over. Its
load of sand swamped the
flames. Within seconds, the
fire was out.

At that moment, the
firefighters arrived. Miss
Creepy and the rest of the
school weren't far behind.

The students found Tammy
lying in an exhausted heap.
"What happened?" cried
Miss Creepy.

As the firefighters made sure
everything was okay, a tired
Tammy told her story.

That evening, Tammy was
the star of a special ceremony
in front of the whole of Creepy
College. But she was too
sleepy to enjoy it.

Perhaps when she woke up,
someone would tell her she
was now a Grade A spook.

Chapter 3

The tale of the haunted TV

One Saturday afternoon, Glen Goggle was watching TV. Suddenly the set made a funny fizzing noise and the screen went black.

Glen's dad called out Mr.
Sparks, the repairman.

Mr. Sparks put the television
in his van and returned with a
battered-looking replacement.
Glen had never seen such an
ancient TV set.

"It's better than nothing," said Mr. Goggle.

Glen's parents had no problems watching the TV. But the first time that Glen tuned in, something strange happened.

Hey! This isn't *Cartoon Club*.

A man in strange clothes appeared on the screen and burst into song.

Harry was a terrible singer. But he was so funny, Glen didn't mind missing the cartoons.

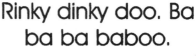

The next time Glen switched on, Harry appeared again. This time he was dressed as a magician.

Prepare to be amazed.

This show was even funnier than the last. Every trick Harry did went wrong.

38

The useless magician made
Glen laugh so much, he had to
turn off the TV to stop his
sides from aching.

39

Next day, Harry tried to dance and kept tripping over his own feet. Although Harry was funny, Glen was starting to miss the cartoons.

Glen was about to switch channels, when Harry fell forward – and came through the TV screen. Then he grew to full size before Glen's astonished eyes.

Whoops!

40

Glen was amazed.

"Sorry," panted Harry. "I should have taken more dance lessons when I was alive."

Glen gulped. "You mean, you're a g...g..."

"I always wanted to be on television," said Harry. "So when I became a ghost, I decided to haunt this set."

You were very funny.

I didn't mean to be.

"I can't rest easy in the spirit world until I'm a star," he sighed.
Glen felt sorry for Harry. He offered to let him stay if he stopped haunting the TV.

Harry spent the next few days moping in Glen's room.

Then one afternoon, Glen showed him a ticket. "Look where we're going," he said, with a grin.

Come and watch

TALENT TIME

The Top TV Talent Contest
being recorded
Saturday October 4 / 3.30pm
at XYZ TV Studios
BIG CASH PRIZE FOR THE TOP ACT!

Harry was full of excitement. He'd never seen a TV show being made before.

Glen wasn't sure if spooks
were allowed in TV studios.
Harry shrank himself down so
Glen could smuggle him inside.

Glen was relieved when he
reached his seat in the audience.
Harry peeked out as the lights
dimmed and the show began.

There were singers, dancers and comedians. Glen thought they were great, but Harry did nothing but grumble.

Glen didn't notice the ghost float away. So he got a shock when a full-size Harry suddenly appeared on stage.

Harry pushed the other contestants aside and went into his act.

He sang terrible songs...

he messed up his magic tricks...

and he finished with his clumsy dance routine.

The audience roared with laughter. Harry won first prize as the star of the show. He called Glen on stage to say thank you.

With a big grin on his face, Harry faded away.
Glen grinned too. Harry had given him the prize money to buy a brand new TV.

Series editor:
Lesley Sims

This edition first published in 2007 by Usborne Publishing Ltd.,
Usborne House, 83-85 Saffron Hill, London EC1N 8RT, England.
www.usborne.com
Copyright © 2007, 2004 Usborne Publishing Ltd.

The Burglar's Breakfast

Felicity Everett

Adapted by Lesley Sims

Illustrated by Christyan Fox

Reading Consultant: Alison Kelly
Roehampton University

Contents

Chapter 1

Breakfast!

Alfie Briggs was a burglar.
But he wasn't a good one.
Tonight, he'd stolen a broken
lawn mower and a bird...

After a hard night, Alfie liked to go home to a tasty breakfast.

Breakfast was his main meal of the day. He always ate at least three courses.

He tried to
make sure he never
ran out of the five
breakfast foods
he liked best.

Cornflakes

Waffles

Buy more fruit

Looking
around his
kitchen, it
was easy to see
what they were.

7

Chapter 2

No breakfast...

Alfie's stomach gave a hungry growl. It was time for breakfast.

Mmm. What shall I have first? Cornflakes I think.

He hunted high...

...and low. But he couldn't find the cornflakes.

Just then, he noticed a
trail of cornflakes leading
out of the door...

...and up the street. It could
only mean one thing.

Someone had stolen Alfie's cornflakes.

He decided to track down the thief and get back his breakfast.

Chapter 3

On the trail

Nose pressed against his magnifying glass, Alfie followed the cornflake trail.

He followed the trail into the park. He followed it to Pets' Corner. The thief would be sorry he'd stolen from Alfie.

13

Suddenly, Alfie came face to face with the thief. The thief looked even grumpier than Alfie. What's more, he had two sharp horns.

"Er, nice goat!" said Alfie. The goat glared. Perhaps he didn't like having his breakfast interrupted.

On his way home,
Alfie thought about what
he'd have for breakfast
instead of cornflakes.

Scrambled egg.
Nice and runny with
lots of butter.

Feeling happier, he strode
along when {crunch!} Alfie
stepped on a broken egg shell
beside the hedge.

"Someone else has had
the same idea!" he said
and grinned.

He thought he knew who
that someone was.

17

Alfie knelt down. He
crawled through a hole in the
hedge. On the other side were
more broken shells and
one happy fox.

19

The fox ran off. Alfie
spotted something.

Alfie was cross. First, his cornflakes had been snaffled by a greedy goat. Now his plan for eggs had been scrambled by a cheeky fox.

He stomped home. He flung open his front door. Then he stormed into the kitchen.

Chapter 4

Cat and mouse

"Right," Alfie said, crossly. "It will have to be sardines. Now, where did I put them... Huh?"

He was staring at an empty plate. All six sardines had vanished. But this time, he had a good idea who the thief was.

TIBBLES! Keep your thieving paws to yourself.

Alfie was furious. First, no
cornflakes. Then, no eggs.
Now, no sardines. He would
have to make waffles.

24

Alfie set the table and
turned on the oven. Then
he went to get
his waffles.

Grrr! Someone had beaten
him to it. Luckily, they'd left
a trail. Alfie followed it.

The thieves hadn't eaten
the waffles. But now Alfie
didn't want to eat them either.

Chapter 5

Sugar shock

Alfie sighed. No cornflakes, no eggs, no sardines, no waffles. Was there anything to eat?

He was in luck. There was
a big juicy grapefruit in the
fruit bowl.

"Mmm, lovely," said Alfie.
He licked his lips. "I'll just
get the sugar..."

It wasn't just one sneaky creep. There were hundreds. But they were very small.

Alfie took out his magnifying glass. He'd soon find out who was making off with his sugar.

Chapter 6

Still no breakfast

By the time Alfie had solved
the mystery, there wasn't a
single grain of sugar left.

Alfie felt hungry and very,
very cross.

Then he paused. Oh dear!
Maybe this was how people
felt when he burgled their
houses. Alfie felt ashamed.

But he also still felt hungry.
There was only one thing left
to do. He would have to go
out for breakfast.

Chapter 7

Paper plan

At Rosie's Café, Alfie ate an enormous breakfast. But even that didn't cheer him up.

I don't want to be a burglar any more. But what else can I do?

As he drank his coffee, Alfie glanced at a newspaper. He read something which gave him an idea.

He took a closer look.

NEED A JOB?

Can you:
Follow trails?
Track down stolen goods?
Catch crooks?
Spot clues?
Keep a cool head?

The STOP-A-THIEF
Detective Agency
needs
YOU!

"Can I follow trails?"
thought Alfie, remembering
his trip to the park.

"Can I track down stolen goods?" he wondered.

"Without even trying!" he said.

"Can I catch crooks?" he asked himself. "I certainly can – and Tibbles won't steal my fish again!"

"Can I spot clues?" he said.
He rubbed his chin. "Ha! I
can spot clues almost invisible
to the naked eye."

Chapter 8

A new job?

"I can do all of those things!"
said Alfie. Then he read the
last line of the list.

"Can I keep a cool head?
Hmmm..."

Alfie shrugged. He hadn't
been cool about the grapefruit.
But who can keep their cool
when they're very hungry?

The Stop-A-Thief Detective Agency gave Alfie a job the same day. The boss had never known anyone like him.

Alfie caught more crooks in his first week than all the other detectives put together.

And he never stole another thing – not even breakfast.

Try these other books in
Series One:

The Dinosaurs Next Door: Stan loves living next door to Mr. Puff. His house is full of amazing things. Best of all are the dinosaur eggs — until they begin to hatch...

The Monster Gang: Starting a gang is a great idea. So is dressing up like monsters. But if everyone is in disguise, how do you know who's who?

Designed by
Amanda Gulliver,
Katarina Dragoslavic
and Maria Wheatley

This edition first published in 2007 by Usborne Publishing Ltd.,
Usborne House, 83-85 Saffron Hill, London EC1N 8RT, England.
www.usborne.com
Copyright © 2007, 2002, 1996, 1995 Usborne Publishing Ltd.

Pinocchio

Carlo Collodi

Retold by Katie Daynes

Illustrated by
Mauro Evangelista

Reading Consultant: Alison Kelly
Roehampton University

Contents

Chapter 1

A piece of wood

Once upon a time there
was... a piece of wood.
Lying in a corner of the
carpenter's workshop,
it looked just like any
other piece of wood.
The carpenter's name
was Mr. Cherry and
he needed a table leg.

"Perfect!" he said, catching sight of the wood. He rested it against his worktop and picked up a chisel.

I'll just chip off the bark...

As the chisel touched the wood, a voice cried out, "Don't hurt me!"

Mr. Cherry looked up in surprise. He was alone in the room. "I must be imagining things," he thought.

But when he tried again,
tapping the chisel against the
wood, someone screamed.

"Who's there?" shouted Mr.
Cherry. There was no answer.

Wood
can't talk,
can it?

He shook the wood and listened
carefully... nothing.
Just then, his friend
Gepetto knocked
at the door.

"I want to make a puppet," announced Gepetto.

"Good for you, macaroni hair," called a voice.

Gepetto went red in the face and glared at Mr. Cherry. "What did you say?" he shouted.

I didn't say a word.

"It must have been you," said Gepetto. "There's no one else here. But give me some wood and I might forgive you."

Mr. Cherry was happy to get rid of the strange piece of wood. The wood had other ideas and jabbed Gepetto in the tummy.

"How dare you!" Gepetto shouted, almost losing his wig. He grabbed at Mr. Cherry's arm and Mr. Cherry pushed him away.

Biff! went Gepetto, knocking off Mr. Cherry's wig. *Boff!* went Mr. Cherry and Gepetto's wig fell to the floor.

After that, the two men looked so silly, they burst out laughing. And then they weren't cross any more.

"Goodbye, my friend," said Gepetto, taking the piece of wood.

"Goodbye, Gepetto," replied Mr. Cherry. He closed the door and breathed a sigh of relief.

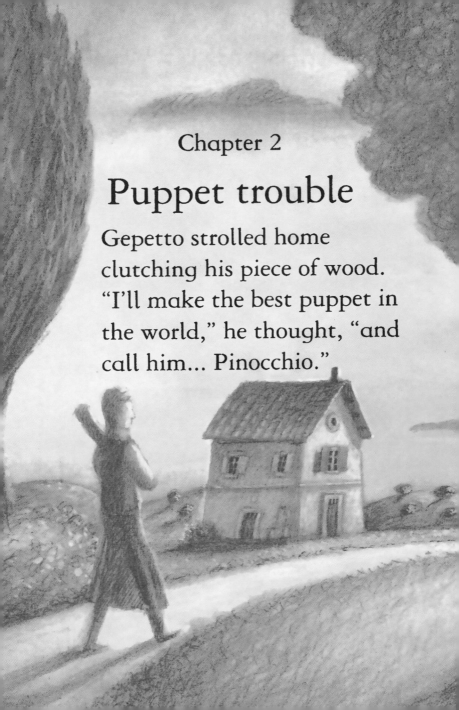

Chapter 2

Puppet trouble

Gepetto strolled home clutching his piece of wood. "I'll make the best puppet in the world," he thought, "and call him... Pinocchio."

First, he chipped at the wood to make a head with hair. Then he gave the puppet two eyes. No sooner were they finished than one of them winked.

Gepetto didn't notice. He had moved on to the puppet's nose. As he smoothed it down, the nose began to grow. Every time he chopped it off, it grew again, longer and longer.

10

Gepetto gave up on the ridiculous

nose and carved out a mouth. Before he'd even finished, the mouth laughed.

"What's so funny?" asked Gepetto. Instead of replying, the puppet stuck out its tongue.

"Behave!" said Gepetto, shaping the puppet's body. "Remember, you're only a piece of wood."

But when the legs and arms were finished, a hand reached out and snatched Gepetto's wig. Before he could say, "Stop Pinocchio!" the puppet jumped up and ran out of the house...

...slap bang into a policeman.

"What's going on here?" asked the policeman. Then he saw Gepetto, waving his chisel, and decided he looked dangerous.

"You're under arrest for threatening a puppet," the policeman said, leading Gepetto away.

13

Chapter 3

Fire!

Pinocchio skipped merrily
back to Gepetto's house.

"How nice to be all by
myself," he said, grinning.

"Cri cri cri, what about me?"
buzzed a cricket.

"Buzz off!" cried Pinocchio.

But the cricket had a lot to say.
He told Pinocchio to respect his
father. "Only good sons have a
chance of becoming *real* boys. And
real boys are better than puppets."

Pinocchio didn't like this bossy
cricket. He covered his ears, but
the cricket kept buzzing. "Shut up,
or I'll squash you!" he cried.

15

"A bad temper will get you nowhere," answered the cricket.

By this time, Pinocchio was very annoyed. He picked up a hammer and threw it at the wall.

"Oh no!" cried Pinocchio. "I didn't mean to hit you!"

The cricket couldn't reply. He was a flattened blob on the wall. Pinocchio felt very guilty for a while. Then he felt hungry.

Searching through the kitchen
cupboards,
the only food
he found was
an egg. He
cracked it
open on the
side of a
frying pan.

But instead of runny egg slipping
into the pan, a chick flew into the
air. "Thank you for freeing me,"
she twittered and
disappeared
out of the
window.

Now there was nothing to eat.
Poor Pinocchio was cold, tired and
absolutely starving. He settled in
the armchair, rested his legs on
the fireplace and fell asleep.

A knock at the door woke
Pinocchio with a jolt. There was
smoke all around him. He jumped
up – and fell down with a bump.
The fire had burned off his feet.

18

"Let me in," called Gepetto.

"I can't walk!" cried Pinocchio.

Gepetto thought the puppet was just being lazy, so he climbed in through the window.

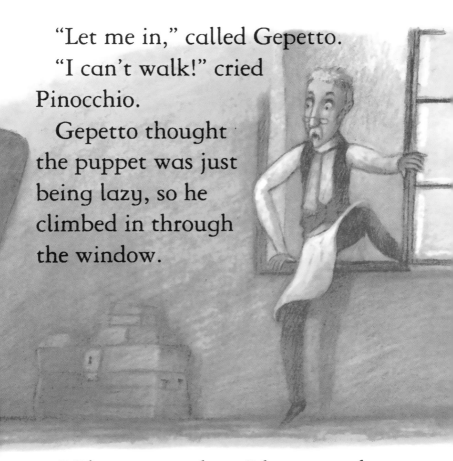

"Oh my poor boy," he gasped, seeing Pinocchio on the floor. He forgot all about his cold night in a prison cell and rushed to help his puppet son.

19

Chapter 4

A puppet show

With a new pair of feet and a full stomach, Pinocchio was a much happier puppet. "Gepetto," he said, "you're a great Dad and I've been a rotten son, but I promise to be good from now on."

Gepetto chuckled. "Really?"

"Well..." said Pinocchio, "it might be easier if I was a real boy."

"I see," replied Gepetto. "Then let's start by sending you to school."

Pinocchio frowned. He didn't like the idea of school.

All boys go to school.

That afternoon, Gepetto sold his only coat to buy his son a school book and some clothes.

In the morning, Pinocchio forced himself to smile at Gepetto as he left for his first day at school.

On the way, he noticed a crowd of people. They were standing outside a brightly painted building.

"What's going on?" he asked.

"A puppet show!" cried a man. "And it begins in ten minutes."

Pinocchio knew he should go to school, but he was longing to see a puppet show.

"I'll go to school tomorrow," he thought, and joined the crowd. When he realized he needed money for a ticket, he almost cried.

"Give me that nice, new book and I'll let you in," said the ticketmaster.

Pinocchio thought of his poor Dad selling his only coat for the book. Then he thought of a real, live puppet show. "OK!" he said, and raced in.

On stage stood the famous
puppets, Harlequin and
Punchinello. Their dances and
tricks made the audience howl
with laughter.

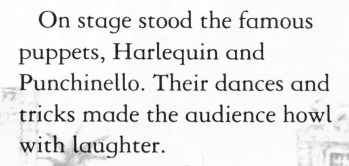

All of a sudden,
the puppets stopped
acting and stared
into the crowd.

"Another puppet!" they cried.
"Come up and join us."

Pinocchio was dragged on stage and surrounded by puppets. They chattered about this and that and completely forgot their show. The people in the audience grew angry and frustrated.

26

Then a scary man stormed onto the stage and everyone fell silent. It was the manager, a fearsome fire-eater. He grabbed the puppets and marched them off.

Backstage, the fire-eater looked sternly at a trembling Pinocchio. "You've ruined my show, puppet!" he yelled. "Now I'm going to use you for firewood."

27

"Don't burn me," begged
Pinocchio, "I don't want to die.
How would my poor old Dad cope
without me?"

"Ah... ah... ah-tishoo!" sneezed
the fire-eater.

The other puppets cheered.
"A sneeze means he feels
sorry for you,"
they cried.

"Take these five gold coins back
home to your father," said the fire-
eater, "and stay out of trouble!"

28

Chapter 5

The fox and the cat

Lucky Pinocchio waved goodbye to his puppet friends and skipped off down the road. He was dreaming of what Gepetto could buy with the gold coins, when he bumped into a fox and a cat.

They were a sorry sight. The fox was lame and had to lean on the cat. The cat was blind and had to be led by the fox.

"What are you smiling about, young puppet?" asked the fox.

"I'm rich," replied Pinocchio. "And my Dad will be so pleased with me."

At the word *rich*, the cat looked up. The fox kicked her with his lame leg and she quickly shut her eyes.

"Why not double your money?" suggested the cat.

"Or triple it!" added the fox.

Pinocchio was confused. "How do I do that?" he asked.

"Come with us to the field of miracles," replied the cat.

Pinocchio pictured himself carrying home bags of gold. "Dad will be thrilled," he cried and followed his new friends out of town.

Just before sunset, they stopped at an inn. The fox and cat ordered everything on the menu, but Pinocchio was too excited to eat.

"Let's sleep here a while," said the cat, showing Pinocchio to the guest rooms.

As soon as Pinocchio's head hit
the pillow, he drifted off into a
wonderful dream. Everywhere he
looked, gold grew on trees.

"Wake up!" called a grumpy
voice. "Your friends have gone
without you and they haven't paid."
Pinocchio rubbed his eyes. It was
the innkeeper. Handing him a gold
coin, Pinocchio rushed outside.

The puppet stumbled blindly in the dark. His only thought was to find the fox and cat.

"Foolish puppet," buzzed a faint but familiar voice.

"Who said that?" whispered Pinocchio.

I am the ghost of the cricket. Now take those coins home.

"Leave me alone," Pinocchio cried. "I'm going to triple my money at the field of miracles!"

"There's no such place," said the cricket. "This lane will only take you to madmen and murderers."

"They don't scare *me*," sniffed Pinocchio. Turning his back on the cricket, he stomped off into the gloom.

Slowly, the moon slipped out from behind a cloud and spread a ghostly glow across the lane. Ahead, Pinocchio could just make out two figures. They looked like... murderers.

Quickly, Pinocchio hid.

"We can see you, puppet," snarled one of the murderers.

"Bring us your gold," purred the other.

A paw brushed past Pinocchio's cheek, so Pinocchio snapped at it – and bit it off!

By kicking, scratching and biting, Pinocchio managed to escape. He fled through the woods, but the murderers sped after him.

Fighting his way through the thick trees, he finally came out into a clearing.

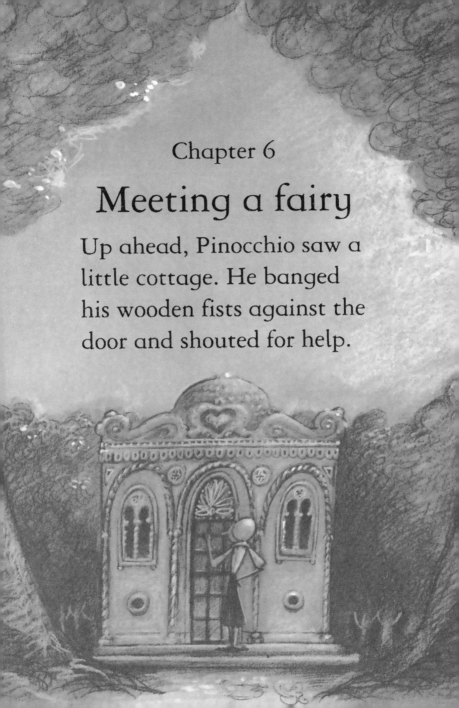

Chapter 6

Meeting a fairy

Up ahead, Pinocchio saw a
little cottage. He banged
his wooden fists against the
door and shouted for help.

Poor Pinocchio could still hear the patter of murderous feet. "HELP!" he shouted again.

A light went on and the front door swung open. The frightened puppet was invited in by a very polite poodle.

"My lady is sleeping," he said, "but do come in. I'll show you to your room."

Relieved to escape certain death, Pinocchio followed him.

"You may sleep here, Master Pinocchio," said the poodle. "Breakfast will be served at eight."

Pinocchio was so pleased to be safe, he didn't stop to wonder how the poodle knew his name.

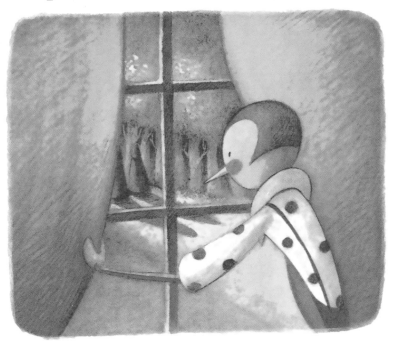

At breakfast, Pinocchio met the lady of the house. She was a silvery fairy who twinkled like starlight. Pinocchio told her about his adventure, from the fire-eater and the gold coins to the murderers in the woods.

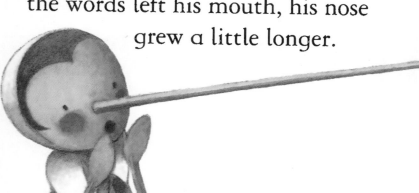

"And where are your coins now?" she asked. "Can I see them?"

"No!" said Pinocchio quickly. "Because I've... er... lost them." As the words left his mouth, his nose grew a little longer.

"Where did you lose them?" asked the fairy, smiling.

"Um... in the woods," lied the puppet. Instantly, his nose doubled in length. "Or maybe I swallowed them," he added. By now, his nose was touching the wall – and the coins were jangling in his pocket.

"You're lying," giggled the fairy.

You'll never be a real boy if you don't tell the truth.

Pinocchio felt very awkward. He tried to run from the room, but his incredibly long nose got in the way.

Soon the fairy stopped laughing and took pity on him. She opened the window and called for three woodpeckers. In no time, they had pecked Pinocchio's nose back to its original size.

A woodpecker whispered something in the fairy's ear.

"Good news!" cried the fairy, turning to Pinocchio. "Your father is in these woods looking for you."

Pinocchio jumped for joy. "I must go and greet him," he cried.

"And give him those coins," added the fairy, pointing to his pocket.

With a sheepish grin, Pinocchio raced outside.

45

Chapter 7

The field of miracles

Before Pinocchio could find Gepetto, who should he bump into but the fox and cat? They were very friendly and apologized for leaving him at the inn.

"Now let's go to the field of miracles!" said the sly fox.

"Not me," said Pinocchio. "I'm off to find my Dad."

"With only four coins in your pocket?" said the cat.

"What a shame," added the fox, "when you could have twenty."

Sixty!

A hundred!

"No! I've made up my mind," said the puppet. "Goodbye."

"Goodbye," called the fox and cat. "See you when we're rich!"

Pinocchio turned to leave, then remembered his dream of golden trees. "Wait for me!" he cried.

But the field of miracles was nothing like Pinocchio's dream. It looked just like any other field.

"You must bury your gold in the middle of the field," said the fox.

"Then take this pebble and throw it in the river," said the cat. "When you come back, your gold will have multiplied."

Pinocchio eagerly dug a hole. He covered the coins with mud, then ran down to the river.

49

When he got back, the fox and cat had disappeared. He rushed to the middle of the field and dug.

"Silly puppet!" squawked a parrot. "Did you really believe their story?"

Pinocchio ignored him and dug deeper and deeper, until he was covered in dirt. The only thing he found was a worm.

I've been tricked!

Chapter 8

Toyland

For hours, Pinocchio sulked in the field. When a huge pigeon called out to him, he didn't bother replying.

"Pinocchio?" cooed the pigeon again.

Pinocchio just sniffed.

"Gepetto is in great danger," the pigeon went on. "Come quickly."

Before Pinocchio could reply, the pigeon scooped him onto her back and soared into the sky. They darted through clouds and arrived at the seashore, just as a huge storm blew up.

A huddle of people stood on the shore. They were pointing to a small boat struggling in the rough sea.

"That poor man," said a woman. "He can't even swim!"

"He only wanted to find his son," sighed another. Suddenly, a huge wave swamped the little boat.

"Dad?" cried Pinocchio. "If I was a good son, you wouldn't be in danger." Then he dived into the frothy water.

Pinocchio swam and swam. Soon the storm died down, but there was still no sign of Gepetto's boat. The wet, miserable puppet was washed onto a sandy beach.

He heard whoops of laughter, then a gang of toys appeared.

"Welcome to Toyland," called a tin soldier.

"Here we only have fun, fun and more fun!" cried a Jack-in-the-box.

"I don't want fun," groaned
Pinocchio. "My Dad has just
drowned and it's all my fault."

"We'll cheer you up!" shouted
the toys.

"Watch out," said a twinkling
voice. "They'll make a fool of you."

Pinocchio looked up, hoping to
see the fairy. All he could see were
grinning toys.

Over the next few days,
Pinocchio tried very hard not to
have fun. But there was so much to
do. The island was one big funfair,
with free rides all day long.

"Whoopee!" cried Pinocchio,
zooming through the air on a
rollercoaster.

"Look at me!" he shouted,
bouncing higher on
a trampoline.

In all the excitement, he
completely forgot about Gepetto.
"You silly wooden toy," said the
fairy voice one afternoon. "You're
no better than a donkey."
This time, Pinocchio ignored her.
What did she know about fun?

The next morning, Pinocchio
woke up feeling itchy all over. His
ears were unusually heavy and he
was growing fur. Nervously, he
looked in the mirror. "Oh no!"
he cried. He was turning into
a donkey.

He couldn't let anyone see him
like this. Without a second thought,
he ran to the beach, jumped into
the sea and swam away.

Chapter 9
Inside the shark

It was hard for Pinocchio to swim as a donkey. He felt very heavy and little fish kept tugging on his coat. Then he realized they were nibbling off his fur.

Soon Pinocchio was a puppet once more. But as he swam to shore, a shark the size of an ocean liner rose above the waves. There was a tremendous WHOOSH, then everything went dark.

Eventually, Pinocchio saw a faint glow in the distance. The glow led him to a man reading by candlelight.

"Dad?" whispered the puppet, hardly daring to believe his eyes. "Pinocchio!" cried Gepetto.

The old man had survived for weeks on food supplies from a ship the shark had swallowed. But now the food had run out. "We're doomed, my son," Gepetto sighed.

"This is all my fault," cried Pinocchio. "If I was a *real* boy, I'd get us out of here." He grabbed Gepetto's hand. "It's OK," he declared. "I'll *still* get us out."

He led Gepetto on a squelchy journey to the shark's mouth, where their exit was barred by teeth.

When it opens its mouth, we'll jump.

I can't swim!

Suddenly, the shark let out a giant burp, throwing Pinocchio and Gepetto into the sea.

The brave puppet towed Gepetto to the shore and, by dusk, they were home again.

That night, the fairy appeared to Pinocchio in a dream. "Well done," she said and kissed him.

Pinocchio woke up in surprise. He rubbed his eyes – and was even more surprised. His hands weren't wooden any more!

Hearing him shout, Gepetto ran into the room. "Son," he cried with joy, "you're a real boy at last!"

Carlo Collodi (1826-1890) was an Italian writer and a schools' advisor. His real name was Carlo Lorenzini but he used Collodi as his writing name, after the village Collodi where he was born.

Series editor: Lesley Sims

Designed by Russell Punter
and Katarina Dragoslavic

First published in 2004 by Usborne Publishing Ltd., Usborne House, 83-85 Saffron Hill, London EC1N 8RT, England. www.usborne.com
Copyright © 2004 Usborne Publishing Ltd.

64

The Snow Queen

Hans Christian Andersen

Retold by Lesley Sims

Illustrated by
Alan Marks

Reading Consultant: Alison Kelly
Roehampton University

Contents

Chapter 1

The magic mirror

There was once a wicked demon who made a magic mirror. This mirror made everything good look twisted and ugly. Anything bad looked even worse.

3

"It's a fine mirror," snarled the demon's students. "Let's show it off to the angels." Flapping their leathery wings, they flew up... and up... until...

Smash!

The mirror slipped from their hands, crashed to the ground and broke into a million tiny pieces.

Some pieces were no bigger than a grain of sand, but they were as powerful as the whole mirror. If a speck flew into someone's eye, everything looked horrible and wrong.

But if a splinter struck a person's heart, that heart began to freeze.

Chapter 2

Gerda and Kay

Not long after the mirror
shattered, a girl named Gerda
was living next door to a boy
named Kay. In all the world,
no two friends were as close.

6

One winter's day, as snow was falling, Gerda's grandmother told them the story of the Snow Queen.

"She lives in the icy north, but in winter she flies around, disguised as a snowflake."

"Beware of her!" the grandmother warned. "She's a wicked woman. But don't worry," she added. "If your heart is pure, you'll always see the queen for who she is."

Wandering home, Kay gazed
at the glittering snowflakes
drifting down. As he stared,
he noticed one flake
seemed larger than
the others.

Then he gasped. The snowflake
was definitely growing bigger...

8

...until it became a beautiful woman. She was astonishing. Her shimmering white clothes were coated in snow and she herself was made entirely of ice.

The woman turned her cold, bright eyes on Kay. He shook his head and she vanished. "I must have imagined her," he thought.

9

Winter passed and Kay forgot all about the Snow Queen. Then one day, while he and Gerda watered the roses in her window box, Kay suddenly cried out.

Kay?
What is it?

Ow! My heart!
And my eye!

He had felt a sharp jab in his eye and another, piercing his heart. But neither Kay nor Gerda could see what had happened.

10

The jabs came from splinters of the broken mirror. At once, Kay began to change and grow cruel.

Seeing Gerda's frightened face made him angry. He jumped up and left. Gerda listened sadly to his boots creaking down the stairs.

After that, Kay saw everything differently. He began to argue and make fun of people in the street. He even mocked Gerda and her roses, though she still loved him.

Next winter, Kay ignored Gerda altogether, and joined the boys on their sleds in the town square.

As they played, a dazzling white sleigh rode into the square. Its driver was dressed in white from her fur hat to her pointed boots.

Everyone but Kay ran away. He shouted, "This looks fun!" and tied his sled to the snow-white sleigh.

The two sharp splinters of mirror had blinded him to danger – for the driver was none other than the Snow Queen herself.

The sleigh picked up speed and Kay laughed with excitement. Hurtling around the square, they dashed out through the city gates.

On and on they flew, through swirling snow. All too soon, the sleigh stopped. As the driver stood up, Kay realized who she was.

The Snow Queen!

You must be frozen. Come and join me in my sleigh.

Quickly, the queen kissed Kay and his icy heart grew colder. She kissed him again and he forgot all about home. He was trapped.

Chapter 3

Gerda's search

In town, no one knew where Kay had gone. All through the cold, dead winter, Gerda was too sad to do anything. But when spring came, with no sign of her best friend, she decided to look for him.

My dear, Kay may not be alive.

I don't believe it!

"The river flows a long way," she thought. "Perhaps the river has passed him on its travels." Putting on her best, red shoes, she went down to the river.

She threw her shoes into the river as a gift, but they floated back to her. So, she climbed into a boat to throw them further in... and the boat swept her away.

She floated for hours. Gerda was afraid but she couldn't turn back. She hoped the river would take her past someone who had seen Kay. But she saw no one.

As dusk fell, she spotted a rose-covered cottage. The boat began to drift to the bank and an old woman hobbled over.

The old woman helped Gerda onto the bank and Gerda told her all about Kay. She described their happy days playing until he suddenly changed.

First he grew mean. Then he disappeared altogether.

Now, the old woman wasn't wicked but she did know a little magic – and she lived a lonely life.

"I'll make sure the girl stays with me," she muttered and cast a spell.

To be extra sure, she made all her roses vanish. She didn't want to remind Gerda of the roses at home and her search for Kay.

Eat as many cherries as you like!

Her magic worked. Gerda played happily in the woman's garden and her old life was soon no more real than a dream.

Even so, sometimes she had a feeling that something wasn't quite right...

Gerda might have stayed in the cottage forever but, one day, she spotted a painted flower on the woman's sunhat. It was a rose!

In that moment, Gerda remembered everything. "Kay!" she cried. "How could I forget you? Oh, I've wasted so much time!"

Without even saying goodbye to the old woman, she ran away.

Chapter 4

Kay in the castle

Meanwhile, the Snow Queen had taken Kay to her magnificent castle in the far north.

Kay was neither happy nor sad. His feelings were frozen inside him. He sat at the queen's feet, on a vast icy lake, so cold he was almost blue. But he didn't notice.

The queen sat sighing on her throne, bored. Looking down on Kay, she decided to play a game with him. "Solve my puzzle and I'll set you free," she declared.

Kay looked at her blankly.

The queen waved a pale hand at some blocks of ice. "If you put those in the right order, they will spell a word," she said, with a cruel smile.

Slowly, Kay's frozen brain realized she was telling him to spell something. He so wanted to please her but he just couldn't do it.

25

The Snow Queen laughed. "You'll never do it, my icicle boy!" she said. Her cold laugh bounced off the walls of the castle. "But it's amusing to watch you try..."

Chapter 5

A helpful princess

Gerda had run for hours to get away from the cottage, with no idea where she was going. At last, stumbling through a gloomy forest, she had to rest.

A curious crow hopped up to her, his head to one side. "Caw!" he croaked. "What are you doing, all alone in the world?"

I'm looking for my friend Kay. Have you seen him?

The crow listened to Gerda's story. "Caw, caw..." he said. "I think I might know where he is."

Gerda couldn't believe her luck. "Tell me!" she begged, excitedly.

"Well now," croaked the crow, "there's a princess in this kingdom and she was looking for a prince. In no time at all, men were lining up to meet her. But no one was good enough."

"Then a young boy appeared from nowhere. His clothes were torn and his boots creaked. But he went inside the palace and – would you believe it – the princess liked him so much, she married him!"

"That must be Kay!" Gerda cried. "He's handsome and clever... and his boots do squeak. Oh, please take me to him!"

"Caw. That's not so easily done," said the crow.

But Gerda pleaded and pleaded with him.

I'll speak to my wife. She works in the palace.

The crow flew off and Gerda waited nervously. Long after sunset, he returned – with good news. Trembling with hope, Gerda followed the crow to the palace. Inside, its grand rooms were draped in the purple night.

As they crept through the
ballroom, shadowy figures swept by.

"Who are they?" Gerda asked,
in a whisper.

"Dreams," replied the crow's wife.

They take the
royal thoughts for
midnight rides.

In the most splendid room of all, two giant flowers hung from a palm tree. The first flower had pure white petals and, curled up in the middle, lay the princess, fast asleep. The flower beside her was red.

Gerda stepped forward and looked in...

Kay? It's me, Gerda!

34

...and the prince woke up. "Who is it?" he mumbled.

Gerda stared at him and burst into tears. It wasn't Kay at all.

Gerda's noisy gulps and sobs woke the princess.

"Who are you?" she cried. Then, as Gerda didn't look dangerous, she gave her a hanky and let her sit down to explain.

That night, Gerda slept in the palace. In the morning, the princess gave Gerda her second-best dress and begged her to stay.

But all Gerda wanted was to search for Kay. "I'll walk around the world if I have to," she said.

The princess smiled and called for her carriage. Gerda gasped. It glistened with golden sugar and inside, the walls were lined with sticky buns and fat cream cakes.

For a second, she simply stared. "Is this really for me?" she asked, pointing to the golden carriage.

"Well, you can hardly walk around the whole world," said the princess, helping her climb in.

Don't worry. I have three more just like it.

The carriage set off and Gerda waved through the window.

"Goodbye! Good luck!" cried the princess.

Chapter 6

The little robber girl

The carriage rolled on into a dark forest. But it shone so brightly that it dazzled a band of robbers, who were hiding among the trees.

"Gold!" they shrieked and rushed to attack.

"Mmm..." said an old robber woman, grabbing Gerda. "She looks tastier than the carriage. Let s eat her!" But, as she raised her knife, something sprang up and bit her ear.

It was the daughter of the chief robber – and she always got her own way.

"I want her for my friend," said the robber girl, pointing to Gerda, "and to play with her carriage."

"Hmph," said the old woman grumpily. The little robber girl pushed Gerda into the carriage and squashed in beside her.

Are you a princess?

No. I'm looking for my friend Kay.

As they rode deeper into the forest, Gerda told her story yet again. By nightfall, they arrived at the robbers' grim, lonely castle.

The little robber girl yawned. "You can sleep with me and my pets," she told Gerda.

Gerda frowned. The robber girl had very strange pets. One hundred pigeons roosted in the rafters and two woodpigeons sat in a silver cage. "They're all mine!" boasted the little robber girl. "But Ba is best of all." And she pointed to a reindeer, who was tied to the wall.

Say hello, Ba!

"Bedtime!" she announced suddenly, flopping down. Gerda stayed awake, watching the robbers polish their knives around the fire. Things were worse than ever. She was stuck here, a prisoner again.

"I'll never find Kay," she sighed. Then the pigeons began talking.

Coo! Did you ever see such a frozen boy?

Coo! His face was like ice.

He'll never thaw now the Snow Queen has him.

"Could the Snow Queen have Kay?" wondered Gerda. "Please, where does the queen live?" she asked the pigeons politely.

"Somewhere north," they cooed. "Ask Ba if he knows."

The reindeer looked up. "Yes," he said, in a slow, deep voice. "I know her home. I'm from there too."

She lives in the far, far north, past Lapland.

The little robber girl, who was still awake, heard everything.

"You don't want to find that rotten old Snow Queen," she said. "You'd be safer here with us." But Gerda was desperate to find Kay.

"Then I shall let you go," said the robber girl, as proudly as a queen herself. "Ba shall take you."

"You'll need food," she went on, finding Gerda bread and ham. With a hard shove, she helped Gerda on to the reindeer's silky-smooth back.

Ba bounded off happily, racing north to his home. The little robber girl stood alone in the moonlight, watching and waving until they were out of sight.

Chapter 7

Journey north

It was a long way even to Lapland. When they arrived, Ba and Gerda were spotted by a Lapp woman.

"You're frozen!" she exclaimed to Gerda, taking them into her hut. "And you've a long way to go," she added, when she heard their tale.

47

"You're in luck," she told them.
"The Snow Queen is away just now,
creating the Northern Lights. You
must go on to Finnmark. I know a
Finn woman who can help."

Gerda watched in surprise as the
woman quickly scribbled a message
to her friend on a dried fish.

Ba galloped off once more across the snowy plains, until they reached the Finn woman's tiny hut.

First, the Finn woman read the fish. Then she listened as Gerda breathlessly told her tale. Nodding, she fetched a parchment from her shelves and studied it.

Finally, she took Ba to one side. "Kay *is* with the Snow Queen," she whispered. "He's under her spell, because of splinters of glass in his eye and his heart. To rescue him, Gerda must get the splinters out."

"But how?" growled Ba. "Can you give her some magic?"

"Gerda has come this far," said the Finn woman wisely. "She is good and sweet and innocent. That will be all the magic she needs."

"Take Gerda as far as the Snow Queen's garden," she went on. "But don't tell her what I've told you." She swept Gerda up and placed her on the reindeer's back.

Go quickly now!

I hope Ba knows where we're going.

Ba galloped until they reached a bush with glossy red berries. There, he stopped and let Gerda down.

Gerda was left all alone in the icy cold. Glittering snowflakes whirled around her, making it difficult for her to move. They were the guards of the Snow Queen's castle.

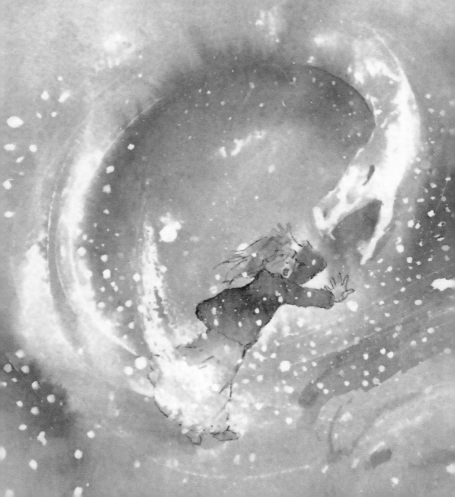

As she hesitated, the guards took on terrible shapes. Huge hedgehogs with vicious spikes, fang-toothed snakes and fierce bears sprang at her. Gerda cried out in fear, but she didn't run away.

Standing boldly before the guards, she told them to leave her alone. Her breath blew out in misty clouds around her. To her astonishment, these clouds became angels, who began to attack the guards.

Seeing the angels gave Gerda
strength. She punched the bear
nearest to her and he melted at her
touch. Then the angels warmed
Gerda's icy feet and hands and she
hurried into the castle.

55

Chapter 8

The snow castle

Inside a cold, empty hall, Kay
was puzzling over the Snow
Queen's challenge. He sat still,
thinking hard... so still that he
seemed frozen stiff.

And that was how Gerda found
him, when she appeared moments
later.

"Kay!" she called, running up to
him. She wrapped her arms around
him, but he didn't move.

Gerda didn't know what to do.
It was like hugging a block of ice.
He was frozen stiff and he didn't
even look at her.

Hot tears dripped from her nose
onto Kay's chest. They reached
right through to his heart, thawing
the ice and washing away the
splinter of glass.

Kay seemed to soften, so Gerda started to talk about the roses back home. Her words and his melting heart brought tears to Kay's eyes too... tears which washed away the splinter there.

He could see clearly again. "Gerda!" he shouted. "Is it really you?" The old Kay was back.

Gerda and Kay laughed and cried and jumped for joy. Even the blocks of ice around them got up and danced. When the blocks fell down again, they spelled the word "Eternity". Kay was free.

Gerda kissed his cheeks so that they glowed.

"Gerda! Yuck!" said Kay, but Gerda kept kissing him until he was completely thawed.

"Let's go!" begged Kay. "The Snow Queen could be back at any minute..."

"She's back now!" said an icy voice, behind them.

Kay and Gerda looked at each other in horror.

"You said if I spelled a word I was free," Kay shouted bravely, "and there it is! I'm going!"

The Snow Queen was furious but there was nothing she could do. She had given her word and she was bound by it.

Laughing with relief, Gerda and Kay tore outside the castle, to find Ba and a friend waiting for them. To Gerda's delight, the reindeer carried them all the way home.

At long last, they arrived at Gerda's house. Her grandmother had given up hope of ever seeing either of them again.

Is it really you? You defeated the Snow Queen?

Gerda and Kay hugged the grandmother over and over.

"This is truly a fairy-tale ending!" cried the grandmother and the roses in the window box nodded their heads, as if to agree.

Hans Christian Andersen was born in Denmark in 1805, the son of a poor shoemaker. He left home at fourteen to seek his fortune and became famous all over the world as a writer of fairy tales.

Designed by Russell Punter

First published in 2004 by Usborne Publishing Ltd., Usborne House, 83-85 Saffron Hill, London EC1N 8RT, England. www.usborne.com
Copyright © 2004 Usborne Publishing Ltd.

Stories of Pirates

Russell Punter

Illustrated by
Christyan Fox

Reading Consultant: Alison Kelly
Roehampton University

Contents

Chapter 1

The pesky parrot

It was Charlie Crossbones' first day as a pirate.

He'd spent the last ten years at Pirate School. Now he was ready to set sail for treasure.

3

He knew how to...

read a treasure map...

unlock a chest...

...and do lots of other piratey things.

4

He even knew how to give a
proper pirate's laugh.

What's more, Charlie had
been lucky enough to inherit
his Grandpa's old pirate ship
and all the gear to go with it.

But as Charlie looked at his outfit, he realized something was missing. He didn't have a parrot.

A moment later, Charlie
spotted just what he needed.

There were parrots of all shapes and sizes. There was only one problem. They were all too expensive.

As Charlie turned to go, the parrot seller called him back. "I suppose you could have this one," he said.

Charlie had never seen such a pretty parrot and he was amazed it was so cheap.

You've got a very special bird there!

going cheap

Now he had his parrot, Charlie wasted no time in setting off on his hunt for treasure.

9

Out at sea, Charlie spotted a ship called the *Fat Flounder*. He knew it belonged to a rich sailor called Captain Silverside.

Charlie waited until the
sailors had gone to lunch.
Then he rowed across to the
ship and sneaked in through
an open window.

Charlie was in luck. He'd
climbed into the cabin where
the captain kept his treasure.

But he had only just begun
to stuff his pockets with gold
coins, when disaster struck.

"Sssh!" Charlie hissed at his
parrot. But it was too late.

Charlie took one look at
Captain Silverside
and ran.

The
captain
and his
men chased
Charlie around
the deck six times before the
poor pirate escaped to his boat.

13

As he rowed back to his ship, Charlie turned to his parrot with a face like thunder.

But every time they went to sea, the parrot caused trouble.

Just as Charlie was about to steal someone's treasure, the parrot let out a warning cry.

Each time, Charlie only
just managed to escape. Soon,
he was a nervous wreck.

Whenever
he tried to
get rid
of the
parrot...

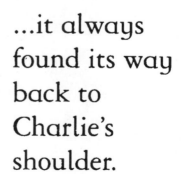

...it always
found its way
back to
Charlie's
shoulder.

16

As Charlie was eating
his supper one evening, he
wondered what he could do.

The Laughing Lobster Inn

Super Deluxe Menu

| Scrummy Scampi | 7 pennies |
| Mouthwatering Mussels | 6 pennies |

Deluxe Menu

| Crispy Cod | 5 pennies |
| Fancy Fishcakes | 4 pennies |

Cheap Menu

| Shrimp on toast | 2 pennies |

Very Cheap Menu

| Bread & cheese | 1 penny |

He had never felt so
miserable. Thanks to that
pesky parrot he was a useless,
practically penniless pirate.

17

Charlie's long face was making the other customers lose their appetites. The landlord tried to cheer him up.

They were so busy talking, neither of them spotted a thief creeping up to the landlord's cash box.

18

The thief was just about to
swipe all the money, when
Charlie's parrot squawked
into action.

19

"What a wonderful bird!" said the landlord. "That thief nearly got away with my cash."

This gave Charlie an idea. Perhaps he could put his parrot to good use after all.

20

The landlord paid Charlie handsomely for his new burglar alarm...

STOP THIEF!

the parrot enjoyed its new job...

...and Charlie had enough money to buy another bird — a quiet one this time.

Chapter 2

Captain Spike

Macintosh Mullet was a poor
fisherman. He lived on tiny
Mullet Island with only his
daughter, Molly, for company.

22

One winter, the weather was so bad that Macintosh didn't catch a single fish.

So, Molly put her father's telescope, her best blue vase and a china cat into a wooden chest and set off for the mainland.

Molly had been rowing for ten minutes when she was spotted by Captain Spike and his band of pirates.

In a flash, they dragged her and the chest on board.

The mean captain tried everything to make Molly talk...

...but she wouldn't give him the key.

"Then I'll smash the chest open!" he cried. As he spoke, a thick fog came down around the ship.

"Help!" cried the pirate who was steering. "I can't see!"

"I know these seas," said Molly. "Promise to let me go, and I'll guide you home."

"Hmm... OK," said Spike. "Shark Island, and step on it!"

An hour passed and the fog began to clear a little.

"I'll take over now," said Spike. "I can't have other pirates see you steer my ship, I'd be a laughing stock."

"Can I go then?" asked Molly.
"No!" said Spike, with a sneer.
"You can walk the plank!"

The sneaky captain had broken his promise. Leaving one of his crewmen at the wheel, Spike forced Molly to walk to the end of a plank, into the shark-filled sea below.

But there was no splash... not even a tiny splish. All the pirates heard was a thud!

At that moment, the fog
cleared as quickly as it had
sprung up.

"This isn't Shark Island!"
growled Spike. "She's tricked
us. Quick lads! Out of here."

It was too late. Before the pirates could move, the port police jumped on board. Soon, Spike and his men were safely behind bars.

But the port police were still worried about the fog. So they built a lighthouse next to Mullet Island and made Molly the lighthouse keeper.

Chapter 3

The Masked Pirate

Sam Sardine had always wanted to be a sailor.

He was desperate to travel the Seven Seas and do battle with bloodthirsty pirates.

As soon as he was old
enough, he joined Captain
Winkle's ship as a cabin boy.

But Sam soon found that life
on board ship wasn't as
exciting as he'd thought.

He spent all day...

mopping
the decks...

peeling
potatoes...

...and
washing
the sailors'
smelly
socks.

33

Finally, he'd had enough.
He went to the captain and
asked for a proper sailor's job.

Captain Winkle thought Sam
was rather rude. But he decided
to put him to the test.

"All right," he said, "Let's see
you sail the ship into port!"

Sam's chest swelled with pride as he took the wheel.

But steering a ship wasn't as easy as it looked.

Luckily, the ship wasn't too badly damaged. Sam begged for one more chance.

"Very well," said Captain Winkle, at last. "You can guard the ship's treasure."

36

That night, while the rest of the sailors snored in their bunks, Sam sat guard.

But he was exhausted after his hard day's work. Soon, he was fast asleep as well.

zzz..!

37

Hours later, Sam was woken from his dreams by a wicked laugh.

He rushed up on deck, to see the dreaded Masked Pirate sailing off with Captain Winkle's treasure.

Sam felt terrible. What would the captain say? He didn't have to wait long to find out.

When Captain Winkle had calmed down, he offered a reward to whoever could track down the thief or his treasure.

But, as the pirate always wore a mask, no one knew what he looked like.

Suddenly, Sam had an idea.

Captain Winkle didn't have much confidence in his cabin boy, but no one else had a plan.

That evening, Sam went to the Spyglass Inn, where the local pirates spent the night.

At breakfast next morning, Sam said in a loud voice, "I heard the Masked Pirate talking in his sleep last night."

One particular pirate sitting in a corner began to look worried. Sam's plan was working.

"Now I know where the treasure is, I'm going to get it for myself!" Sam went on.

Hearing this, the pirate rushed out of the inn. Sam followed close behind.

The pirate jumped into a boat and rowed to an island just off the coast.

Sam ran to Captain Winkle.

When they arrived
on the island, they
found the pirate
hurriedly
digging up
a treasure
chest.

The captain recognized it at once. It was *his* treasure chest. Taking a flying leap, he landed on the pirate.

"Take my ship and fetch help, Sam my boy!" he roared.

"You trust me to sail?" cried Sam. "Aye aye, Captain!"

There are lots more great stories for you to read:

Usborne Young Reading: Series One
Aladdin and his Magical Lamp
Animal Legends
Stories of Dragons
Stories of Giants
Stories of Gnomes & Goblins
Stories of Magical Animals
Stories of Princes & Princesses
Stories of Witches
The Burglar's Breakfast
The Dinosaurs Next Door
The Monster Gang
Wizards

Usborne Young Reading: Series Two
A Christmas Carol
Aesop's Fables
Gulliver's Travels
Jason & The Golden Fleece
Robinson Crusoe
The Adventures of King Arthur
The Amazing Adventures of Hercules
The Amazing Adventures of Ulysses
The Clumsy Crocodile
The Fairground Ghost
The Incredible Present
Treasure Island

Series editor:
Lesley Sims

This edition first published in 2007 by Usborne Publishing Ltd.,
Usborne House, 83-85 Saffron Hill, London EC1N 8RT, England.
www.usborne.com Copyright © 2007, 2003 Usborne Publishing Ltd.

Stories of
Wizards

Christopher Rawson
Adapted by Gill Harvey

Illustrated by
Stephen Cartwright

Reading Consultant: Alison Kelly
Roehampton University

Contents

Chapter 1

Long, long ago

Long ago, lots of people believed in wizards. They thought there were good ones, who helped people...

...and bad ones, who cast evil spells.

They thought there were old wizards, with long white beards...

...and young ones, who were still learning their magic tricks.

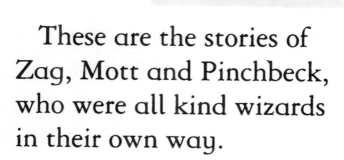

These are the stories of Zag, Mott and Pinchbeck, who were all kind wizards in their own way.

The mean man

Zag was a wonderful wizard. He looked after children who had nowhere else to live. The children adored him.

But Zag was so busy caring for the children that he didn't do any magic. In fact, he forgot his spells. Until, one day...

Look! Not even a button.

"We don't have any money left," he said sadly.

"What are we going to do?" asked Tom, one of the boys.

"Don't worry!" said Zag. "I know how we can make some money."

I'll teach you some tricks.

The children were excited. Did Zag mean magic tricks?

But Zag didn't teach the children magic. First, he taught them how to juggle.

Then he taught them clever jumping tricks, and acrobatics.

Finally, the children put on
a show for the villagers. It
was a great success! Everyone
laughed and clapped and gave
the children money.

Well, almost everyone.

One man walked past, muttering to himself. He didn't give them any money — even though he had bags of gold.

His name was Mervin the Miser and it suited him.

He was a miser – as mean as his name.

Tricks, indeed. Stuff and nonsense.

Mervin stomped off to his house before anyone could spot him. Safe inside, he shut the door with a bang.

The money from the show didn't last. By Christmas Eve, it had run out completely. Outside, it snowed. Inside, the children's tummies grumbled.

And Zag had run out of ideas. "I'm sorry, children," he said. "Maybe we should all just go to bed."

Zag was very old and tired. The children knew he'd done his best.

But they didn't give up.
"Let's go to Zag's Secret
Room," they whispered.

"Maybe we'll find a magic
spell to help us."

The children crept into the
room. Zag hadn't used any
spells for a long, long time.
The room was covered in dust
and cobwebs.

Jack, one of the older boys, found a rusty can. "Laughing powder!" he whispered. "Do you think it works?"

16

There was only one way to find out...

The children slipped out of the wizard's house and into the snowy night. They headed for Mervin the Miser's house.

Mervin was fast asleep.
Jack tiptoed to his bed, and
sprinkled laughing powder
all over him.

Do you think that's
enough?

Mervin didn't stir. He just
grunted in his sleep.

Then Alice pulled a feather from the pillow. She reached for Mervin's toes...

...and tickled them. Mervin woke up at once! The children jumped back, afraid.

"Ha ha!" cried Mervin, with a huge smile. He started to laugh. He laughed until the tears rolled down his cheeks.

"HA! HA! Stop!" he begged. "I haven't felt this happy for years. Tomorrow is Christmas Day! Let's have a party!"

And that's what they did.
Even the mayor was invited.
After that, Mervin made sure
that Zag and the children
never went hungry again.

Chapter 3

The man with a lump on his nose

Egbert had a lump on his nose.
It had been there for five days.
It just wouldn't go away.

"Go and see Mott the wizard,"
said his wife.

So Egbert went to find Mott.
Mott looked hard at the lump,
from many different angles.

Mott took out his book of
spells. He hunted for the page
about lumps.

"Do you want a cheap cure, or an expensive one?" he asked.

"Cheap, please!" said Egbert. "I only have one penny."

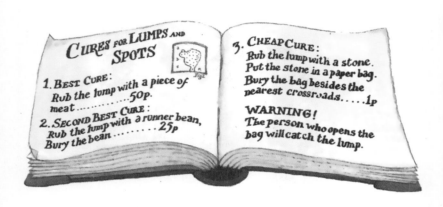

Mott took the penny. He gave Egbert a stone, and told him what to do.

Egbert rubbed his nose with the stone. Then he put the stone  into a paper bag, and buried the bag near a crossroads.

Right away, Egbert's nose felt better. "Hurray!" he cried. "Three cheers for Mott!"

Egbert was thrilled. He
went home and sat down with
a book. He'd just reached an
exciting part when his wife
stormed in.

"Egbert!" she shouted. "Look
what you've done!"

26

"But... I haven't done anything dear," Egbert said, in a small voice.

"Yes you have!" cried his wife. "I heard a man had buried a bag by the big tree. I thought it was treasure, so I dug it up. And now I have the lump!"

Chapter 4

The band of robbers

Pinchbeck the wizard and Pogo the goblin were walking together in the woods.

28

They were talking about a magic spell.

"The mushrooms must be picked at midnight," Pogo told Pinchbeck.

I spy a bag of gold!

They were so busy talking, they didn't see a robber creeping up behind them.

Suddenly, the robber jumped
out. He hit Pinchbeck over
the head with his club.

"Give me your gold!"
he shouted.

Pinchbeck dropped the gold.
Pogo just ran.

30

The robber tied Pinchbeck to a tree. Three hours later, Pogo came back.

"My head hurts," groaned Pinchbeck.

Let's go to the castle for help.

Slowly, Pinchbeck and Pogo climbed to the castle. They stopped in front of a huge wooden door and knocked.

Inside, the king and queen were having tea.

"Who's there?" called the king.

"Pogo!" said Pogo. "With Pinchbeck the wizard."

"We were robbed in the woods. Please let us in."

"That's terrible!" said the king. "Come in at once."

The queen made some fresh tea, and wrapped Pinchbeck's head in bandages.

"The robbers came here too," she said.

"And they're coming back tomorrow," the king added. "If we don't give them two more bags of gold, they'll take over our castle."

And we don't have any gold left...

That night, Pinchbeck and Pogo stayed in the castle. They wished they could do something to help.

"My head's thumping too much," sighed Pinchbeck. "I can't think of any spells."

But Pogo had an idea. Early
the next morning, he sneaked
out of the castle.

He found two sacks in a
shed and tiptoed through
the garden.

If he tried hard enough, he might be able to work a spell. As fast as he could, he stuffed both sacks with leaves.

Almost there...

Then he hurried back to the castle.

When Pinchbeck saw the sacks, he clapped his hands with glee.

"Pogo! You've helped me to remember a spell!"

Umpi-grumpi,
do as you're told.
Fool those robbers and
turn into gold!

Yellow smoke filled the air, then...

39

Rat-a-tat-tat! The robbers were banging on the door.

"Open up!" they yelled. "We know you don't have any gold. The castle's ours!"

The queen began to cry.
"But we have nowhere to go,"
she sobbed.

"Tough!" said the robbers.

Just then, the robbers
heard another voice. It
was Pinchbeck.

The robbers couldn't believe
their eyes. They blinked, and
stared, then blinked again.

"Take your gold," said Pinchbeck. "And make sure we never see you here again."

"Ha! We're rich now," said the chief robber. "Why would we come back?"

43

And they set off. They rode
for five days and five nights.
The sacks were getting lighter
but the robbers didn't notice.
At last, they stopped to rest.

Tired and hungry, they
decided to cheer themselves
up. "Let's count our gold,"
they said.

"It's a trick!" shouted the
chief robber. "We'll go back!"
But it was no good. They'd
come too far and were lost.

At the castle, Pinchbeck's head healed and his spells returned. It was time to go.

But before he left, he gave the king and queen a magic sack of gold which would never run out.

Goodbye!

Then he and Pogo headed back into the woods, the way they had come.

Try these other books in
Series One:

The Burglar's Breakfast: Alfie
Briggs is a burglar. After a hard
night of thieving, he likes to go home
to a tasty meal. But one day he gets
back to discover someone has
stolen his breakfast!

The Dinosaurs Next Door: Stan
loves living next door to Mr. Puff.
His house is full of amazing things.
Best of all are the dinosaur eggs —
until they begin to hatch...

The Monster Gang: Starting a
gang is a great idea. So is dressing
up like monsters. But if everyone
is in disguise, how do you know
who's who?

Series editor: Lesley Sims

Designed by
Katarina Dragoslavić

This edition first published in 2007 by Usborne Publishing Ltd.,
Usborne House, 83-85 Saffron Hill, London EC1N 8RT, England.
www.usborne.com
Copyright © 2007, 2002, 1980 Usborne Publishing Ltd.

Romeo & Juliet

William Shakespeare

Adapted by
Anna Claybourne

Illustrated by Jana Costa

Reading consultant: Alison Kelly
Roehampton University

Characters in the story

Old Montague,
head of the
Montague family

Count Paris,
a nobleman

Prince Escalus,
ruler of
Verona

Romeo
Montague

Mercutio,
Romeo's friend

Benvolio,
Romeo's cousin

Friar Laurence, an old monk

Juliet's mother

Friar John, Friar Laurence's friend

Old Capulet, head of the Capulet family

Juliet Capulet

Juliet's nurse

Tybalt, Juliet's cousin

Contents

Chapter 1

Capulets and Montagues

It was a warm summer's afternoon in the pretty town of Verona. People were busy shopping and chatting in the sunshine when suddenly...

5

Two gangs of young men tore across the market square, fighting, kicking and rolling in the dust. The townspeople ran for cover.

The gangs belonged to two of Verona's richest families – the Capulets and the Montagues. The families were sworn enemies, and they were always fighting.

In minutes, Verona's ruler Prince Escalus arrived with his soldiers to break up the fight. The prince was furious.

"I've had enough of this feud!" he raged. "It's got to stop. From now on, anyone caught fighting will be put to death!"

Old Montague, the head of the Montague family, hurried into the market square, searching for his son Romeo. But he only found Benvolio, Romeo's cousin.

Where's Romeo? Is he safe?

"Don't worry, uncle," said Benvolio. "Romeo wasn't fighting. He's too sensible."

Soon after that, Romeo himself
wandered by. Benvolio was telling
him what had happened, when
someone spoke behind them.

Have you heard?
Old Capulet's holding a
masked ball tonight.

"Did you hear that, Romeo?" whispered Benvolio. "A party at the Capulets' house. Let's go! If we wear disguises, no one will guess who we are."

That's a brilliant idea!

Excitedly, the two young Montagues went to find their friend Mercutio, to invite him along.

10

Chapter 2

Falling in love

At the Capulets' mansion, the
place was buzzing with excitement.
Servants raced around, laying the
tables and lighting candles, putting
the finishing touches to the party.

Upstairs, Juliet Capulet's nurse was helping her dress, when Juliet's mother came in.

"Now Juliet," she said. "A man named Count Paris is coming tonight. I hope you like him. Your father and I want you to marry him."

But I'm only thirteen!

"Oh Juliet, sweetheart," squealed her nurse. "You're to be married! How exciting!"

Juliet was horrified. She wasn't ready to get married. And what if she *didn't* like Count Paris?

But there was no time to argue. The party was about to start. Straightening her dress, Juliet went down the grand marble staircase to the banqueting hall.

13

A little later, three surprise guests arrived. Benvolio and Mercutio wanted to dance, but Romeo stood still.

He had spotted a beautiful girl in a pink and cream dress and he couldn't take his eyes off her.

Who is that girl? She's lovely.

Juliet's cousin Tybalt recognized the three friends and went straight to Old Capulet. "Uncle, there are Montagues here!" he declared. "Let's kick them out."

"No, Tybalt," said his uncle. "Remember the prince's warning."

We don't want to start a fight.

Romeo saw the girl leave the hall and followed. Shyly, he went up to her. "I don't know who you are," he said, "but I've fallen in love with you. You're beautiful!" And he kissed her.

Juliet had left the hall to escape from Count Paris. She didn't like Paris at all. But when Romeo kissed her, she felt her heart fluttering. She fell in love with him at once.

"Who are you?" Juliet murmured.

"He's Romeo Montague!" snapped Juliet's nurse, who had come to look for her. "And Old Capulet would have a fit if he saw his daughter with a Montague. Come on," she urged, taking Juliet away. "Count Paris wants to dance with you."

You're Juliet *Capulet*?

Romeo groaned. "She's a Capulet? What am I going to do?"

17

When the party ended, Romeo
sneaked outside and hid in the
Capulets' garden.

As the moon rose, he saw Juliet
step onto a balcony. "Oh, Romeo!"
she sighed. "It's you I love. If only
you weren't a Montague!"

"Juliet," Romeo called to her. "I'm
here in the garden. And I love you."

"You do?" said Juliet.

"With all my heart," Romeo replied. "I'd marry you, if I could."

"But my parents are going to make me marry Count Paris," Juliet wailed.

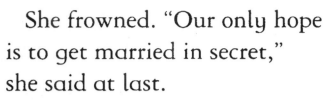

She frowned. "Our only hope
is to get married in secret,"
she said at last.

"Then we will," said Romeo.

"I'll ask my nurse to help
us," Juliet decided. "Send me
a message tomorrow."

"I will," Romeo promised,
"but now I'd better go.
Goodbye Juliet!"

Chapter 3

A secret wedding

The next morning, Romeo went to
visit Friar Laurence. The friar was
a wise monk who made medicines
and helped people with problems.

21

"What can I do for you, Romeo?" Friar Laurence asked.

"I'm in love with Juliet Capulet," Romeo explained. "I know our parents won't like it, but we really want to get married."

"Then I'll help you," the friar said, kindly. "When your parents find out you're married, it might help stop the fighting. If you both come to my house this afternoon, I'll marry you in secret."

Romeo was delighted. He ran to the market square to find Juliet's nurse and give her the message.

The nurse rushed off to tell Juliet
what Romeo had said. She hated
to see her beloved Juliet unhappy.

Friar Laurence
will marry you this
afternoon!

Juliet couldn't stop smiling. "I'll
tell my parents I'm going to see the
friar about my wedding to Count
Paris," she decided.

As the clock struck two, Juliet arrived at Friar Laurence's house. Romeo was waiting for her and the friar performed the secret wedding at once.

Romeo and Juliet were married.
But Juliet's parents were expecting
her back and she had to go
straight home.

So Romeo went to look for Benvolio and Mercutio.

He found them in the market square, arguing with Tybalt Capulet. "What's the problem?" Romeo asked.

27

"You Montagues are the
problem," snarled Tybalt, turning
to Romeo. "You sneaked into our
party and I'm going to make you
pay. I challenge you to a duel!"

"I refuse," Romeo replied. "You
know the prince said no fighting."

"You're afraid to fight!" Tybalt
taunted him.

"Don't speak to my friend like that!" said Mercutio.

"Oh, so you want to fight instead, do you?" Tybalt shouted, drawing his sword. Mercutio drew his too, and they started fighting.

"Stop it!" yelled Benvolio. He and Romeo frantically tried to pull the pair apart. They were too late. Tybalt stabbed Mercutio, who slumped to the ground – dead.

Romeo was so upset, he grabbed Mercutio's sword. Without thinking, he ran at Tybalt and stabbed him too.

Benvolio stared in horror as Tybalt sank to the ground. "Romeo, what have you done?" he gasped. "Quick, go before the prince comes!"

Romeo dropped the sword and ran for his life.

Chapter 4

Escape to Mantua

When Prince Escalus arrived,
Benvolio told him about the fight.
The prince was angry but he could
see Tybalt was mostly to blame.
"Romeo shall not die," he said.
"I'll banish him instead."

31

Being banished meant Romeo would have to leave Verona and never come back. It was better than being put to death — but not much.

Oh no! Poor Juliet!

Gossip spread fast in Verona and the nurse soon heard what had happened. With tears in her eyes, she went to tell Juliet.

Juliet was heartbroken. "Cousin Tybalt is dead," she sobbed, "and I'll never see my Romeo again!"

"Don't cry," begged the nurse. "I'll bring Romeo to see you before he leaves. He's hiding at the friar's house."

"Yes, please find him," Juliet said, wiping her eyes. "Ask him to come and say goodbye."

33

The nurse went straight to the
friar's house. Romeo looked as if
he'd been crying too.

"Romeo, you should be grateful,"
said Friar Laurence. "The prince
has spared your life."

"But I'm banished," Romeo said.
"And I want to be with Juliet."

"Go and see her tonight," said the friar, "but make sure you leave Verona by dawn. Head for the city of Mantua. After a while, I'll talk to the prince. I'll ask him to forgive you and let you come home."

The nurse smiled at Romeo. "And I'll tell Juliet you're on your way."

That night, Romeo went
again to the Capulets' garden
and climbed up the ivy to
Juliet's balcony.

Juliet!

Romeo!

But before dawn,
Romeo had to leave.
"It's not time yet,"
Juliet pleaded.
Romeo sighed.
Giving his new wife
one last kiss, he
climbed down the
balcony, sped from
the garden and set
off for Mantua.

36

All that morning, Juliet cried
and cried. Her nurse tried to
comfort her, but she couldn't stop.
Suddenly, her mother and
father swept in.

"Poor Juliet," said her mother,
going over to her. "You're still upset
about Tybalt. But this will cheer
you up. You're to marry Count
Paris. The wedding's on Thursday!"

"Thursday?" Juliet gasped. It was so soon. "And I don't want to marry Count Paris. Please don't make me." Her father scowled.

"I won't marry him," Juliet shouted. "No, no, no!"

"What do you mean, no?" said her father angrily. "You'll marry Count Paris on Thursday and that's that!" And her parents left.

"But I'm already married," wept Juliet. "What am I going to do?"

"Well, you can't tell your parents about Romeo," said her nurse.

I think you'll have to marry Count Paris.

The nurse bustled away and Juliet realized only one person could help her. "I must go and see Friar Laurence," she thought.

Chapter 5
The magic potion

Friar Laurence
was planting herbs
in his garden when Juliet arrived.

"Oh friar, please help me," she
begged. "My father says I have to
marry Count Paris on Thursday!"

"But you can't," said the friar.

"You have to help." Juliet was desperate. "I'd rather die than marry Paris. Is there anything you can do?"

The friar thought for a while. "Well," he said finally, "there is one thing that might work."

What is it?

"I'll give you a magic herbal potion," the friar said. "When you drink it, you'll go into a coma. Your body will be cold and it will look as if you're dead. But really, you'll just be in a very deep sleep, which will last for two days."

How will that help?

"Drink the potion tonight. In the morning, your parents will find you and think you're dead. They'll put your body in the Capulet family tomb while they arrange your funeral."

"Then what?" asked Juliet.

"I'll send a messenger to Mantua to tell Romeo the plan," the friar went on. "Two nights from now, you'll wake up. Romeo can come to Verona to rescue you -- and you can run away together!"

"I'll do it," said Juliet, bravely.
She held the bottle in a trembling
hand. "Thank you, Friar Laurence."
Clutching the potion tightly, she
turned and ran home.

Back at the Capulet mansion,
Juliet went to talk to her parents.

"I'm sorry I was rude to you," she
said sweetly. "I was upset about
Tybalt. Of course I'll marry Count
Paris on Thursday."

"Good girl," said her mother.

That night, Juliet sat on her bed.
Carefully, she uncorked the bottle
Friar Laurence had given her and
drank every last drop of the bitter
potion.

I hope
this works.

A few moments later, she fell into
a deep, deep sleep.

Chapter 6

Romeo returns

It was
just as the friar
had promised. The next morning,
Juliet's nurse found her cold body
lying on the bed and screamed.
"She's dead! Juliet's dead!"

"There'll be no wedding for my daughter," said Old Capulet, trying to hold back his tears. "Instead, we must prepare for a funeral. Carry her body to the family tomb."

Meanwhile, Friar Laurence wrote a letter to Romeo, explaining everything. He sealed up the letter and gave it to his friend, Friar John, to deliver.

But the news spread fast. Soon, people for miles around had heard about Juliet's death. In Mantua, a servant told Romeo that Capulet's daughter had died.

"I'll go back to Verona and find Juliet in the tomb," Romeo sobbed. "Then I'll lie beside her and drink poison, so I die too. That way, we can be together."

51

Romeo went to find an apothecary. "I need the strongest poison you have," he said.

"You can't buy poison in Mantua. It's against the law," the man told him. But Romeo saw he was poor and offered him forty gold coins. The apothecary quickly handed over a tiny bottle.

One sip of this could kill 20 men. Be careful.

Romeo put the poison in his bag
and headed for Verona
as fast as his horse
could carry him.

By the time Friar John arrived in
Mantua, Romeo had already left.
So the friar set off back to Verona,
without delivering the letter.

Late that night, Romeo arrived in Verona. He crept to the Capulets' house and found the entrance to the tomb. But someone else was already there.

Count Paris!

"What are you doing here, Montague?" demanded Count Paris. "Juliet is dead because of you. You killed her cousin Tybalt and she died of grief."

"That's not true!" Romeo cried. "I loved her more than you did."

"You're trespassing," snapped the Count, drawing his dagger. "Get out." He lunged at Romeo.

Romeo drew his dagger too and fought back. Count Paris gasped and fell to his knees, dying.

Oh! I am slain!

Romeo stepped over the body and went to find Juliet. She was lying inside, as cold as the stone beneath her. Romeo took her hand and wept as he kissed her cheek.

She still looks so beautiful – almost as if she's not dead at all.

Back at Friar Laurence's house, Friar John had returned. "I went to Mantua, but I couldn't deliver the message," he announced. "Romeo wasn't there."

Friar Laurence felt sick. "But Juliet will wake up alone in the tomb," he said. "I must rescue her!" And he rushed from his house, heading for the Capulet tomb.

In the tomb, Romeo took out his bottle of poison. He drank it all, lay down beside Juliet and kissed her one last time.

Thus with a kiss, I die.

The poison worked fast. In a few moments, Romeo lay still.

Not long after that, Juliet awoke. She rubbed her eyes and sat up. "Where am I?" she wondered. Then she remembered the magic potion and Friar Laurence's plan.

"Romeo?" she called. "Oh no!" she cried, as she saw his still body. She noticed the poison bottle in his hand and shook his shoulders. He didn't stir.

Juliet realized what he'd done. "Oh Romeo," she sobbed. "I can't live without you. I'll kiss your lips and poison myself too."

Just then she heard a noise. Someone was coming.

Juliet grabbed Romeo's dagger. Before anyone could arrive to stop her, she plunged it into her heart and collapsed on top of Romeo.

Friar Laurence burst into the tomb, followed by soldiers and servants. They were too late. Romeo and Juliet were dead.

The friar summoned the Capulets, the Montagues and Prince Escalus and told them the whole sad story.

The prince turned to the two families. "See what your hatred has done," he said. "Romeo and Juliet have paid the price for your feud."

Old Capulet and Old Montague agreed to bury Romeo and Juliet side by side. Wiping away their tears, they promised that their families would never fight again.

For never was a story of more woe,
Than this of Juliet, and her Romeo.

William Shakespeare
1564 - 1616

William Shakespeare was a writer who lived in England around 400 years ago. He wrote lots of plays, telling tales of love, marriage, murder, ghosts, witches and kings.

Shakespeare worked at a playhouse in London, called the Globe, where his plays were performed. Later, people collected the plays and made them into books.

Shakespeare didn't make up most of his stories. He got them from old books, folktales or real life, and retold them to make exciting plays. The story of Romeo and Juliet may have been based on real people who lived long ago in Italy.

Today, there is a replica of Shakespeare's Globe in London, where you can see his plays performed.

Series editor: Lesley Sims
Cover design: Russell Punter
Digital manipulation: Mike Olley

Internet links

For links to websites where you can find out more
about Shakespeare, go to the Usborne Quicklinks
Website at **www.usborne-quicklinks.com** and type
the keywords **YR Shakespeare**. Please note that
Usborne Publishing cannot be responsible for the
content of any website other than its own.

First published in 2006 by Usborne Publishing Ltd.,
Usborne House, 83-85 Saffron Hill, London EC1N 8RT, England.
www.usborne.com
Copyright © 2006 Usborne Publishing Ltd.

The Wind in the Willows

Kenneth Grahame
Adapted by Lesley Sims

Illustrated by
Mauro Evangelista

Reading Consultant: Alison Kelly
Roehampton University

Contents

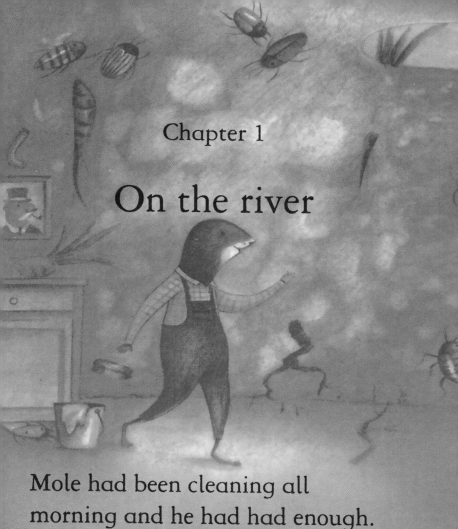

Chapter 1

On the river

Mole had been cleaning all morning and he had had enough.

"Bother!" he cried at last, flinging down his brush and heading for his tunnel to the outside world.

He scratched and he scrabbled
and he scraped with his paws, until
POP! he was out in the sun.

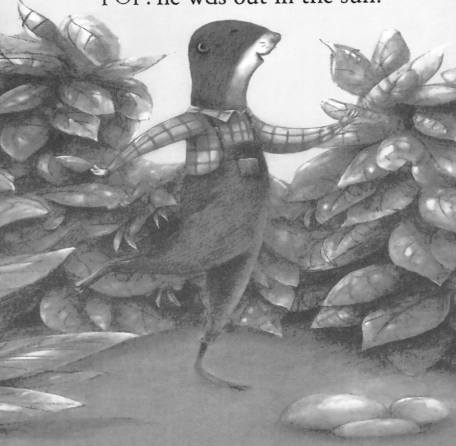

"This beats spring-cleaning!" Mole
cried, dancing around a hedge.

4

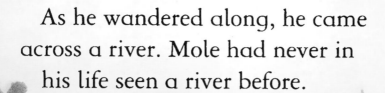

As he wandered along, he came
across a river. Mole had never in
his life seen a river before.

It chuckled and gurgled, rippling
with glints and gleams and
sparkles. Mole was bewitched.

He was gazing at the river, when
a small brown creature appeared
on the opposite bank. Then it
winked – it was the Water Rat.
  Mole and Rat looked at each
other for a moment.

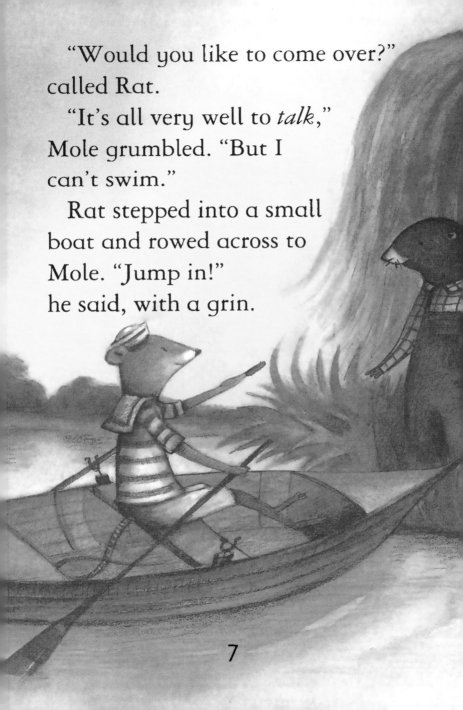

"Would you like to come over?" called Rat.

"It's all very well to *talk*," Mole grumbled. "But I can't swim."

Rat stepped into a small boat and rowed across to Mole. "Jump in!" he said, with a grin.

Mole took Rat's paw and carefully climbed aboard. He smiled in astonishment. "I've never been in a boat before."

"What?" cried Rat. "Never? What have you been doing then?"

"Is it as nice as all that?"
asked Mole, shyly.

"*Nice?*" said Rat.
"There's simply
nothing better..."
He drifted off
into a dream and
crunch!

The boat struck the bank.
"Oops!" Rat said, laughing,
and pulled away down the river.

9

Mole sat back, trailing a paw in the water and enjoying the gentle sway of the boat.

"What's over there?" he asked, sitting up and pointing to some trees in the distance.

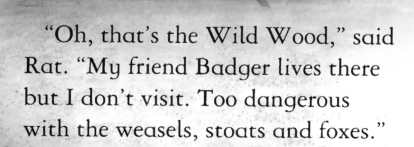

"Oh, that's the Wild Wood," said Rat. "My friend Badger lives there but I don't visit. Too dangerous with the weasels, stoats and foxes."

Before Rat could say more,
Mole spotted a stream of
bubbles and Otter's
wet, brown head
popped up.

"Everyone's on the river
today," he gasped. "I've just
seen Mr. Toad in his new boat
– new outfit, new gear, new
everything! Can't stop." And,
with a splash, Otter was gone.

11

Rat frowned. "Typical," he said.
"Toad's a great fellow, but he
always wants something
new. Then, as soon as
he has it, he's bored."

They stayed on the river until the
sun sank in the sky. Mole watched
Rat pulling the oars and decided
he wanted to row.

12

Excited, he jumped up and snatched the oars.

Then he plunged them into the water...

slipped, flew into the air...

and landed oomph! on Rat.

In a panic, Mole grabbed at the side of the boat. Sploosh! The boat went over and he was in the river – a very cold, wet river.

Coughing and spluttering, Mole was going under when a firm paw reached out to haul him to safety.

"Oh Ratty," he sobbed, a soggy lump of misery. "I am so s-s-sorry." Rat smiled. "Don't think any more about it. But how would you like to stay with me for a while? I could teach you to swim and row."

Mole was so pleased, he could only nod as they squelched home.

Chapter 2

The open road

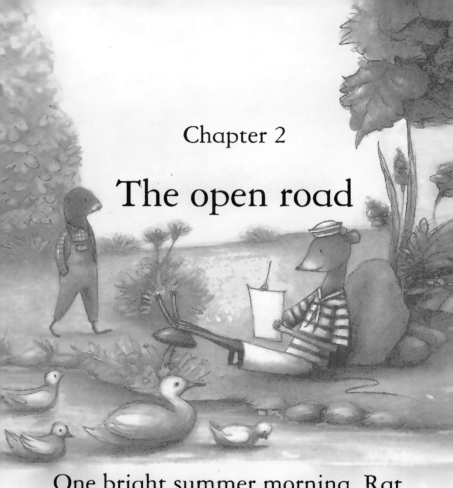

One bright summer morning, Rat was writing a poem about ducks when Mole appeared.

"Ratty," he said, "can we visit Mr. Toad?"

"Of course!" cried Rat, jumping up. "We'll row there at once. It's never the wrong time to visit Toad."

Mole gasped as he saw Toad Hall – a grand house with a lawn that went right down to the river.

Toad was in his garden, studying a map. "Hooray!" he said, as Rat and Mole strolled up. "You're just in time for a trip in my new caravan."

"I thought you had a new boat?" said Rat.

"Oh pooh!" said Toad, rudely. "Boats are boring. Wait until you see my wonderful caravan."

There was no doubt it had
everything they might need for a
few days away, and all so cleverly
stored. Soon, they were on the open
road. Even Rat, who missed his
river, enjoyed ambling
along the narrow
lanes.

He and Mole were walking
beside the caravan, talking of this
and that, when Poop! Poop! A car
swept past, throwing up a cloud
of dust and knocking the
caravan over.

Rat jumped up and down in fury,
waving his fist at the car. "You
villains!" he shouted. "Scoundrels!"
Toad didn't say anything but,
"Poop! Poop!"

Mole went to calm the horse and check the caravan. "It's ruined," he said sadly. "Oh Toad..."

"Who cares about that horrible little cart?" scoffed Toad. "A car is the only way to travel."

And he talked of nothing else, all the way back to Toad Hall.

Chapter 3

The Wild Wood

After their ruined caravan trip,
Mole and Rat stayed quietly by the
river. Many of Rat's friends looked
in for a chat, but never Badger.
Leaves fell and chill winds blew.
Rat stayed inside, snoozing
by the fire.

So, one cold afternoon, Mole slipped out to visit Badger himself. He felt quite cheerful as he entered the Wild Wood... until dusk fell.

The wood, already dark, grew darker. Strange shadows danced about him. Then a whistling began – faint, shrill and all around.

In a panic,
Mole began to
run, bumping into
things and falling
over. Shaking with fear,
he hid in the hollow of an
old oak tree — lost, worn out
and very, very scared.

Meanwhile, Rat had woken up.
"Moly!" he called but there was no
answer. He saw Mole's coat and
boots were gone and went outside.

There, in the mud, were Mole's
tracks – leading straight
into the Wild Wood.

Horrified, Rat grabbed a stick
and set off, calling for his friend
the whole time.

At last, he heard a little cry.
"Ratty, is it really you?" Mole
whimpered, from his hiding place.
"It really is," said Rat. "Come
on. We must go home."

But it had started to snow. Flakes whirled around them, covering the trees and hiding the path.

Rat shivered. "We may have to stay here after all."

They were looking for shelter, when Mole fell over a door-scraper.

To Mole's surprise, Rat laughed and began to dig in the snow.

"I don't see why you're so happy," grumbled Mole. "I've just scraped my shin."

"Don't you see?" panted Rat. "You've found the entrance to Badger's burrow!"

And Mole had.

"Badger!" yelled Rat, banging on the door. "It's Rat and my friend Mole, lost in the snow."

"Ratty?" said Badger, when he opened the door at last. "What are you doing out there? Come in and get yourselves warm."

He led them to a snug kitchen, found them dry clothes and made supper. Over steaming cocoa and oatcakes, they began to talk.

"Tell me all the news," said Badger. "How's Toad?"

Ratty frowned. "Going from bad to worse. He had another car crash last week."

"He's been taken to the hospital three times," added Mole, "and paid out a fortune in fines."

"He's a hopelessly bad driver," finished Rat, with a yawn. "If he carries on like this, he'll be killed."

"In the spring, we shall take him in hand," said Badger firmly. "But now it's time for bed."

The next morning, after a big breakfast to keep out the cold, and then lunch to keep up their strength, Badger waved them off.

"That's enough adventure for me for a while," thought Mole, as they headed for home.

Chapter 4

Talking to Toad

Early next spring, Badger arrived one morning, just as Mole and Rat were finishing breakfast.

"It's time to take Toad in hand!"
Badger declared. "We must go to
Toad Hall at once."

Up at Toad Hall, a shiny red car
sat on the drive. Toad was at the
front door, adjusting his
driving goggles.

"Hello!" he called cheerfully.
"You're just in time for a jolly, um
jolly..." He paused as he saw his
friends' stern faces.

"Inside," ordered Badger. "We're
going to your study for a talk."

"Talking won't work," muttered
Rat.

Almost an hour later, Badger and Toad came out of the study.

"Toad is very sorry for his foolishness with cars," said Badger. "Aren't you, Toad?"

"No!" Toad said. "Not sorry at all. In fact, the very next car I see, poop-poop! Off I shall go."

"Then we shall hide your keys and lock you in your bedroom until you see sense," said Badger. "We'll take turns keeping watch."

Rat was on duty when Toad
asked for a doctor and a lawyer.
"Oh Ratty, I feel so... oh dear,"
Toad moaned faintly.

Rat was alarmed. "Toad must be really ill," he thought, racing from the room and locking the door behind him. "I'd better get help."

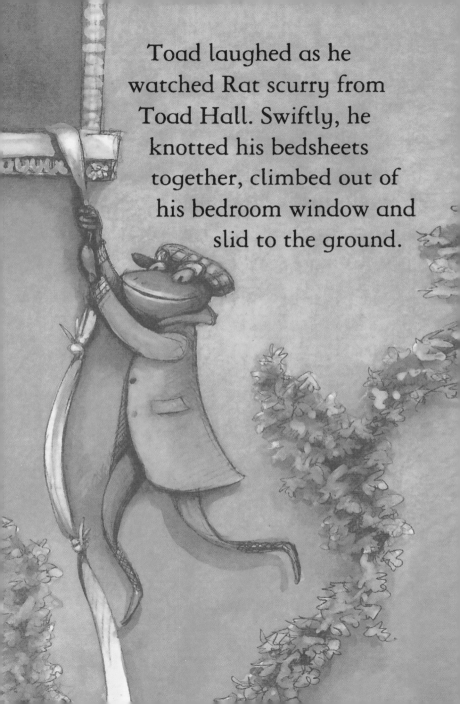

Toad laughed as he watched Rat scurry from Toad Hall. Swiftly, he knotted his bedsheets together, climbed out of his bedroom window and slid to the ground.

"I'm just too clever for Ratty!"
Toad thought as he briskly
walked away. "He's no
match for me."

Feeling very pleased
with himself, he went
on until he reached an
inn. Outside, was the
most magnificent car
Toad had ever seen.

"There's no harm in just *looking* at it," he said to himself. And then, "I wonder if it starts easily?"

As if in a dream, Toad started the engine...

as if in a dream, he climbed into the driver's seat...

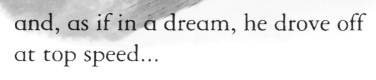

and, as if in a dream, he drove off at top speed...

41

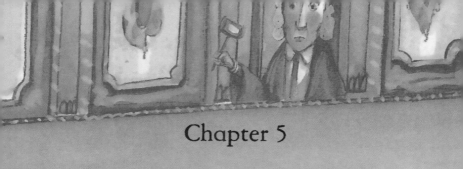

Chapter 5

Toad's adventures

The very next day, he was in court.
"Toad," said the Judge fiercely,
"you stole a valuable car. You
drove it very badly. *And* you were
rude to a policeman. I am sending
you to prison for twenty years!"

"This is the end of everything," Toad sobbed, as he sat in a lonely dungeon. "Oh wise Badger, oh clever Rat, oh sensible Mole. And stupid, stupid Toad."

Toad was too miserable to eat. The jailer's daughter noticed and it made her sad to see him so thin and unhappy.

"Cheer up Toad," she said. "See what I've brought you," and she handed him a plate piled high with hot buttered toast.

Toad dried his eyes, nibbled at the toast and began to feel better.

The jailer's daughter started to
visit regularly. As the days went
by, she grew to like him.

"Toad," she began, on one visit,
"my aunt is a washerwoman..."

"Never mind," said Toad.

"Do be quiet," she said. "My aunt
does the prisoners' washing and I
think she can help you escape..."

That night, a small, stout figure hurried from the prison in the dress and shawl of a washerwoman, hidden behind a pile of washing.

"Goodnight ma'am," said a prison guard.

Toad chuckled to himself. "'Night!" he squeaked in reply.

Toad stumbled through fields,
over ditches and under
hedges, until he was too
tired to go on.

With a huge yawn,
and pulling the shawl
tight around him, he
collapsed by a tree
and slept.

When Toad woke up the next
morning, he wondered where he
was. Then, with a leap of his heart,
he remembered — he was free!

He stood up, stretched
and marched
out into the
morning sun.

Before long, he reached a canal.
A solitary horse was plodding along
the tow path, pulling a yellow
barge with a smiling bargewoman.

Toad barely heard her friendly
greeting.

"Is anything wrong?" she asked.

"Well ma'am," he replied, "I
need to get to Toad Hall to do the,
um, washing and-"

49

"This is a bit of luck!" the woman interrupted. "I'm going that way now – and I have a pile of washing to be done."

"You are?" said Toad. "Pile of washing..." he added, doubtfully.

"Climb on," she said. "I'll give you a lift and you can do my washing on the way."

Toad stepped aboard with a
grin. "I am so clever," he thought.
"Washing's in the cabin," said
the bargewoman.
Toad shrugged. "How hard can
washing be?" he muttered.

After half an hour of fighting the
clothes, Toad was hot and drenched
but the clothes were as dirty as ever.
The bargewoman laughed.
"You're not a washerwoman at all."

"How dare you laugh at me,"
Toad roared. "I'll have you know
I'm a very distinguished Toad."

The bargewoman screamed.
"A slimy toad? On my barge?
Never!" And, grabbing him
by an arm and a leg, she
flung him overboard.

Toad went flying through the air and landed with a loud splash in the canal. Gasping for breath, he struggled to the bank, fighting his dress all the way. "It's all over," he wailed. "I shall be caught again."

"What's wrong?" asked a voice. Toad looked up to see a familiar face. A small brown face with whiskers. "Ratty?" he said.

"Toad?" said Rat. "Is that you?
Whatever happened?"

"I've had such trials," boasted
Toad. "Thrown into prison, then
escaped. Come to Toad Hall and
I'll tell you the whole amazing tale."

"Oh Toad, we can't," said Rat.
"The Wild Wooders have
taken it over."

Chapter 6

A surprise attack

A shocked Toad followed Rat home.
"Now don't worry," said Rat,
once Toad had dried off. "Badger
has a plan to recapture Toad Hall."

Just then, Mole and Badger came in. "Ratty, we attack tonight!" said Mole. "They're having a party and Badger knows a secret tunnel that leads right into Toad Hall and..."

He stopped as he saw Toad. "Toad, you're home! Whatever happened?"

"It's quite a story..." Toad began.

"No time for that now," said Badger. "We must prepare."

That night, armed with sticks and swords, the four of them crept into the secret tunnel. They groped and shuffled along, until at last Badger stopped. "We ought to be under the Hall now."

As they paused, they heard a murmur of shouting, cheering and stomping from above.

The tunnel sloped up and they came through a trap door, into the kitchen. Such a noise was coming from the main hall, there was little danger they'd be overheard.

"NOW boys!" shouted Badger
and they ran into the hall.

59

Squealing and screeching filled
the air as terrified weasels dived
through windows and startled
stoats shot under the table.

Badger, Mole and Rat dashed
around, bopping anyone who got
in their way. As for Toad, he went
straight for the Chief Weasel
and sent him flying.

In five minutes, it was all over.
"Well done everyone!" said
Badger. "I think we should have
a party of our own to celebrate."

"Dear friends," Toad said, over
a jolly supper. "Thank you for all
your help. I wouldn't have my
home back without you."

And, from that night, Toad was a changed animal. Instead of being boastful or reckless, he was content to live a quiet life by the river with his three best friends.

Kenneth Grahame (1859-1932)

Kenneth Grahame spent part of his childhood with his grandmother, in Cookham Dene, Berkshire, in England. He loved playing in her garden by the river, and exploring the nearby woods.

When he grew up, he worked for the Bank of England, but he wrote in his spare time. *The Wind in the Willows* was written for his son, Alastair, and first published in 1908.

Designed by Hannah Ahmed

First published in 2007 by Usborne Publishing Ltd., Usborne House, 83-85 Saffron Hill, London EC1N 8RT, England. www.usborne.com
Copyright © 2007 Usborne Publishing Ltd.

THE SORCERER'S APPRENTICE

Retold by Fiona Chandler

Illustrated by
Poly Bernatene

Reading Consultant: Alison Kelly
Roehampton University

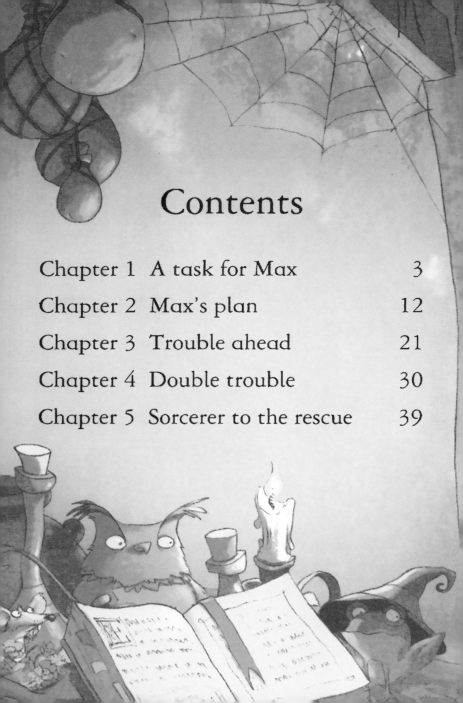

Contents

Chapter 1

A task for Max

Max had spent all morning cleaning the sorcerer's workshop – and he still hadn't finished.

Wash this...
Polish that... I'm
fed up with it.

"How will I ever learn to be a sorcerer like Sticklewick?" he moaned. "He never lets me do any magic."

Just then, Max heard footsteps on the stone staircase. "Uh-oh, that's him! Back to work."

4

A moment later, Sticklewick
appeared. "Max, I have to go
into town," he announced,
waving a long shopping list.

5

Max was astonished.
Sticklewick had never left him
alone in the castle before.

"I can explore the dungeons
and swim in the moat," he
thought. "Or just sit in the sun
and do nothing at all."

"There's plenty to do while I'm out," Sticklewick went on. "For a start, this floor could do with a good scrub."

Look! I've just stepped on a toadstool.

"But fill up the water tank first. It's almost empty."

8

Max groaned. It always took hours to fetch enough water to fill the tank. And it was such hard work.

"Oh, and one more thing,"
Sticklewick added.
"Don't try any spells!"
He frowned.

"Or I'll... I'll turn you into a
tadpole," he threatened, his
bushy eyebrows bristling.

10

With that, there was a flash
of light and a puff of purple
smoke. The sorcerer was gone.

Chapter 2

Max's plan

"Well, don't just stand there!"
croaked a little voice. "You
have work to do." It was
Tabitha, Sticklewick's toad.

"Oh, hop it!" said Max, crossly. "I've been working all morning. I need a rest first."

"There's no need to be rude," said Tabitha, hopping onto a broomstick.

13

Max didn't reply. Seeing Tabitha perched on the broom had given him a brilliant idea.

Last week, Sticklewick had cast a spell on a broomstick. It had come to life and done everything the sorcerer asked.

"I'm sure I can remember the words," Max thought, concentrating.

"You're up to something," said Tabitha. "You'd better not try any spells. You heard what Sticklewick said."

"Don't be such a spoilsport," said Max. "What harm can it do? Anyway, he won't know."

Max closed his eyes and thought for a moment. Taking a deep breath, he said the magic words...

Root and branch of old oak tree, bring this broom to life for me!

All at once, the broom began to twitch. It shook and it shuddered, then... slowly... it grew two skinny arms and two skinny legs.

Wow! I did it!

"Now," Max ordered the broom, "fetch me some water. And be quick about it!"

18

The broom ran off. In no time, Max heard it coming tap-tap-tap down the steps. It poured the water into the tank and set off for more.

Feeling very pleased with himself, Max flopped down in the sorcerer's chair. "Time for a snooze," he yawned.

Soon, he was fast asleep.

Chapter 3

Trouble ahead

Max woke up to find Tabitha hopping on his lap. "What is it?" he mumbled, sleepily.

"Quick!" croaked Tabitha. "The tank is overflowing and the broom won't stop!"

Max jumped to his feet. Water was sloshing over the sides of the tank... and the broom was clattering down the steps again.

"Stop!" he shouted. "That's enough!" But the broom took no notice. Streams of water poured across the floor.

"Great stuttering sorcerers,
just say the spell!" begged
Tabitha.

"What spell?" asked Max,
puzzled. Then he remembered.
Of course! He needed a spell
to make the broom stop.

"Oh no," he groaned. "I... um... I don't think I actually know it."

Oh boy!

By now, the water was ankle deep. And still the broom was fetching more.

"I know!" cried Max, splashing across the floor. "I'll look in Sticklewick's spell book. Let's see..."

How to cure smelly feet

How to turn cabbage into chocolate

How to make it Christmas every day

Max flicked through
page after page.

"This is hopeless," he wailed.
"There are thousands of spells
here. I'll *never* find the right
one. What am I going to do?"

"You could chop the broom
up," said Tabitha, helpfully.

"Good thinking!" said Max. He grabbed a hatchet, lifted it high above his head and swung it down hard.

With a loud CRACK, the broomstick split in two.

Chapter 4

Double trouble

"That was close," said Max, with a sigh of relief. "Thanks Tabitha, you're brilliant! Tabitha? What's wrong?"

"Look at the broom!"
Max's eyes opened wide. The two pieces of the broom were moving... and each piece was growing new arms and legs.

Faster than ever, the brooms
raced off for more water.
"I'm in big trouble now,"
thought Max, glumly.

In no time, the brooms
were back, sloshing water
everywhere.

Max tried to stop them.

He tried
tripping
them.

He even tried to sit on them.
But it was no use.

"I give up," said Max, miserably. "Sticklewick is going to be furious."

I wonder what it's like to be a tadpole...

Meanwhile, the brooms were still dashing in and out, up and down the steps. All the time, the water was getting deeper.

Soon it reached Max's knees... then his waist... then his chest.

I wish I could swim.

SPLASH! SPLOSH! The brooms flung a few more pails of water into the room. Waves washed across the workshop.

Tabitha shot past, trying
to surf.

"I warned you not to try any spells," she spluttered, spitting out water. "Maybe next time you'll listen to me."

37

"If this goes on, there won't *be* a next time," muttered Max, desperately. "Help!" he yelled, climbing onto the table.

Somebody help!

But he knew there was no one around to hear.

Chapter 5

Sorcerer to the rescue

Suddenly, there was a loud pop. Sticklewick appeared in a shower of green sparks.

What on earth...?

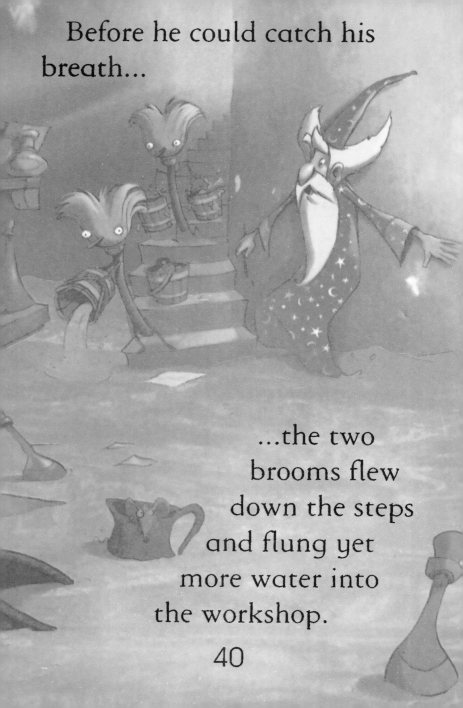

Before he could catch his breath...

...the two brooms flew down the steps and flung yet more water into the workshop.

40

"Galloping goblins!" cried the sorcerer. "What *has* that boy been doing?"

Quickly, he raised his wand and spoke the magic words.

Eye of bat and tooth of boar, return to how you were before!

In a flash, one of the brooms vanished. The other whizzed across the room and stood neatly to one side.

Finally, with a loud glug-glug-glug, the water began to drain away.

42

Nervously, Max climbed
down from the table. His
knees felt weak.

I'm in for
it now.

Sticklewick glared at him.
"Well? What have you got to
say for yourself?"

"Um... I'm really sorry..."

"Not good enough!" roared the sorcerer. "I warned you. Now it's tadpole time."

Max dived behind the water tank. "*Please* don't turn me into a tadpole," he cried. "I won't ever meddle with magic again."

"No, you won't," snapped
Sticklewick. "Tadpoles can't do
simple spells and they certainly
can't do tricky ones..."

He paused and thought for a
second. Max didn't dare move.

Hmm... that was
quite a difficult
spell you did...

Just then, Tabitha spoke.
"He might be a good sorcerer
one day... Maybe you should
start teaching him magic."

He is your
apprentice
after all...

"Maybe..." said Sticklewick,
"but first he cleans up here."
He turned to Max. "And if you
ever disobey me again, you'll
be frogspawn in the moat."

From that day on, Max was
a perfect pupil. Soon he learned
how to do spells properly. And
when he grew up, he became a
great sorcerer...

...although he was always a
little afraid of broomsticks.

The tale of *The Sorcerer's Apprentice* has been around for almost 2,000 years. It was first written down by a Greek named Lucian of Samosata. This version is based on a poem composed in 1797 by the German writer, Johann Wolfgang von Goethe.

Series editor: Lesley Sims
Designed by Katarina Dragoslavic

First published in 2007 by Usborne Publishing Ltd., Usborne House, 83-85 Saffron Hill, London EC1N 8RT, England. www.usborne.com Copyright © 2007 Usborne Publishing Ltd.
Printed in China. UE. First published in America in 2007.

Macbeth

Based on the play by
William Shakespeare

Retold by Conrad Mason

Illustrated by
Christa Unzner

Reading consultant: Alison Kelly
Roehampton University

Characters in the story

Macbeth

Lady Macbeth

Banquo

Macduff

Ross

Duncan, King of Scotland

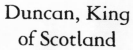

Malcolm

Three witches

Contents

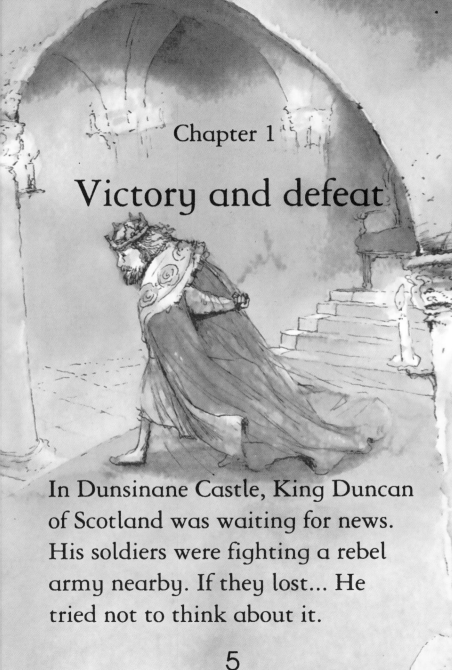

Chapter 1

Victory and defeat

In Dunsinane Castle, King Duncan
of Scotland was waiting for news.
His soldiers were fighting a rebel
army nearby. If they lost... He
tried not to think about it.

5

The doors to the throne room crashed open, and Duncan's son staggered in, supporting a wounded warrior.

"Father," Prince Malcolm panted, "this man has just come from the battlefield!"

"What news?" asked the
king, nervously.

"Victory sire," the warrior gasped,
"thanks to your general, Macbeth."

He killed the
rebel leader.

King Duncan sighed with relief.

7

"Find the man a doctor," he
ordered, as Malcolm helped the
warrior out of the room.

Then Duncan called for his
trusted advisor, Lord Ross. "Go to
Macbeth," he said, "and tell him I
shall reward him for his bravery."

From now on,
Macbeth shall be
Lord of Cawdor.

Chapter 2

The witches

Meanwhile, Macbeth and his friend Banquo were riding home from the battlefield.

All at once, a mist sprang up, swirling around them, and the sky grew dark.

Macbeth pulled up his horse with a yell of fright.

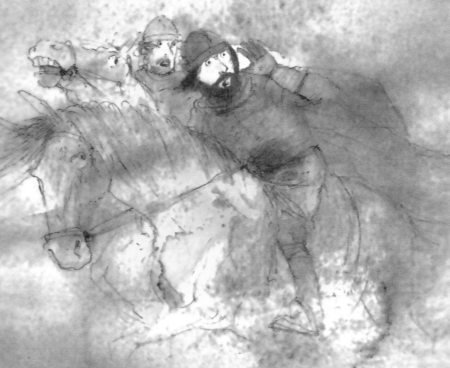

In front of them, three figures loomed out of the mist.

They were old, ugly hags,
all dressed in black cloaks.

"Who are you?" cried Macbeth.
He tried to sound brave, but inside
he was terrified.

"Hail Macbeth, Lord of Cawdor,
and future king of Scotland!" the
hags cackled.

"Wait, what do you mean?"
demanded Banquo. "Who says
Macbeth is the Lord of Cawdor?"
But the figures had vanished.

Macbeth's eyes grew wide.
"Were they witches?" he whispered.

Before Banquo could reply, a
horseman rode out of the mist.
It was Lord Ross.

"Macbeth," he called. "I bring
great news. King Duncan has
made you Lord of Cawdor."

14

Banquo was amazed. "So they were right after all," he thought. He turned to look at his friend.

But Macbeth was gazing into the distance, lost in thought.

Chapter 3

Murderous plans

In the tallest tower of Inverness
Castle, Lady Macbeth was reading
a letter from her husband.

"Well, well, three witches said
you'd be king!" she murmured.
"But are you brave enough to
make our dreams come true?"

As she pondered, the door opened
and Macbeth came in.

Welcome home!

He threw his sword and helmet
on the bed and hugged his wife.

17

She stepped back and looked into his eyes. "My husband," she said, "if you're to be King of Scotland, only one man stands in your way – and that's Duncan."

Macbeth shut his eyes. Ever since meeting the witches, he had been haunted by thoughts of killing Duncan. He wanted to be king, just as they had promised.

But the thought of murder filled him with dread.

"No," he said, turning away.

I can't kill him. I won't do it.

"You coward!" spat Lady Macbeth. "This is your chance to be king. Everyone knows you deserve it. What's more, Duncan is coming to visit this very night!"

Macbeth thought again. He couldn't do it – could he? The thought of a glittering crown filled his heart with excitement and greed.

Chapter 4

Death in the night

The great hall of Inverness Castle rang with music and laughter. At the end of the table, King Duncan chatted with Lady Macbeth.

Meanwhile, Macbeth stood alone in the moonlit courtyard. His mind was made up – Duncan would die. He just wished that it was over and done with.

Slowly, he walked back to the great hall, praying that the hours would pass more quickly.

At long last, Duncan and his lords went to bed, and the servants put out the torches. Silence filled the dark castle.

Macbeth took a deep breath, and wiped his brow. It was time.

24

But as he approached the steps
to Duncan's room, he stopped
dead. Was his mind playing tricks?
In the darkness he could see a
dagger, dripping with blood.

Can it
be real?

He shook his head. Nothing
there. Clutching his own dagger,
Macbeth climbed the steps...

The next morning, the castle
woke to a terrible howl from
Duncan's room.

"Murder! Murder!"

Everyone jumped out of bed and
rushed to see what was happening.

Oh horror!

They soon found
King Duncan – dead.

"Who did this?" thundered
Macbeth. No one had an answer.
Only Macbeth knew the truth, and
he kept it to himself.

In silence, the lords stared at their
dead king.

Chapter 5

To kill a friend

A week had passed. Macbeth sat
alone in the great throne room at
Dunsinane Castle, thinking.

After Duncan's murder, Prince Malcolm had gone missing, and the lords had crowned Macbeth instead. He was king!

Now he had everything he wanted. But he wasn't happy. He was thinking of Banquo. Banquo knew about the witches. What if he guessed who killed Duncan?

There was only one solution —
Banquo would have to die, too.
Macbeth rang for a servant.

You sent for me,
my lord?

"Listen closely," Macbeth told
him. "Tonight I am holding a feast
for all my lords. Find Banquo, and
make sure that he never arrives."

The servant bowed and left. Alone again, Macbeth thought of his best friend Banquo, who would soon be dead.

A sick feeling swept over him, made up of fear, sadness, and terrible, terrible guilt. His life was turning into a nightmare.

That night, two horsemen trotted
through a gloomy forest, on their
way to the feast. It was Banquo
and his son, Fleance.

Fleance shivered, and pulled his
cloak tighter around his shoulders.

"Looks like rain,"
grumbled Banquo.

"Let it pour," said a voice from
the bushes.

Before Banquo could react, he was on the ground, with someone's knee on his chest. Men stood all around, their daggers gleaming in the dark.

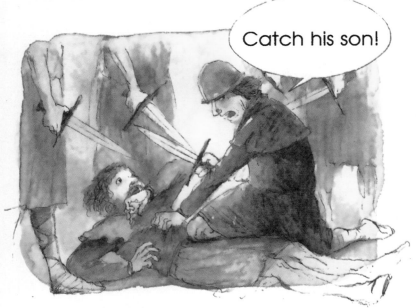

"Run!" Banquo howled at Fleance. The terrified boy turned his horse and sped off as fast as he could.

Banquo reached for his sword, but it was too far away. There was nothing he could do. He closed his eyes as the daggers came closer...

Chapter 6

The haunting

Macbeth's feast was nearly over
when something terrible happened.

He looked around at the happy
guests and smiled. Then he froze.
There, at the end of the table,
was Banquo.

Macbeth stumbled to his feet and
cried out in fear. At once, everyone
stopped talking.

"What's wrong, my dearest?"
asked Lady Macbeth.

"You should be dead!" croaked
Macbeth, pointing at Banquo.

The lords couldn't see
Banquo – just an empty place.

Banquo's face was deathly
white, and his clothes were stained
with blood. He glared at Macbeth,
saying nothing.

"A ghost!" stammered Macbeth.
"It wasn't me! I didn't kill you!"
But the ghost had gone.
Murmurs ran around the table.

"Get out!" shouted Macbeth.
"All of you. Leave me alone."
The puzzled lords stood and
hurried out, casting worried
glances at their king.

In minutes, only Macbeth and
his wife were left. He turned to her,
and saw that her eyes were filling
with tears.

"Can we ever
      forget what we've done?"
she wept.
      Macbeth took her hand
and tried to comfort her,
but she wouldn't look at him.
Murder was driving them apart.

Chapter 7

Three prophecies

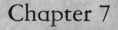

The wind howled across the moor,
and rain fell in thick sheets.

"I need to speak to you, witches,"
called Macbeth. "Where are you?"

At once, they appeared.

"What's to become of me?"
Macbeth demanded.

"Fear Macduff, the Lord of Fife," cried one.

"Fear nothing," said the second, "until Birnam Wood comes to Dunsinane Castle."

Macbeth sighed with relief. "That can never happen," he smiled. "I'm safe."

"Fear no man," said the third witch, "that was born of a woman."

"Then I really have nothing to fear," said Macbeth, laughing. "Every man was born of a woman – even Macduff."

The witches gave no reply. They faded into the rain, and were gone.

"My lord?"
Macbeth turned to see a messenger, waiting patiently with his horse. "Yes?" he asked.

"Lord Macduff has found Prince Malcolm, in England," said the messenger. "He hopes to bring him back and make him king."

Macbeth went pale. "So be it!" he raged. "Macduff will pay for his treachery. Order my men to enter his castle, and kill his wife and children."

Chapter 8

The tide turns

In England, Prince Malcolm sat
with Lord Macduff beside a stream.
It was a beautiful day. Birds flew
overhead, and the sun shone.

"It's time for you to come back to Scotland," said Macduff, gravely. "You should be king. It was Macbeth who killed your father – I'm sure of it."

Malcolm said nothing. He was deep in thought.

Then his face broke into a
smile. He had spotted Lord Ross
approaching across the meadow,
and he leaped up to greet him.

"Lord Ross, my father's friend!"
he cried.

But Ross didn't seem happy to
see Malcolm.

"Lord Macduff, I have something
dreadful to tell you," he said. "The
tyrant Macbeth has killed your
wife and children."

Macduff's face twisted with grief and fury. Then he spoke, his voice calm and cold. "Now you see why you must return," he said.

"Very well," said Malcolm. "Macbeth must be stopped. Tomorrow we march to Dunsinane."

Chapter 9

Macbeth's last stand

When news spread that Malcolm was on his way, the lords of Scotland flocked to join him. By now, everyone guessed that it was Macbeth who had killed Duncan.

At Birnam Wood, Malcolm halted his army. "Cut branches from the trees," he ordered. "We'll hide behind them when we attack Dunsinane Castle."

As the army advanced, hidden behind their shield of leaves, it seemed as if the great forest itself was moving.

From the battlements, Macbeth watched in panic. Just as the witches had promised, Birnam Wood was coming to Dunsinane.

A moment later, a horrible scream came from inside the castle, and a servant rushed out, his hands covered in blood. "My lord," he stammered, "it's your wife. She's killed herself."

Macbeth went white. He understood at once – guilt had driven his wife to this. He felt lonely, and numb with fear.

But there was no time to grieve.
"Bring me my sword," he roared.
"I don't care if Birnam Wood has
come to Dunsinane. No man can
kill me. Open the gates!"

The battle was fierce. But within minutes, Malcolm's soldiers had taken the castle. Everywhere, men lay dying.

Macduff crept down a corridor, hunting for Macbeth.

Macduff spun and saw Macbeth, his eyes blazing and his sword dripping with blood.

"You can't kill me," sneered Macbeth. "No one born of a woman can hurt me."

"Then prepare to die, you murderer," said Macduff grimly. "For I was never born! I was cut from my mother's dead body."

Macbeth threw back his head and laughed. "So, the witches tricked me," he snarled. "Very well. At least I'll die fighting!" And he ran at Macduff.

The two men fought like demons. Their swords flashed through the air, and clashed against each other.

Then all at once, Macbeth
slipped. He reached out to steady
himself, but it was too late.
Macduff's sword was raised, ready
to strike.

In a moment the blade came
slicing down, and it was all over.

"Hail Malcolm, King of Scotland," Macduff panted.

Macbeth lay dead on the ground, where his greed for power had brought him. His bloody deeds had led to the bloodiest of ends.

William Shakespeare
1564-1616

William Shakespeare was
born in Stratford-upon-Avon,
England, and became famous
as an actor and writer when he moved to
London. He wrote many poems and almost forty
plays which are still performed and enjoyed today.

Internet links

You can find out more about Shakespeare by going to the
Usborne Quicklinks Website at www.usborne-quicklinks.com
and typing in the keywords 'yr shakespeare'.
Please note that Usborne Publishing cannot be responsible
for the content of any website other than its own.

Designed by Michelle Lawrence

Series designer: Russell Punter

Series editor: Lesley Sims

First published in 2008 by Usborne Publishing Ltd., Usborne House,
83-85 Saffron Hill, London EC1N 8RT, England. www.usborne.com
Copyright © 2008 Usborne Publishing Ltd.

Stories of Princes and Princesses

Christopher Rawson
Adapted by Lesley Sims

Illustrated by
Stephen Cartwright

Reading consultant: Alison Kelly
Roehampton University

Contents

Chapter 1

The clumsy prince

Colin was the clumsiest prince in the kingdom. Other princes fought dragons. Colin fell over them. Other princes battered villains. Colin bumped into them.

3

One day, he tripped in front
of a sad princess. She thought
he was so funny, she wanted
to marry him on the spot.

Are you princely
enough to marry my
daughter?

Her father had other ideas.
He gave Colin three tests, tests
he knew Colin would not pass.

4

First, Colin had to show
how polite he could be. But
he was so busy talking
politely to the queen...

...that he didn't see the butler.

Next,
he had to
take the
princess
out. But
somehow,

he lost the royal boat.

Then he had to ride the royal
horse like a prince.

"He rides like a clown!" said

the king.
"He must
leave the
palace
tomorrow."

6

That night, Colin couldn't sleep. Suddenly, he heard a scream. It was the princess!

Help! I'm being kidnapped!

Colin jumped. What was going on? Was someone stealing the princess? He leaned out of his window and sent a flower pot flying...

Oww!

...straight onto the head of the man stealing the princess.

The princess thief fell to
the ground with a thud.
  Colin raced from the tower
and swept up the princess.

The king and queen raced
out too.

"What's going on?" cried
the king. "What has Clumsy
Colin done now?"

"He's rescued me!" said the
princess.

"Really?" said the king.

"Really!" she said.

The king smiled. "Well, the reward for rescuing a princess is to marry her," he said.

So Colin lived clumsily, but happily ever after.

Chapter 2

The princess who wouldn't get married

Prue liked being a princess, except for one thing. She didn't want to marry a prince.

"You have to," said her dad. "It's what princesses do."

12

The king asked three princes
to visit. "Choose one," he
told Prue.

But Prue didn't want to.
"Princes are boring!" she said.

Prue did like the third prince. But she didn't say so.

Too hairy!

The king was angry.

If you won't marry a prince, you'll marry the first man who comes to the castle!

The very next day, a beggar
arrived, playing an old violin.

Prue and the
beggar were
married on
the spot.

With his beard, the beggar
reminded Prue of someone.
Whoever he was, she didn't
want to marry him. But the
beggar took Prue home
as his wife.

Welcome
to your new
home!

"Cheer up!" he said. "If you
married a prince, you'd have
to live in a boring castle."

The beggar was kind, but very poor. They wore old rags and never had enough to eat. Prue was used to servants. Now, she did everything.

One day, the beggar
brought home some straw.
"We can make baskets to
sell," he said. But the straw
cut Prue's hands.

"You must get a job," said the beggar. "Prince Alec is getting married. Perhaps you can work in the castle over the hill."

The castle cook was pleased to have help. She took pity on Prue and gave her some food.

Prue was going home when she passed the ballroom. She sighed. There was Prince Alec, giving a speech to his guests.

Perhaps it wouldn't have been so bad to marry a prince...

Just then, the prince turned around and saw her.

"You're the hairy prince!" cried Prue.

Prue tried to run away and the food fell from her apron. The guests began to laugh.

"I'd like to dance with you!"
said the prince and he reached
for her hand.

Just one dance.

Prue burst into tears. She pulled her hand from

the prince and fled.

But Prince Alec caught up with her. Prue looked at him closely. It was her beggar.

Don't you recognize my violin?

He took her back to the
ballroom.

"Would you marry a
prince now?" asked Alec.

"I would," said Prue. "But
I'm already married to you!"

Chapter 3

The princess and the pig boy

Once, a poor prince named Sam lived in a tiny castle. All he owned were a beautiful rose tree and a lovely nightingale.

Sam fell in love with a rich princess named Sara. So, he sent her his beautiful tree and the lovely nightingale.

But Sara was not pleased. "A silly tree and a noisy bird?" she said. "Send them back!"

Sam didn't give up. He went
to Sara's palace and got a job
taking care of the palace pigs.

But Sam missed his home.
He especially missed the
lovely songs of his nightingale.
So, he made a rattle which
played magical tunes.

It's put
the pigs to
sleep!

Sara was out with her maids when she heard the rattle.

"I want it!" she said.

"It costs one hundred kisses," said Sam.

"Never!" said Sara. But she did want the rattle. "I'll give you ten kisses," she said.

"The price is one hundred," said Sam. Sara had to give in.

31

The king was on his balcony, when he heard giggling. It was coming from the pig sty.

The king hurried down. He
crept up behind Sara's maids
and looked over their shoulders.

The king was very angry.
"Princesses don't kiss pig
boys!" he shouted. "Both of
you must leave at once."

Go and never come back!

Sam and Sara had to leave
the palace.

"I don't even like pigs," said Sara. "I wish I'd married that poor prince."

Sam quickly changed his clothes behind a tree. "You can!" he cried.

The poor prince!

The happy prince!

Sam took Sara to live in his tiny castle. Sometimes, she even watered the rose tree.

Chapter 4

The smelly prince

Percy was the rudest, dirtiest, smelliest prince in the country.

He lived all alone in his dirty old castle. He didn't like children. He hated animals. He had no friends, not one.

Even his soldiers called him Smelly Perce – though not to his face.

He was a very lonely prince, until one day, he had an idea. He would capture a princess and marry her.

Percy grabbed the first princess to come along. He was taking her home when they passed some moles. There were mole hills all over his field. Percy was very angry.

Percy locked the princess in a tower. But she had already agreed to marry someone else – a clean prince named Harry.

"I shall rescue her at once!" Harry said...

...but he couldn't get into Percy's castle.

Just then, a mole popped its
head above ground.

"Percy smashed our homes,"
it said. "We'll help you."

Don't worry, your
highness. We'll soon get
you into the castle.

The moles dug all night.

They dug all of the next day too. By the following evening, they'd built a tunnel.

It ran all the way under the moat and into the castle.

Prince Harry was delighted.
The tunnel took him into
Percy's dungeons.

Harry set the prisoners free.
Then he went to find Percy
and the princess.

Percy tried to stop Harry.
But his sword was so rusty,
it bent. He was no match
for Harry.

As if that wasn't bad
enough, Harry's soldiers
decided Percy needed a bath.

To Percy's surprise, he
found being clean was fun.
And people were friendlier.

Harry rescued the princess and married her. Even Percy was invited to their wedding.

The invitation said: "Please come – but take a bath first!"

Try these other books in
Series One:

Wizards: One wizard looks after orphans, one sells cures and one must stop a band of robbers.

Giants: Two huge stories – about a kind giant called a troll and how three mean giants meet a grisly end.

Witches: Three bewitching tales: one witch loses her broomstick, another loses her temper, and the third loses her cool with a clever farmer.

Dragons: Stan must outwit a dragon to feed his children, while Victor must persuade two dragons not to eat him.

Designed by
Katarina Dragoslavić

This edition first published in 2007 by Usborne Publishing Ltd.,
Usborne House, 83-85 Saffron Hill, London EC1N 8RT, England.
www.usborne.com
Copyright © 2007, 2003, 1980 Usborne Publishing Ltd.

48

Stories of Magical Animals

Retold by
Carol Watson

Adapted by Gill Harvey

Illustrated by Nick Price

Reading consultant: Alison Kelly
Roehampton University

Contents

Chapter 1

Pegasus

Long ago in Greece, there lived
a handsome prince named
Bellerophon*. He was strong,
brave, and loved by everyone...
except the king.

* say bel-**lair**-o-fon

The king wanted to get rid of
Bellerophon. So, he thought up
a plan and sent for the prince.

"Think you're brave, do you?"
he sneered. "We'll soon see
about that."

You must kill the
Chimera*, a terrible
beast that keeps eating
my people.

4

* say ki-**meer**-a

Eager to obey his king, Bellerophon set off to find the monster. On the way, an old lady stopped him.

"First, you must catch the winged horse, Pegasus," she said.

"Find Pegasus and you will be safe from the beast. Pegasus is strong and swift and flies like a bird."

After searching for days,
Bellerophon found the horse
high up in the mountains.
"What a beauty," he gasped.

Pegasus was wild and free,
with powerful beating wings.
Catching him wouldn't be easy.

In a flash of silvery light,
the goddess Athene* appeared.
She held out a golden bridle
to Bellerophon.

This is a magic bridle. It will help you catch Pegasus.

"If you put this over the horse's head, Pegasus will become tame," she said.

7

Bellerophon thanked Athene and hid behind a rock near a river. When Pegasus came to drink, Bellerophon tiptoed out.

Very quietly, he crept up to Pegasus and slipped the bridle over the horse's head.

Startled, Pegasus reared up.
"Steady," said Bellerophon.
The horse calmed down and
Bellerophon climbed onto
his back.

Spreading his wings, Pegasus
soared into the sky.

9

As they flew on, the air grew hot, steamy and smelly.

"Ugh!" said the prince as he sniffed. "That's disgusting! We must be near the Chimera."

They flew down in time to see the beast leaving its cave.

The Chimera didn't have just one head. It had two: a goat-head, with terrible horns, and a lion-head which breathed fire.

Even its tail was an evil-looking snake. It spat at Bellerophon, trying to sting him with poison.

11

Pegasus flew closer and the prince fired his arrows. The lion roared. Huge flames shot from its mouth.

Pegasus rose above the fire
and Bellerophon shot more
arrows. They struck the goat-
head and the snake-tail.

Then the prince took out his
spear and stuck a lump of lead
on the end of it.

The mouth of the lion-head opened wide to roar and Bellerophon plunged his spear down the lion-head's throat.

As the lead melted, the lion-head gave a howl of pain and the beast collapsed. The Chimera was dead.

Bellerophon went back to the king and told him the good news.

The king wasn't too pleased, but his people were delighted.

"Bellerophon's a hero," they cried. "He's like a god!"

All this praise made
Bellerophon big-headed.

"Maybe I
am a god,"
he said. "If
I beat the
Chimera, I
must be!"
So he flew
to Mount
Olympus,
where the
gods lived.

Time to
go home.

Zeus, the king of the gods, was annoyed to see the prince and sent a bee to sting Pegasus. The horse reared up, throwing Bellerophon off.

Bellerophon fell through the clouds to the ground and was killed in an instant.

Then Zeus caught Pegasus and rode him home to Mount Olympus.

Faster, Pegasus, faster!

From that day on, Pegasus lived with the gods, pulling Zeus across the sky in a chariot made of gold.

Chapter 2

The greedy
griffin

Hassan was a farmer, but the
only animals on his farm were
his two beloved oxen.

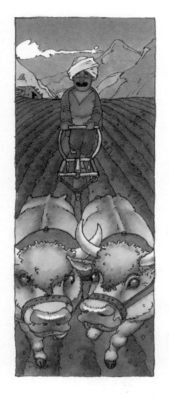

One day, he was working in the fields when, suddenly, the sky went dark.

Hassan looked up. Was it about to rain? But he didn't see a cloud overhead...

...he saw a griffin! A griffin was a terrifying creature. It had the head and wings of an eagle, but the body of a lion.

20

Swooping down, the griffin snatched up the two oxen in its lion's claws.

Hassan ran away in terror. With a few flaps of its giant wings, the griffin was gone.

Back at home, Hassan sat down and wept.

"There is no hope," he sobbed. "The griffin will eat my oxen. I have nothing." His friends tried to cheer him up.

We'll go and rescue them!

Feeling a little better, Hassan and his friends set off to find the griffin. For hours they climbed, higher and higher into the mountains.

All at once, Hassan stopped.

Higher up the mountain still, they came across what they thought was a strange plant.

"What a funny tree," said one of the men.

Hassan shook his head. "It's not a tree," he said.

It's a griffin's feather!

24

Just then, they heard a loud noise. *Ahhhhhhh... uhhhhh.*

"W-w-w-what's that?" the men whispered, looking over the rocks.

There was the griffin, fast asleep and snoring, with the ox trapped by its paw.

"Quick, before it wakes!"
cried Hassan. As fast as they
could, the men put arrows
to their bows and fired them.

The griffin woke up with
a mighty bellow. But it was
too late.

A hail of arrows struck its chest. As the griffin fell back, Hassan's ox jumped up and ran to safety.

And, from then on, whenever Hassan worked in his fields, he checked for strange clouds first.

Chapter 3

The evil cockatrice

There was once a farmer
named Zak. He and his wife,
Beela, were happy but very
poor. Their only animals were
a few hens and a rooster.

One day, the rooster began running around and around in circles, while crowing loudly.

"Beela! Come and look at this!" called Zak.

Cock-a-doodle-doo!

The rooster sat down and
ruffled its feathers.

"He looks
like he's
about
to lay an
egg," said
Beela.

"But roosters can't!" said
Zak.
They
stared.
This one
had laid an
egg and it
was huge.

A few minutes later, the egg began to crack. A tiny

rooster comb appeared.

The rooster stared at the egg with its beady eyes. Suddenly it gave a great squawk and rolled over, dead.

Zak and Beela gasped in
horror as a snake crawled out
of the egg. It sat up proudly
and looked around.

Beela saw its beady red eyes
and pointy rooster's comb.

"A cockatrice!" she
screamed.

"What's a cockatrice?" asked Zak.

"It's a very evil creature," said Beela. "It's only born when a rooster lays an egg."

The cockatrice slithered off. Everything it touched was burned, leaving a horrible scorched trail.

Anything that looked into the creature's creepy red eyes died immediately.

"We must warn everyone!" cried Beela. She and Zak ran to the village leader.

The cockatrice is dangerous!

34

The village leader sent a brave soldier to kill the cockatrice. The soldier wore a helmet to protect his eyes and blindfolded his horse, too.

We'll catch the nasty beast...

"Do be careful!" Beela called out, as he left.

The soldier rode along,
looking for the cockatrice.

When he found a scorched field, he knew it was near. Then he saw it.

Charging up, he raised his spear and stabbed the cockatrice as hard as he could.

As the spear went in, the
soldier shouted out in pain. It
was as though poison had shot
up the spear into his arm.

My arm! It's
burning!

He fell from his horse and
lay still, unable to move. The
cockatrice wasn't hurt at all.

The villagers were terrified that the cockatrice would kill them all.

"Perhaps the old priest can help," said Zak.

Let's see... You'll need a mirror.

"To kill the creature, you must show it a reflection of itself," the priest said.

Zak and Beela ran off to fetch the biggest mirror they could find. Then they hid behind some rocks, to wait.

When the cockatrice arrived, they crept forward, holding the mirror in front of them.

As soon as the cockatrice saw itself, it let out a desperate shriek.

Zak and Beela peeked around the mirror. The cockatrice was dead on the ground. Its evil eyes had claimed their last victim.

Chapter 4

Unicorn magic

Once, there was a king who believed unicorn horns were magic. "Find me a unicorn!" he cried to Toby, his page. "And don't come home without one."

Toby hunted all over the world, but he couldn't find a unicorn anywhere.

The king is crazy! I don't believe unicorns exist.

Days became weeks...
weeks became months...
months became years...

Toby grew old, but he didn't dare go home empty-handed. He had just one place left to try – the mountains of Tibet.

There, he met an old man whose granddaughter knew where a unicorn lived.

I know the way, but it's a long trek.

For days they journeyed.
Toby's feet hurt and his bones
ached.

Finally, the girl said, "The
unicorn lives around this bend.
But if I show you, you must
promise to leave him alone."

Toby didn't say anything. There, in front of them, was a unicorn. At last, he could go home.

But Toby went home alone. Even if the king was angry, he couldn't touch the unicorn.

When Toby told
the king, he was
shaking with fear.
"Oh well,"
said the king.
"If I can't have
a real unicorn,
I'll put them on my banner."
"You might have thought of
that before!" said Toby, but he
said it to himself.

Try these other books in
Series One:

Animal Legends: The secrets of the animal kingdom revealed. Find out why cats hate rats, why monkeys live in trees and how rabbits took their revenge on a grumpy crocodile.

Dragons: Stan must outwit a dragon to feed his children and Victor must persuade two dragons not to eat him.

The Burglar's Breakfast: Alfie Briggs is a burglar, who discovers someone has stolen his breakfast!

The Dinosaurs Next Door: Mr. Puff's house is full of amazing things. Best of all are the dinosaur eggs — until they begin to hatch...

Series editor: Lesley Sims

Designed by
Katarina Dragoslavic

This edition first published in 2007 by Usborne Publishing Ltd.,
Usborne House, 83-85 Saffron Hill, London EC1N 8RT, England.
www.usborne.com
Copyright © 2007, 2003, 1982 Usborne Publishing Ltd.

Around the World in Eighty Days

Jules Verne
Adapted by Jane Bingham

Illustrated by Adam Stower

Reading Consultant: Alison Kelly
Roehampton University

Contents

Chapter 1

The journey begins

Over one hundred years ago, there
lived a man named Phileas Fogg.
For many years, he led a very quiet
life. He spent every day at his club,
which was where rich men went to
meet their friends.

3

Every morning, he left his house at exactly 11:30 and walked 576 steps to his club.

Then he ate lunch.

After lunch, Fogg read three newspapers from cover to cover. Then he ate supper. After that, he played cards with friends.

You've beaten us again, Fogg!

On the stroke of midnight, he went home to bed... before doing exactly the same the next day.

But one Wednesday everything changed. Fogg read some amazing news in his paper.

"Listen to this," he announced to his friends. "It says it's possible to travel around the world in only eighty days!"

I don't believe it!

You'd jump from train to ship to train again non-stop.

Despite his friends' laughter, Fogg was convinced he could do it.

When one friend bet that it couldn't be done, Fogg replied, "I will bet twenty thousand pounds that I can go around the world in eighty days or less!"

Everyone thought he was crazy but Fogg had made up his mind.

"I shall be back on December 21st," he said.

See you in eighty days!

As soon as he arrived home, Fogg asked Passepartout, his butler, to pack a small bag. Luckily, Passepartout had been an acrobat and could move quickly.

In less than ten minutes, they were on their way to the station...

and at 8:45 exactly, the train pulled out. Fogg and Passepartout were off on their great adventure.

They were heading for the coast, where they could catch a boat to France. But they were also heading straight for trouble.

Chapter 2

Arriving in Africa

Dangerous thief

Wanted
dead or alive!

While Phileas Fogg was crossing
Europe, the police were hunting a
runaway thief. Only a few days
before, he had stolen the huge sum
of fifty-five thousand pounds from
the Bank of England.

An inspector named Fix was
convinced the thief would escape
by sailing from Europe to Africa.
He was waiting on the quay when
Fogg reached Suez in North Africa.

Fogg sent Passepartout to get his
passport stamped. "I need proof of
the trip," he explained.

Quite by chance, Passepartout
happened to ask Inspector Fix the
way to the passport office.

When Fix saw the passport, he gasped. Fogg's description exactly matched the description of the thief. Fix was certain he'd found his man.

But he couldn't act at once. First, he needed some papers, which would allow him to arrest the thief.

So, Fix found out where Fogg was
going and sent an urgent message
to London. "Am on the trail of the
thief. Following him to India. Send
arrest papers to Bombay."

Fix quickly packed a small bag
and boarded the ship for India.

The voyage was rough, but Fogg stayed as calm as ever. He ate four meals a day and played cards. He might have been at home.

Two days early, the ship steamed into Bombay. Inspector Fix was ready to make his arrest, but the papers had not arrived.

"My only hope," Fix decided, "is to stop Fogg from leaving India." Later that day, he saw his chance.

Passepartout had visited a temple but he didn't realize he was supposed to take off his shoes. When a priest tugged them from his feet, he started a fight.

Fix was delighted. "Now I've seen that butler break the law, I can make sure he's arrested and jailed here – along with his master!"

Fix followed Passepartout to the station and watched him catch a train. "See you in Calcutta," Fix muttered to himself. "I'll get your Mr. Fogg there."

Chapter 3

Fogg to the rescue

The train puffed its way through
India, passing magnificent temples
and fields of coffee and cotton.
Passepartout saw it all, amazed.
Fogg found a man to play cards.

But halfway through the third day, the train came to a stop.

"The track ends here," a guard announced. "It starts again in fifty miles at Allahabad."

Passepartout was furious. "How will we reach Calcutta in time?" he demanded.

Fogg didn't seem worried. "I've allowed time for delays," he said quietly. "We simply need to find another way to travel."

Passepartout rushed off. Soon, he was back with the answer.

Look! An elephant!

The elephant was expensive but Fogg didn't mind. He invited his card-playing friend to join them.

Then he hired a guide and, half
an hour later, they were lurching
through the jungle. Passepartout
bounced up and down with glee.
Every now and then, he tossed the
elephant a
sugar
lump.

They journeyed for hours,
crossing forests of date trees and
sandy plains. That night, they
camped in a ruined bungalow.

They were off again at six the next morning, breakfasting on bananas picked from a tree.

They had almost crossed a thick forest, when they heard music and voices. A large procession was snaking its way through the trees.

In the middle of the procession, a group of warriors carried the body of a dead prince. Behind them, two priests were pulling a beautiful girl.

Passepartout was shocked. "What are they doing?" he cried.

"It's the custom," their guide explained. "When a prince dies, his wife must die too, so they can go to heaven together."

"Tomorrow, Princess Aouda will be burned to death beside her husband."

Passepartout was horrified. Even Phileas Fogg, who let nothing disturb him, seemed upset.

"I have twelve hours to spare," he observed. "Let's save her."

By nightfall, the procession had reached a small temple. The princess was locked firmly inside. Everything seemed hopeless, until Passepartout had an idea...

Next morning, Princess Aouda
was laid beside her husband. Then
the priests lit a huge fire, watched
by a silent crowd. Suddenly, the air
filled with screams. Some people
even flung themselves to the ground.
The dead prince was sitting up.

25

His ghostly figure rose through the smoke and grasped Princess Aouda in his arms. Then he strode off into the jungle.

"Let's go!" the ghost called to Fogg. It was Passepartout, who had disguised himself as the prince. Fogg and his friend chased after them, dodging bullets and arrows as they ran to safety.

Chapter 4

Tricked!

At Allahabad, Fogg gave the
elephant to their guide and jumped
on a train. But Fix had reported
Passepartout's fight at the temple.
As they arrived in Calcutta, Fogg
and Passepartout were grabbed by
police and taken to court.

Fogg and Passepartout faced a week in jail. The poor butler felt terrible. Then Fogg offered the court two thousand pounds.

"Very well," said the judge. "You may go free for now. But we'll keep the money if you don't return."

Aha... He's spending all the stolen money!

Fogg caught his next ship, to Hong Kong, with an hour to spare.

Fix was furious. "But Hong Kong belongs to Britain," he thought. "I can arrest Fogg there."

Princess Aouda, who hoped to find her cousin in Hong Kong, went too. When the ship stopped for coal in Singapore, Fogg and the princess went for a carriage ride.

They drove past pepper plants and nutmeg trees, grinning monkeys and grimacing tigers.

Near the end of the voyage, the ship battled against a raging wind. Fogg remained perfectly calm, but Passepartout was in a panic. "We'll miss our next ship, I know it!"

29

In the end, they reached Hong Kong one day late. Fogg had missed his next ship, which was to Yokohama in Japan.

"I knew it!" cried Passepartout.

Fix was delighted. "Now Fogg's stuck here and I can arrest him!" But luck was not on Fix's side.

It turned out that the ship to Yokohama had also been delayed, so Fogg hadn't missed it at all. Even worse, Fix's arrest papers still hadn't arrived.

Fix was desperate. Somehow, he had to keep Fogg in Hong Kong until the papers came.

Fogg booked a hotel for that night and set off to find Aouda's cousin. He sent Passepartout to reserve three cabins on their ship.

On the quay, Passepartout heard that the ship was sailing that very evening – and so did Fix.

We'll leave at six tonight.

"I must find my master!" the butler cried. But Fix invited him to a smoky inn for a drink first.

"I'm a detective and your master is a thief!" declared Fix, at the inn.

"Nonsense!" said Passepartout.

"Fogg mustn't know his ship sails tonight," thought Fix and bought the butler several drinks.

Before long, Passepartout was snoring and Fix had slipped away.

Fogg was on the quay early next morning and Princess Aouda was still with him. Her cousin had already left Hong Kong – and so, of course, had their ship. There was no sign of Passepartout either.

I'm afraid the ship left last night. I missed it too!

The next steamer wasn't leaving for a week. But Fogg did not give up easily. Instead, he looked for another boat to take him to Japan.

34

Finally, Fogg found a captain of a small boat who agreed to take them to Shanghai. "You can catch another steamer for Yokohama from there," he said. Seeing Fix on the quay, Fogg offered him a lift.

Before the boat left, Fogg searched all over Hong Kong for Passepartout. But his butler had vanished.

Where can Passepartout be?

I don't know. But I've left some money for him with the police.

For two days, the little boat sped through the waves. Then a great storm blew up and gigantic waves crashed upon the deck. The boat was tossed around on the sea like a ball.

When at last the wind dropped, they had lost precious time. Even with all the sails hoisted, the boat couldn't go fast enough.

Then Fogg spotted a steamer.

"That's the one from Shanghai to Yokohama," said the captain.

"Signal her," said Fogg.

With a bang, a rocket soared into the air and the ship steamed over. As soon as it reached them, Fogg, Aouda and Fix clambered aboard.

But, in the meantime, what had happened to Passepartout?

He had woken up just in time to catch the ship to Japan. Rushing on board at the last minute, he discovered – to his horror – that Fogg wasn't there.

When they landed at Yokohama, Passepartout didn't know what to do. He was wandering around in despair, when he saw a poster.

"Maybe I could join the acrobats!" he said to himself. "They're going to America and that's where Fogg is heading next."

"Can you sing, standing on your head, with a top on your left foot and a sword on your right?" asked the owner of the group. Passepartout nodded. "You're in!"

That evening, he took part in his first show, at the bottom of a human triangle. The crowd loved it. But suddenly...

all

the

acrobats

collapsed

in

a

heap.

Passepartout had spotted Phileas
Fogg, jumped up and run over.

Chapter 5

Racing home

They had no time for explanations.
Fogg and his beaming butler raced
to catch their next ship, for San
Francisco. Princess Aouda, who
had nowhere else to go, came too.
She grew fonder of Fogg each day.

As the ship steamed on, Passepartout began to think Fogg would win his bet. But one day he saw Fix on deck. The inspector had secretly followed them.

I'm sorry I tricked you.

Passepartout hit him.

"Wait!" cried Fix. "It might have seemed I was against you before—"

"You were!" said Passepartout.

"Well, yes," agreed Fix, "and I still think Fogg's a thief. But now I want him in England. It's only in England I can arrest him."

Passepartout didn't want to worry Fogg, so he kept quiet about Fix. But when Fogg went to get his passport stamped in San Francisco, he bumped into the inspector too.

"What a surprise!" lied Fix and joined them on the next stage of the journey, crossing America by train.

The Pacific Railroad steamed right across the country to New York. It had every luxury on board, from shops to restaurants, but it still had to wait when a herd of buffalo crossed the track.

44

The next obstacle was a shaky
bridge. "I'll cross at top speed!"
said the driver. He went so fast the
wheels barely touched the tracks.

The train reared up and jumped
across. As it landed on the other
side, the bridge crashed into
the river.

Soon after that, they hit real trouble. The train was steaming by some rocky cliffs, when a band of Sioux warriors jumped onto its roof. The warriors quickly took over driving the train.

Passepartout sped into action.

Crawling under the train, he wriggled and swung all the way to the engine, without being seen.

Then he unhooked the engine and the train slowly came to a halt... just beside the station.

But when Fogg looked for his butler a few seconds later, he'd gone.

"The warriors took him when they fled!" shouted a guard.

Calling over some soldiers, Fogg went into the hills to look for him.

It took all day to find and free Passepartout. They had to camp out overnight and only got back to the station the following morning.

By then, their train had long since left and the next one wasn't due until that evening.

"I've done it again," wailed the butler. But Fix came to the rescue.

"I've just met a man who owns a land yacht," he announced.

Soon, they were gliding over the snow. Wind filled the yacht's sails and it whizzed over the icy plains.

They caught up with the train for New York at the very next station. It puffed across the country at top speed. Fogg still had a chance.

They finally stopped at a station by the steamship pier, on the bank of the Hudson River in New York. But the ship to England had already left – only forty-five minutes earlier.

No other steamers could take them across the Atlantic Ocean in time. Passepartout was crushed, but Fogg just visited every ship in the port. Once again, he found a captain who would take passengers.

The ship was sailing to France but that didn't worry Fogg. He simply locked the captain in his cabin and changed course.

The ship was fast but it was now winter and the weather was terrible. Then the engineer gave Fogg more bad news.

"The coal for the boiler is running out!" he said grimly.

"Even my clever master can't solve this," thought Passepartout.

Once again, Fogg surprised him.
He ordered the sailors to cut down
the mast and chop it into logs.

Then he told the astonished men
to burn the wood in the ship's boiler.

Over the next three days, the
sailors burned the ship's bridge...

the
cabins...

and even
the decks.

By the time they reached
England, only the ship's metal
hull was left.

They landed in Liverpool, with just enough time for Fogg to catch a train to London and win his bet. But, as Fogg stepped off the ship, Fix made his move.

"Phileas Fogg," the detective announced, "I arrest you for stealing fifty-five thousand pounds."

Fogg was thrown into prison and there was nothing Princess Aouda or Passepartout could do.

Three hours later, they were waiting for news, when Fix rushed in. His hair was a mess and he looked ashamed. "I've made a dreadful mistake," he cried.

The real thief was arrested three days ago!

Fogg was free again. But he had only five and a half hours left.

Fogg paid for a special train which roared down to London. As it pulled in, he checked the station clock – 8:55. Fogg had lost his bet by just ten minutes.

I don't believe it! We came so close...

Chapter 6

What next?

Phileas Fogg did not show any sign
of how he felt. He simply left the
station with Passepartout and
Aouda and drove home. The next
day, he stayed in his room, adding
up all the money he had lost.

At seven o'clock, Fogg visited Princess Aouda in her room.

"Madam," he said sadly, "When I brought you to England, I planned to give you a fortune. But I am afraid now it is not possible."

"My dear sir," the princess replied gently, "I don't want your money... just you."

You want to marry me?

Fogg was overjoyed and, for the first time in his life, it showed. "Passepartout!" he called. "Run to the church and book our wedding for tomorrow!"

Monday morning?

Monday morning!

59

Meanwhile Fogg's friends at his club had spent the last few days in a fever of excitement. They had not heard a word from Fogg since he left on October 2nd.

On the evening of December 21st, they waited eagerly to see if he would show. And, as the hands on the clock reached 8:44, they heard a knock on the door.

Here I am, gentlemen!

It was Phileas Fogg in person. But how had he done it? Well, Passepartout had returned from the priest with incredible news.

"Not Monday tomorrow," he gasped. "To-tomorrow, Sunday. Today is... SATURDAY!"

Going around the world to the east had gained Fogg an extra day. He'd had ten minutes left to get to the club and win his bet.

Fogg won twenty thousand pounds but, as he had spent nearly nineteen thousand pounds on the way, he wasn't much better off.

On the other hand, he did find a wife and happiness on his trip. Most people would go around the world for less!

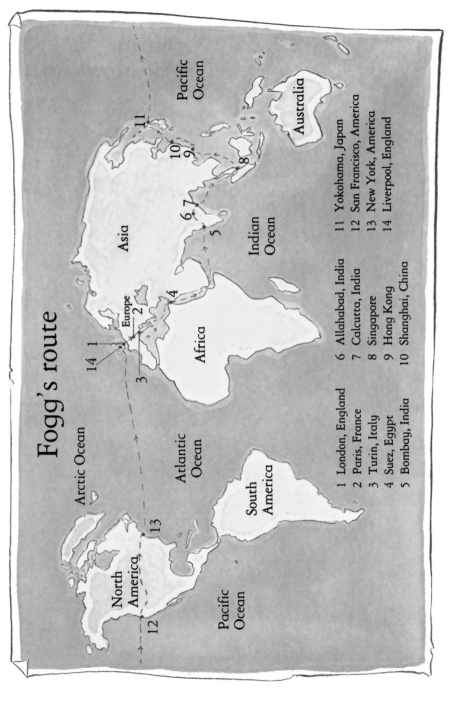

Fogg's route

1 London, England
2 Paris, France
3 Turin, Italy
4 Suez, Egypt
5 Bombay, India

6 Allahabad, India
7 Calcutta, India
8 Singapore
9 Hong Kong
10 Shanghai, China

11 Yokohama, Japan
12 San Francisco, America
13 New York, America
14 Liverpool, England

Jules Verne (1828-1905) was a French writer
who loved science and travel. He combined them with
adventure in his stories. His first book, *Five Weeks in a
Balloon*, was published in 1863. Ten years later, he
wrote *Around the World in Eighty Days*. Another of his
famous stories is *Twenty Thousand Leagues Under the Sea*.

Series editor: Lesley Sims

Designed by
Russell Punter

This edition first published in 2004 by Usborne Publishing Ltd.,
Usborne House, 83-85 Saffron Hill, London EC1N 8RT, England.
www.usborne.com
Copyright © 2004 Usborne Publishing Ltd.

Stories of

WITCHES

Christopher Rawson
Adapted by Gill Harvey

Illustrated by
Stephen Cartwright

Reading Consultant: Alison Kelly
Roehampton University

Contents

Chapter 1

The lost broomstick

This story begins with a witch called Bess and an invitation to a party. Bess loved parties. There was just one problem.

It's a long way away.

3

Bess couldn't remember where she had put her broomstick. She looked everywhere.

Boots... spare cauldron... hmmph. No broomstick.

But it was no good. The broomstick was lost. At last, Bess had to give up.

Now what could she do? She couldn't fly without her stick and it was too far to walk.

Then she had a great idea. "My magic rope!" she cried.

"I can turn someone into a horse and ride to the party. I just need to find someone."

Bess hid behind a tree and waited. Soon, a man came along. His wife walked behind him, carrying all their heavy bags.

Bess let the man pass. "He's no good, he's limping," she said. "Besides, his wife will be strong from carrying all those bags."

She jumped out and threw her rope over the woman.

At once, the woman turned into a horse. Bess climbed onto her back.

"Now for the party. Giddy-up!" she cried.

The man kept limping. At first, he didn't notice what had happened. But when he looked back...

...all he could see were his bags, and a horse galloping off in the distance.

The man went to get the bags, but he couldn't find his wife. Nobody had seen her.

Crossly, the man picked up the heavy bags. "I'll just have to carry these myself," he said.

A long way away Bess had stopped. The horse was worn out – and so were her shoes.

At the next village, Bess took her to a blacksmith. With four new horseshoes, the horse was ready to go.

At the party, the other witches pointed to the horse.

"Look at Bess without a broomstick!" they said and cackled with laughter.

Look, it's Bess on a horse. Ha, ha!

But Bess didn't mind. It was a wonderful party. The witches skipped around a cauldron, singing silly songs...

...before casting spells on each other, just for fun.

All too soon, the party was over. The other witches flew off on their broomsticks. Bess untied her horse and set out for home.

Bess was nearly home when she met the man she had seen before. He was still carrying the heavy bags.

You look tired!

"Hello," she said. "Would you like to buy this horse? I don't need her anymore."

"What a good idea!" said
the man. "Then I won't have
to carry these bags. I lost my
wife, you see."

Bess said nothing. She
just smiled.

The man gave Bess a bag
of gold and climbed onto
the horse.

With the horse to carry him, the man was home in no time. He took the horse to a stable.

"What a fine beast you are," he said, patting her. He took off the rope...

...and jumped back with surprise. The horse had turned into his wife – just like that!

But...
but how?

She was pleased to see that being a horse hadn't changed her too much. But there was one difference...

18

...which meant she couldn't carry the bags anymore. From then on, every time they went shopping, her husband had to do it.

He kept asking her to turn back into a horse, just to show him the secret. She never did.

Chapter 2

Dog spell

Early one morning, Farmer Crumb and his wife set off to work in the fields. Their daughter Kate carried a picnic basket, full of food.

They worked hard all morning. Then Farmer Crumb looked up. "Time for lunch!" he said.

Kate ran off to the barn where she had hidden their picnic basket.

But before she reached the barn, Kate heard a strange sound. *Zzzzzzz*, it went. *Zzzzzz...*

She peeked inside. An old witch was lying in the hay, fast asleep. And she'd found the picnic basket.

Kate was very angry. "How dare you!" she cried.

The witch woke up with a jump. Kate shouted at her some more.

You greedy old woman! We're hungry!

"How dare you speak to me like that," snarled the witch. "I'll teach you a lesson!"

Before Kate could move, the witch had cast a spell. "Maxi-baxi-jollybee-hog, get on the ground and bark like a dog!"

Poor Kate crawled back to her mother and father.

"Woof!" she barked. She couldn't say anything else.

"What happened?" cried her mother.

Farmer Crumb chased after the witch. "Come back here!" he yelled. "What have you done to my daughter?"

Change her back, or I'll...

The witch just laughed. "You can't catch me!" she shouted, as she flew off on her broomstick.

Farmer Crumb and his wife took Kate home.

"What can we do?" they asked their friends. Mrs. Crumb was very upset.

My little Ka-Ka-Kate...

Woof!

But no one knew how to help.

"We must go to Rimpole," said Farmer Crumb, at last. Rimpole was an old wizard who lived on a hill. "If anyone can help us, he can."

Woof-woof!

She's done nothing but bark for three days!

Kate had to crawl to his house on her hands and knees. "Please help," begged her dad.

Rimpole frowned. "I can't break the spell," he said. "But I might be able to catch the witch for you."

He stared into his crystal ball. "Aba-doo-well! Who cast the spell?" he cried.

The witch's face appeared in the ball. "Ah, it's *you*, is it?" muttered Rimpole. "I might have known."

Rimpole fetched toadstools, nails, mustard powder and red berries. He mixed them and he pounded them. Then he added a splash of ketchup.

He heated the brew until it bubbled gently. "Perfect!" he said. He looked into his crystal ball again.

But the witch wasn't scared of anyone — especially Rimpole.

As the brew began to bubble
more fiercely, the wizard
chanted a spell.

Tongues of fire,
flames of might, give the
nasty witch a fright!

At once, the cork flew out
of the bottle and flames shot
up the chimney.

33

That wiped the smile off the witch's face. She began to look very worried indeed.

She saw the flames creeping up on her. "Help!" she squealed and began to run...

But the flames were too
quick for her.

"Oh, stop them, stop them!"
cried the witch.

As soon as the witch made her promise, Kate jumped to her feet. She wasn't a dog anymore.

The family never saw the witch again. But, after that, Kate was always careful where she hid the picnic basket.

Chapter 3

The farmer's revenge

Farmer Jones had a big brown cow. Every day, she gave him five buckets full of the creamiest milk in the village.

In the same village, there lived a greedy witch. She didn't have a cow, but she did love creamy milk.

One day, she had an idea for a wicked spell. "From now on, the milk will all be mine!" she cackled.

Next morning,
Farmer Jones
took the buckets
of milk to his
milk churn,
as usual.

But as he
poured it, he
got a shock.
The milk just
disappeared. Not
a drop was left.

Farmer Jones was furious.
"Calm down, dear," said
his wife. "That
won't bring the
milk back. I'm
sure we can
find out what
the problem is."

I'll soon
sort this out!

And she
set off for
the village,
to see
what was
going on.

The witch
was pumping
water at the
village pump.

"That's funny looking
water!" muttered Mrs. Jones.

The witch
filled her
bucket. She
walked off,
grinning.

The naughty witch hadn't
pumped water at all.

"Aha!" cried Mrs. Jones
and ran all the way home.

When she told her husband
about the witch, he smiled.

"I know what to do," he
said. "I have a sneaky plan."

This problem
needs sorting out!

The next time he went to
milk his cow, he took a big
box with him.

He emptied the milk
into the churn. It
disappeared,
just as before.
But then
he did
something
else.

Ha-ha! See how
that tastes, witch!

He opened
the box and
tipped in
lots of white
powder, too.

In the village, the witch
filled her bucket with milk.
She dipped her mug into it.

"Lovely milk!" she cried,
and took a big gulp.

But the milk began to bubble and froth. The witch began to splutter and cough. Farmer Jones had added soap powder to it.

Soon, the witch was burping bubbles. She had soapy hiccups for a week — and she never stole milk again.

Try these other books in
Series One:

Giants: Some giants are naughty, some are foolish, but they're all enormous. These stories tell how a kind giant called a troll helped a poor fisherman, and how three wicked giants met a grisly end.

The Monster Gang: Starting a gang is a great idea. So is dressing up like monsters. But if everyone is in disguise, how do you know who's who?

Wizards: Here are three magical tales about three very different wizards. One is kind, one is clever and one knows more secret spells than the other two together.

Series editor: Lesley Sims

Designed by
Katarina Dragoslavić

This edition first published in 2007 by Usborne Publishing Ltd.,
Usborne House, 83-85 Saffron Hill, London EC1N 8RT, England.
www.usborne.com
Copyright © 2007, 2002, 1980 Usborne Publishing Ltd.

48

The Clumsy Crocodile

Felicity Everett

Adapted by Rebecca Treays

Illustrated by Alex de Wolf

Reading Consultant: Alison Kelly
Roehampton University

Contents

Chapter 1

Everglades

Cassy Green was on her way to work. It was the very first day of her new job.

She was going to work at
Everglades, the biggest and
best store in town.

It sold things you just couldn't buy anywhere else. So, when Cassy got a job there, she was as pleased as punch.

- Toy Department
- China Department
- Exotic Pet Department
- Robot Department
- Luxury Goods Department
- Food Hall

First, Cassy was sent to work in the China Department. After only ten minutes, she had sold sixty cups and saucers to a very rich lady. She was doing well.

Cassy packed the china carefully into a box. She was as gentle as a crocodile can be, but maybe just a little slow. The lady began to get impatient.

Cassy quickly tied a big bow on the box. She didn't want the lady to be cross, not her very first customer. But as Cassy picked up the box, disaster struck!

She'd packed it upside down.
Sixty cups and saucers smashed
onto the floor.

The customer stamped her foot
angrily and left.

Next Cassy was sent to the Toy Department. She hoped there was less to break. She didn't want any more accidents.

"I must put this ball away," she thought. "Someone could trip over it and have a bad fall."

But as she bent down, her
tail swung out behind her. The
Toytown Express was knocked
right off its rails.

So she was sent to the Food Hall.
But there, things went from bad
to worse.

Cassy tripped over a stool. A
bowl of salad flew into the air
and landed...

...on Ernest Everglade's head. Ernest Everglade owned the department store. He was Cassy's boss and he was not a happy man.

"Go to my office," he yelled. "NOW!"

Trembling, Cassy obeyed.

Chapter 2

A cross boss

Ernest Everglade was
furious. He liked salad,
but not on his head.

14

"Go and don't ever come back," he told Cassy. "I don't want a clumsy crocodile in my store."

Cassy begged and pleaded.
She pleaded and begged.
"Just give me one more
chance. I'll be very careful,"
she promised.

But Mr. Everglade was more
interested in his newspaper. He
wasn't even listening to Cassy.

16

At last, he looked up. "I don't have time for you," he sighed. "Some jewel thieves are in town, the famous Greedy Boys."

Cassy gasped. Everyone had heard of the Greedy Boys. But she still wanted her job back. She began to cry.

Now, Mr. Everglade couldn't stand crying. He would do anything to stop it.

"OK, OK," he said. "Go to the Luxury Goods Department first thing Monday morning."

Oh thank you!
You won't regret it.
I promise.

Chapter 3

Getting it right

The next day was Sunday.
Cassy worked hard at home,
getting ready
for Monday.

She emptied her cupboards and stacked everything inside them. She stacked every pot, plate, cup, and saucer in the house.

The stacks got wobblier and wobblier...

and higher...

and higher...

Next she found paper, scissors, ribbon and tape. She wrapped everything she could get her hands on.

When she'd finished wrapping, Cassy was exhausted. All she wanted to do was sit down.

But when she looked for her comfiest chair, there was just one small problem...

So she set up her mirror and
served imaginary customers.

"A flying pig? Try the pet
department sir... I'm sorry,
madam, we don't sell crocodile-
skin handbags."

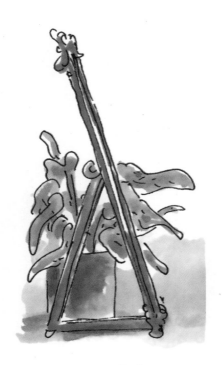

"You don't like your spotted socks, sir? I'll change them at once."

And she smiled her toothy crocodile smile until her whole face ached.

Can I help you?

Finally, Cassy put on her
Everglades badge and admired
herself in the mirror. She
looked perfect!

27

Chapter 4

Cassy in charge

On Monday morning, Cassy
was the first to arrive in the
Luxury Goods Department.

28

Only the security guard was there. He had been guarding the store during the night.

The guard was finishing his breakfast. He was very pleased to see Cassy. Now he could go home to bed.

30

Cassy was nervous. She didn't want to be left alone in the store.

"You'll be fine," said the guard. "Just keep an eye on the Everglades Emerald."

The guard left. Cassy wasn't nervous any more. She felt important. She was in charge.

The Everglades Emerald was the most expensive thing in the store. It was kept in a case of extra strong glass.

Cassy thought it was the most beautiful jewel she had ever seen.

But Cassy wasn't the only one admiring the emerald. Hiding behind a pot were Nigel and Rupert – the Greedy Boys!

"What a beauty," sighed Nigel.

"But look at that case," said
Rupert. "How will we ever
break the glass?"

"Never fear," Nigel whispered.
And as Cassy wandered away
from the emerald, Nigel took
something from his pocket.

Chapter 5

Disaster!

Nigel held up a small whistle.

"My secret weapon," he said. "It can't be heard by humans, but it can..."

He put the whistle to his lips and blew. The case exploded.

"...shatter glass!" he finished.

He grinned. The Everglades Emerald was theirs for the taking.

"At last," gasped Rupert. "I can't wait to get my hands on it!"

Nigel and Rupert sneaked
out from their hiding place.
Their eyes glittered
with greed.

"Now to collect our prize,"
said Nigel.

41

The thieves crept closer to the emerald. But Nigel had made a big mistake.

He was right about humans not being able to hear his whistle. What he didn't know was that animals could hear it...

"Hey!" thought Cassy. "The Toytown Express!" She spun around, ready to race to the Toy Department... forgetting her tail, which swung around too.

43

This time it hooked a priceless
pearl necklace.

Cassy tugged her tail.

Oops!

The necklace snapped, pearls
went everywhere and Cassy
went flying.

So did the Greedy Boys. The
rolling pearls sent them skidding
to the floor. They tumbled to the
ground, bringing the Everglades
Emerald with them.

Cassy turned to see the Greedy
Boys lying in a heap.

"Oh no! Customers!" she cried
and rushed over to help them up.

Please let
me help. I am
so sorry.

Rupert was groaning in agony. Nigel still had his eye on the emerald. He wouldn't let a clumsy crocodile ruin his plans. He'd waited years to steal this giant gem.

In her hurry to help, Cassy
tripped. She slid across the floor,
her arms thrust out...

48

and collided nose first with
a table, a table which held
Everglades' Ancient Treasures.

The table wobbled... the
treasures wobbled...

Then they crashed to the floor.

Cassy got up. She was horrified. What had she done?

One of the ancient pots had toppled off the table...

...straight onto her customers' heads.

51

At that moment, the boss walked in. Cassy started to explain. But Mr. Everglade wasn't listening.

He had just seen the Everglades
Emerald lying on the floor.

Then he saw the pot. And the legs. And the bag lying next to them. And he quickly put two and two together.

He was no longer a cross boss. He was a very pleased and excited boss.

He picked up the emerald and
beamed at Cassy.

"Well done! You've saved the
Everglades Emerald."

Cassy was puzzled. Mr.
Everglade pointed to the pot.

"And you've caught the Greedy Boys," he added.

"Oh? So I have!" said Cassy.

Chapter 6

Cassy the hero

That afternoon the boss
gave a party for Cassy.

The whole town was invited,
except for the Greedy Boys.
Nigel and Rupert were both
safely behind bars.

It was the best party ever.
There was singing and dancing,
cake and ice cream – and fantastic
fizzing fireworks.

Then Cassy was given a medal.
It was the proudest moment of
her life. She was a hero.

After the party, Mr. Everglade smiled at Cassy.

"I've got a new job for you," he said. He didn't want Cassy to be an assistant anymore.

Instead, she became Everglades'
Chief Taster and Tester – with her
tail tucked firmly beneath her.

Try these other books in
Series Two:

The Fairground Ghost: When Jake
goes to the fair he wants a really
scary ride. But first, he has to teach
the fairground ghost a trick or two.

The Incredible Present: Lily gets
everything she's ever wished for... but
things don't turn out as she expects.

Gulliver's Travels: Gulliver sets sail
for adventure and finds a country
beyond his wildest dreams...

Series editor: Lesley Sims

Designed by Katarina Dragoslavić
and Maria Wheatley

This edition first published in 2007 by Usborne Publishing Ltd.,
Usborne House, 83-85 Saffron Hill, London EC1N 8RT, England.
www.usborne.com
Copyright © 2007, 2006, 2002, 1995, 1994, Usborne Publishing Ltd.

The
Emperor's
New Clothes

Retold by Susanna Davidson

Illustrated by Mike Gordon

Reading Consultant: Alison Kelly
Roehampton University

Contents

Chapter 1

Nothing to wear

Once upon a time there was an emperor who *loved* clothes. He really didn't care about anything else.

3

He ignored his soldiers...

4

avoided his advisors...

hated plays...

5

...and only liked riding in the park so he could show off his amazing outfits.

But the emperor had a
problem. The royal procession
was in two weeks' time, and
he had nothing to wear.

I know.

"You must have something, Your Excellence," said Boris, his servant. "You already have seven thousand, three hundred and twenty-two outfits."

"But I've worn them all before," moaned the emperor.

"I want to look so amazing, so fantastic, so *splendiferous*, that people will talk about me for years to come."

"I see," said Boris, looking rather glum. It was Boris who had to take care of all the emperor's clothes.

9

"Are you sure this one won't do?" Boris asked hopefully, picking a velvet and gold suit from the pile.

"Boris," said the emperor, in a stern voice.

"Er, yes, sire?" said Boris.

"Who is the emperor here?"

"You are, Your Excellence," replied Boris.

"Right. And if I say I want new clothes, then I mean it!"

"Go and find me the finest clothes-makers in town," ordered the emperor. "At once!"

"I'm off to have a snooze," the emperor added. "It's been a very tiring morning."

Chapter 2

Slimus and Slick

URGENT!
Emperor needs
tasteful
and elegant
new outfit!
Clothes-makers
apply here.

Boris spent all day looking for an incredible outfit. He wasn't having much luck, until...

...two strangers rushed up to him. "We're the finest clothes-makers in the world," they said. "Take us to the emperor at once."

When they arrived at the palace, the strangers pushed past the palace footmen and burst into the emperor's room.

"Who are you?" shouted the emperor, angrily. He was busy choosing his afternoon coat and hated being interrupted.

15

"We are Slimus..."

"and Slick..."

"...at your service," they said, and bowed.

The emperor just stared
at them.

"Haven't you heard of us?"
said Slimus, looking shocked.

We're world-
famous!

"Um, well... no," admitted
the emperor. He hated not
knowing things.

17

"We make magical clothes!"
said Slimus.

"Magical?" said the emperor,
sounding interested.

"Yes," said Slick, with a sly
smile. "Our clothes can only
be seen by clever people."

18

"They will be absolutely invisible to anyone stupid," Slimus explained.

"Anyone who can't do their job properly won't be able to see them either," Slick added.

Boris gulped. "What if I can't see the clothes?" he thought.

The emperor was very excited. "Make me a magic suit this minute," he cried.

"It won't be cheap," said Slimus and Slick. "We only use the very best material."

"Take this," said the emperor, handing them a sack of money. "You can work in the palace – take anything you want. Only get to work. I want that suit!"

Chapter 3

The two cheats

As soon as they were alone,
Slimus and Slick laughed until
their bellies ached and their
faces turned purple.

"The fool believed us!" cried Slimus. "We're going to have lots and lots of *lovely* money."

They set up their looms in the palace and ordered in the finest silks and the most expensive gold thread.

But they didn't use any of it. Instead they sold it all for lots more money.

"Is there anything else you need?" asked the emperor.

"Yes," Slick replied. "Five fudge cakes, ten tubs of vanilla ice cream and a constant supply of chocolate. That would really help our work."

"But you mustn't see a thing until it's finished," Slick told the emperor. "We want it to be a fantastic surprise."

Every day the emperor crept past their door, listening to the loom going back and forth. He was desperate to know how the suit was coming along.

"I know," he thought. "I'll send Boris along to find out."

But when Boris went in, he could see nothing but empty looms.

"What do you think of our wonderful work?" asked Slick.

"Such a charming pattern, isn't it?" said Slimus.

25

"Oh crumbs," thought Boris.
"I can't see a thing. I must be
stupid."

"Well," demanded Slimus.
"Have you got nothing to say?"

26

Boris gulped. "It's, er, fantastic," he lied. "Absolutely, um, great. I'll tell the emperor I'm very pleased with it."

I wish I could see it!

He hurried off to tell the emperor how fabulous his new clothes were. Slimus and Slick smiled to themselves, and went back to eating cake.

Chapter 4

The emperor's visit

Word quickly spread through
the kingdom that the emperor
had ordered some amazing
and mysterious new clothes.

And the emperor couldn't wait a moment longer to see them. He called for Boris and the palace footmen, and went to see Slimus and Slick at work.

29

"Oh Your Excellence," said
Slimus, bowing low. "We're so
pleased to see you!"

The emperor looked at the
loom, then looked again.
"This is terrible," he thought.
"I can't see anything. I'm not
worthy of being emperor!"

But aloud he said, "It's magnificent."

"Really very tasteful," added Boris.

The palace footmen were worried. Each thought the other could see the magic material. "Splendid," they said in unison.

Slimus and Slick pretended
to take the material down
from the loom. They made
cuts in the air with huge
scissors and sewed using
needles without any thread.

Everyone clapped loudly.
The emperor even gave Slimus
and Slick a gold medal each
for their excellent sewing.

On the morning of the royal procession, the emperor went to put on his new clothes. He was filled with nervous excitement.

33

"Would Your Majesty care to undress?" said Slimus. "Then we'll put on your clothes in front of the mirror."

"I'll bring over the cloak," said Slick. "Boris, pick up the train, will you?"

"This is your shirt, Your
Majesty," said Slimus. "See,
it's as light as a spider's web."

Wonderful!

Slick smiled. "Oh it fits *so*
well," he said.

Then the palace footmen bent down, just as if they were picking up a train. The emperor admired himself in the mirror one last time.

Gosh...

"Well, I'm ready," he said. "Don't I look splendid, Boris?"

"Yes, Your Excellence," said Boris, looking straight up at the ceiling.

"Then open the palace doors," said the emperor. "Let the royal procession begin."

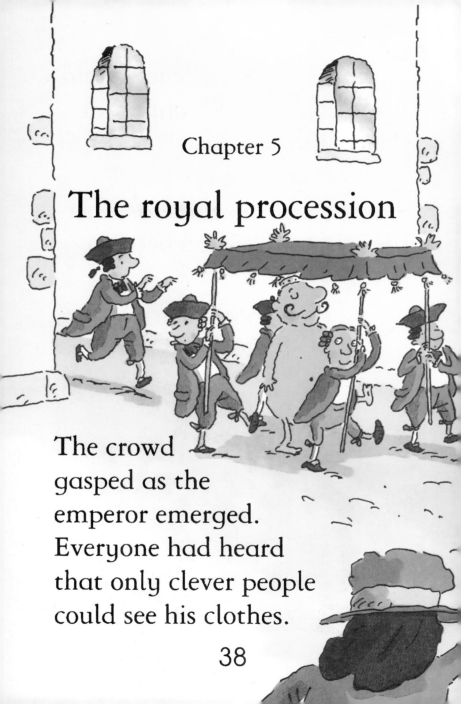

Chapter 5

The royal procession

The crowd
gasped as the
emperor emerged.
Everyone had heard
that only clever people
could see his clothes.

"What a wonderful outfit," they cried.

"Such a magnificent pattern," said a woman.

The emperor smiled to himself. "These are my most successful clothes ever," he thought, and added a spring to his step.

"Let me see him," cried a small child, who was stuck at the back of the crowd.

The child was lifted up on his father's shoulders, so he could see the emperor in all his glory.

"Ooh!" said the child. "The emperor's got nothing on!"

Everyone around the child fell silent and looked at the emperor again.

Soon the whole crowd was chanting. "The emperor's got no clothes on!"

The emperor's got no clothes on!

The emperor heard their words and shivered. Suddenly, he felt very cold.

He looked down. To his horror, the emperor saw that they were right.

Then he blushed bright red — all over.

"I must carry on," he thought. "This is the royal procession – and *I* am the emperor."

The emperor held his head high and walked more proudly than ever.

Meanwhile, Slimus and Slick were packing their bags full of money, getting ready to flee the palace forever.

"We tricked him!" they cried, and cackled with glee.

As for the crowds – they were enjoying the best procession ever. Boris, of course, wasn't having such a good day...

"Oh well," he thought, as he followed the emperor home. "At least one thing turned out as he wanted. People *will* talk about the emperor for years to come."

The Emperor's New Clothes was first told by Hans Christian Andersen, who was born in Denmark in 1805. He was the son of a poor shoemaker but grew up to write hundreds of fairy tales.

Series editor: Lesley Sims
Designed by Natacha Goransky
Cover design by Russell Punter

First published in 2005 by Usborne Publishing Ltd., Usborne House, 83-85 Saffron Hill, London EC1N 8RT, England. www.usborne.com
Copyright © 2005 Usborne Publishing Ltd.

The Magic Gifts

A folk tale from Korea

Retold by Russell Punter

Illustrated by Gabo León Bernstein

Reading consultant: Alison Kelly
Roehampton University

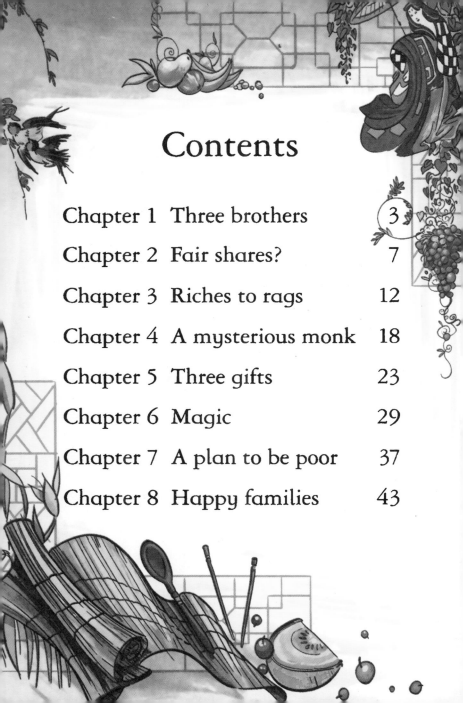

Contents

Chapter 1

Three brothers

Long ago, a man called
Chang lived with his three
sons – Yong, Chin and Ying.

Chang was very old and
very rich. One day, he called
his sons to his bedside.

"I want you to make me a
promise," he croaked.

4

"When I die, I want you to share my fortune equally. You must live together happily."

5

Chin was glad to agree. But his older brothers didn't sound so happy.

Chapter 2

Fair shares?

Not long after, Chang died
and the brothers shared out
his fortune.

"I'm the oldest," said Yong, grandly. "I should have the largest share."

"I'm nearly as old as you," whined Ying. "I deserve a large share too."

8

So Yong and Ying each took a big share of the fortune. "The rest is yours," they told Chin.

Chin was left with a tiny bag of silver coins.

"Thank you," said Chin. Unlike his greedy brothers, he didn't care for money.

Ying and Yong couldn't wait to spend their cash. Soon the house was full of new furniture.

"There's no room for you, Chin," said Ying. "You'll have to move out."

So Chin bought an old hut in the village. His home was simple but he was happy.

Chapter 3

Riches to rags

Chin spent his days with the poor villagers. He used his money to help them.

He bought
them food...

new
clothes...

and even paid
their rent.

He never spent a penny
on himself.

13

Meanwhile, Chin's brothers used their share of the fortune to make even more money.

They bought a
huge house...

silk
clothes...

and sparkling
jewels.

They spent every single
penny on themselves.

15

One day, Ying and Yong
saw a man dressed in rags. He
looked familiar.

Is that Chin?

It can't be.

It was Chin. He had given
away all his money and was
the poorest man in the village.

16

"You can't go around like that," said Yong.

"You're making our family look bad," added Ying.

"Leave the village right now," said Yong. "And don't come back until you're rich."

Chapter 4

A mysterious monk

Chin didn't want to upset his brothers, so he left the village. He walked for miles and miles.

At last, he came to a wide
stream. He took off his shoes
and dangled his tired feet in
the cool water.

"Excuse me," said a voice.
Chin jumped. Behind him
stood an old monk.

"I'm on my way back to my temple," said the monk. "But I can't get across the stream."

The bridge has broken.

Chin was tired, but he was happy to help. "No problem," he said. "Jump on my back."

The old man held on tightly.
Chin carefully waded through
the rushing water.

The monk and his bundle
were heavier than they looked.
But Chin kept going.

When Chin reached the
other side of the stream, the
monk gave a weak sigh.

"Could you carry me back to
my temple?" he asked.
"No problem," puffed Chin.

Chapter 5

Three gifts

After a long walk, Chin and the monk arrived at a lonely, deserted temple.

23

"Where are the others?"
asked Chin.

"I'm the only one here," said
the monk. "It's a hard life."

Chin felt sorry for him. "I'll
stay and help you," he said.

Chin spent the next few months sweeping floors...

mending things...

and copying out books.

One day, the monk noticed
Chin looking sad. "What's the
matter?" he asked.

"I miss my brothers and the
villagers," sighed Chin.

"Then you must return," said the monk. "I'll be alright on my own."

The next day, Chin got ready to leave.

"I have three gifts for you," said the monk.

The monk handed Chin
an old straw mat, a wooden
spoon and a pair of chopsticks.

"They might come in
useful," said the monk, with
a smile.

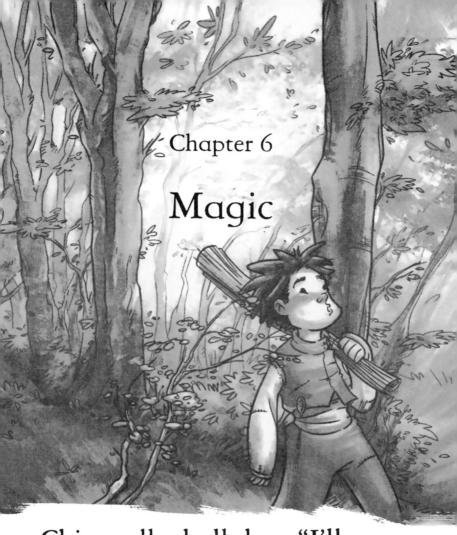

Chapter 6

Magic

Chin walked all day. "I'll
spend the night in this forest,"
he thought.

He spread out the straw mat and lay down on top. It was thin and worn, but Chin soon fell asleep.

When Chin woke up, he couldn't believe his eyes.

The forest had disappeared
and he was lying in a big bed
in a beautiful room.

Chin poked his head out of
the window. He was in the
tower of a grand castle.

Chin saw the old straw mat
under the mattress of the bed.

Chin picked up the spoon.
It made him think of food. "I
wish I had something to eat,"
he sighed.

Fruit came pouring out of
the spoon. Grapes, cherries,
plums, peaches and pineapples
piled up on the floor.

As he munched the fruit, Chin looked down at his torn clothes.

"I wish my suit was as fine as this castle," said Chin, taking a spoonful of cherries.

34

Chin suddenly found he was
dressed in silk robes. "The mat
and spoon must be magic," he
thought.

"I wonder if the chopsticks
are magical too," thought Chin,
tapping them together.

Suddenly, four beautiful
maids appeared. They sang
and danced for Chin.

"If only my brothers could
see me now," thought Chin.

Chapter 7

A plan to be poor

That very day, Ying and Yong passed Chin's castle.

"I've never seen this place before," said Ying.

"It's enormous," cried Yong. "The owner must be even richer than us."

The two nosy brothers sneaked inside. When they saw Chin, they were amazed.

Chin told them all about the monk and the magic gifts. Ying and Yong were jealous.

"Maybe if we were poor, the monk would give us magic gifts," Ying whispered to Yong.

"I'm sure he would," said Yong. "Let's get started."

When they got home, the two brothers gave away their sparkling jewels...

new furniture...

and silk clothes.

They even gave away their huge house.

All they had left were the
clothes they stood up in.
  "Let's visit the monk and
collect our gifts," said Ying.

Soon we'll
be super, super
rich!

Chapter 8

Happy families

When the brothers arrived at
the temple, there was no sign
of the monk.

They waited all day. But the old man never appeared. "Let's stay a little longer," said Ying.

They waited and waited. The days turned into a week.

The weeks turned into a month.

And the months turned into a year.

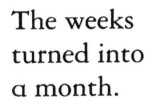

But the monk never returned.

Finally, the brothers gave up. They trudged back to the village, tired and penniless.

Chin saw them from the window of his castle. "Come inside," he called.

Chin welcomed Ying and Yong into his home and shared his fortune with them.

At last, the three brothers lived happily together – just as their father had wanted.

The Magic Gifts is based on an old
Korean folk tale.

Series editor: Lesley Sims

First published in 2009 by Usborne Publishing Ltd., Usborne House,
83-85 Saffron Hill, London EC1N 8RT, England. www.usborne.com
Copyright © 2009 Usborne Publishing Ltd.

THE
MONSTER
GANG

Felicity Everett
Adapted by Gill Harvey

Illustrated by Teri Gower

Reading Consultant: Alison Kelly
Roehampton University

Contents

Chapter 1

One rainy Saturday

Micky + Ben when we went to the beach

Me + Goldie

Ruby on her skates

Tas pulling faces

Micky, Lee + all their comics

It was too wet to play outside, so Ellie was looking at her photo album.

At last, the rain stopped. As Ellie went out, Tas zoomed up on her bike.

"Ben, Lee and Micky are on their way," Tas added.

"They're slow because Ben's wearing his new boots."

Just then, Ruby spun past.
She was learning how to do
cartwheels.

Look! I've got
the hang of it
now.

"Hi Ellie! Hi Tas!" she said.
"What are you doing?"

Ellie felt a plop of something wet on her cheek. She sighed. It was raining again.

"Looks like we're going inside," she said.

Do you want to come to my room?

Chapter 2

A great idea!

In Ellie's room, they lay
around. They played games...

10

...they drew pictures of space men and monstrous aliens...

...they played more games...

...then they were bored.

It was still raining outside.
There was nothing left to do...

...until Ben had a fantastic idea.

Let's start a gang!

Chapter 3

The new gang

"A gang needs a good name," said Ellie.

They each tried to think of one. It was tricky. But, in the end, everyone had an idea.

They wrote their ideas on
pieces of paper.

Then they folded the papers
up and put them into Tas's
bike helmet.

"You pick one out, Ben," said Lee. "The gang was your idea."

Ben closed his eyes and put his hand into the helmet. He swirled it around the papers... dug deep... and fished one out.

16

Ben read what was on the paper. "The Monster Gang!" he said. He looked very pleased with himself.

Everyone agreed it was a perfect name.

"What do Monster Gangs do?" asked Ruby.

"They look scary," said Lee.

"We'll have to dress up!" cried Ellie.

No non-scary costumes allowed.

"Gangs need a place to meet," said Micky. "And monsters need a den... I know! My grandad's got a treehouse. How about that?"

Let's all meet tomorrow morning.

A treehouse was a great den. Now, they were a real gang.

Chapter 4

The first meeting

The next morning, six
monsters clambered
into the treehouse.

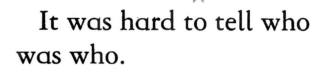

It was hard to tell who
was who.

The treehouse hadn't been used for ages. Inside, it was covered in dust. And it didn't look much like a monster den.

So, they drew scary pictures.

They made creepy bats out of
paper and cobwebs out of string.
"I know how to make scary
spiders," said the spotty blue
monster. "Look!"

Then they stuck everything up. It took ages to pin up the cobwebs.

"Whew!" said the green
monster. "That was hard
work. I'm hungry now."

Luckily, two of the gang
had brought monsterish food to
eat. They had a monster feast!
The monsters munched away.

Then the blue monster, who was Ben, decided to find out who the other monsters were.

As he handed out drinks, he started to guess.

Ah! Scraped knees...

Ruby's bruises gave her away.

"Is this hair real?" asked
Ben. He gave it a tug, just
to be sure.

"Sorry, Tas," said Ben. "I
didn't mean to hurt you."

Micky was easy to guess. He couldn't see without his glasses and had to wear them over his costume.

"I'd know those glasses anywhere," said Ben.

The red monster had a
comic poking out of his back
pocket.

Ben didn't really need a clue,
with Lee's face grinning at him.

29

"That just leaves one," said
Ben. The last monster smiled
down from the tree, and
reached for a drink.

"You must be Ellie," said Ben.
"There's no one else left."

"Come on down, Ellie," said Ruby. "Let's take a closer look at your costume."

It doesn't *look* much like Ellie...

Chapter 5

A perfect disguise

The monster climbed down
from the tree. Tas pulled her
ear to make her mask move.
But it stayed firmly in place.

Micky got down on his
hands and knees to inspect the
monster's feet.

"It must be an all-in-one
suit," said Ruby. "It's great!"

They all decided that Ellie's costume was the best.

It's fantastic, Ellie!

Everyone agreed that she should be their gang leader. After all, Ellie was the only one who looked like a real monster.

They made her a Monster Gang Leader badge. She grinned and ate a chocolate muffin to celebrate.

Chapter 6

Gang business

Now they had a leader, they needed a secret sign. They tried lots of different ones.

Too silly...

...too hard...

...too rude...

But this one was just right.

"Gangs need rules," said Micky. "Let's make some up."

Making up the rules was fun. Their gang leader wrote them down, eating another muffin.

Just then, they heard a
voice. A voice they all knew!

Chapter 7

Who's there?

"It can't be Ellie," said Ben.
"She's already here. She's our
gang leader!"

They rushed to the door to peer down from the treehouse.

It was Ellie... with her dog, Goldie, wagging his tail by her side.

The rest of the gang stared at her. How could she be in two places at once?

Sorry I'm late! I had to take Goldie for a walk.

43

They scrambled back into
the treehouse. Ellie hurried
after them. But their gang
leader had vanished.

"Look! There's a note," said
Ellie. She picked it up. "Oh...
it doesn't make sense."

Ruby guessed how to read the note. "It's mirror writing!" she said.

When they held the note up to a mirror, everything became clear.

Did you guess my secret? I'm a real monster! I hope I can come to the next meeting of the Monster Gang.

Love
Ug
XXX

Try these other books in
Series One:

The Burglar's Breakfast: Alfie
Briggs is a burglar. After a hard
night's thieving, he likes to go home
to a tasty meal. But one day he gets
back to discover someone has
stolen his breakfast!

The Dinosaurs Next Door: Stan
loves living next door to Mr. Puff.
His house is full of amazing things.
Best of all are the dinosaur eggs —
until they begin to hatch...

Series editor: Lesley Sims

Designed by
Maria Wheatley and
Katarina Dragoslavić

Black Beauty

Anna Sewell

Adapted by
Mary Sebag-Montefiore

Illustrated by
Alan Marks

Reading Consultant: Alison Kelly
Roehampton University

Contents

Chapter 1

In the beginning

When I was very young my life was gloriously happy. I galloped with other colts by day and slept by my mother's side at night.

But when I was four years old, a man named Squire Gordon came to talk to my master, the horse breeder. He stroked my black coat and the white star on my forehead. "Beautiful!" he exclaimed. "Break him in and I'll buy him!"

Then he touched the white patch on my back. "It's like a beauty spot," he said. "I'll call him Black Beauty."

I shook with fear. I was going to be sold! Would I have to leave my mother? And what was *breaking in*?

"You must learn to wear a saddle and bridle," my mother explained. Then the groom thrust a cold steel bar into my mouth and held it there, with straps over my head and under my throat. There was no escape.

At first the bar frightened me, but with kind words and treats of oats I learned to get used to it.

Just before I was taken to Squire Gordon, my mother spoke to me for the last time. "Now, Black Beauty," she whispered, "be brave. All young horses must leave their mothers to make their way in the world.

Just remember – never bite or rear or kick. And whatever happens, always do your best."

7

When Squire Gordon's groom
arrived, he jumped on my back and
we rode away. I cantered through
twisting villages until we
reached a long drive.
Apple orchards
stretched out on
either side.

The groom led me into a large,
airy stable with plenty of corn and
hay. A friendly whinny from the
next stall made me look up.

8

A fat little pony with a thick mane and tail was poking his head over the rail. "I'm Merrylegs," he said. "Welcome to Birtwick Park.

That was John who rode you here," Merrylegs went on. "He's the best groom around – and Squire Gordon is the best owner a horse could have. You'll be happy here."

9

A tall chestnut mare glared at Merrylegs. "Trouble is, no one knows how long a good home will last," she snapped. "I've had more homes than you've had hot oats."

"Meet Ginger," said Merrylegs. "She bites. That's why she keeps getting sold, even though she's so handsome."

Angrily, Ginger tore at wisps of hay in her manger. "You don't know anything," she muttered. "If you'd been through what I have, you'd bite too."

"Poor Ginger!" I thought. "What could have made her so unhappy?"

Chapter 2

Ginger's story

Over the next few days, John took me out. At first we went slowly... then we trotted and cantered, and ended up in a wonderful speedy gallop.

"Well, John, how is my new horse?" asked Squire Gordon.

"First rate, Sir," replied John, grooming me carefully. "Black Beauty's as swift as a deer, as gentle as a dove and as safe as houses."

"A lady's horse, perhaps?" asked the Squire's wife, feeding me pieces of apple.

"Oh yes, Mrs. Gordon. He'll be a good carriage horse too. We could try him out with Ginger," John suggested.

14

So I was paired up with Ginger to pull the carriage. During our journeys, she told me the story of her life.

"If I'd had your upbringing, I might be good tempered like you," she began. "My first memory is of a stone being thrown at me."

"Poor you!" I said, but Ginger hadn't finished. "When my first owner broke me in, he shoved a painful bit in my mouth," she went on.

Do as I say!

"I reared up in pain and he fought me with his whip until blood poured from my flanks...

...and then he cut off my tail."

"Why?" I cried. I'd noticed Ginger had no tail, but thought she must have lost it in an accident.

Delightful!

"Fashion," Ginger replied bitterly. "Some people think horses look better with a stump. Now I have nothing to whisk flies away with."

She sighed. "It's agony when they crawl on me and sting."

"Horrible!" I snorted.

"That's not all. My first owner sold me to a rich London gentleman who put me in a bearing rein."

"A what?" I asked.

"It's a tight rein that pulls your neck all the way back. Imagine your tongue pinched, your jaw jerked upright and your neck on fire with pain.

Everyone thought I looked wonderful, but oh, how it hurt! Kindness wins us, not painful whips," said Ginger.

"But we're lucky here," she said, at last. "Squire Gordon hates bearing reins, and John is teaching young Joe, our new groom, to be just as good as he is.

And I'm *trying* to behave now, because everyone's so kind."

Chapter 3

Horses know best

Soon after this, Mrs. Gordon fell ill. We didn't see her for weeks. Then one stormy night John rushed to the stables.

"Best foot forward, Beauty," he
cried. "We must ride as hard as we
can to fetch the doctor. Mrs.
Gordon is at death's door."
   We galloped into lashing rain,
while thunder and lightning raged
around us.

Leaves and twigs danced in the air, torn from their branches by a savage wind.

As we got to the main road, a terrible splitting sound crashed through the darkness. A huge tree had fallen in our path.

23

Gathering all my strength, I jumped – and sailed over it.

At last we reached the bridge.
I could hear the river roaring.
But the moment I stepped onto
the bridge, I stopped.

"Come on, Beauty," John urged. I couldn't move. I could tell something was wrong. John gave me a light touch of the whip, but I stayed like a statue.

Just then, the moon lit up the bridge. We saw the far end had collapsed into matchsticks, tossing in the raging water.

"Well done, Beauty!" John cried.
"We would have been killed. But
I'm afraid it's ten miles to the
next bridge. We'll have to hurry."

You understand
me, don't you Black
Beauty?

"Gallop and get there…" I
murmured to myself. "Gallop and
get there…" The faster I said it,
the faster I went.

I raced home with both John and the doctor on my back. I'd never been so tired in my life.

"You're steaming like a kettle," said young Joe. "You're too hot for your blanket. Here, have some ice-cold water."

All through the night I shivered and sweated and longed for John to come. When he arrived, he was horrified. "Joe! You've nearly killed Beauty!" he shouted. "He's caught a bad chill.

You should have put on his blanket – and that icy drink did him no good at all."

29

"I didn't know," Joe muttered sulkily.

"Didn't know?" yelled John. "You should make it your business to know. If you don't know, ask!"

"I'm sorry," wept Joe. "I didn't mean to hurt him."

With careful nursing, I recovered, but Joe never forgot the lesson he had learned.

Chapter 4

A terrible time

Mrs. Gordon got better too, but the doctor said she must live in the sun to be really well.

Goodbye Ginger.

Everything was to be sold –
Birtwick Park, Merrylegs, Ginger
and me. Merrylegs went to
the priest.

We said goodbye under the apple
trees, where we'd talked and
played so happily. I never saw
Merrylegs again.

Ginger and I were sold to Lord and Lady Richmore. John had tears in his eyes when he handed us over to Reuben, our new groom.

Next day, Lord and Lady
Richmore came to inspect us.

"They look very nice, Reuben,"
announced Lady Richmore. "They
can pull my carriage. But you
must put their heads up. High."

"Squire Gordon never used a
bearing rein," Lord Richmore
reminded her.

"Well, I won't have horrible,
common-looking horses," snapped
Lady Richmore.

Reuben pulled my head back
and fixed the rein tight. I felt
red-hot pain. Ginger tried to jerk
her head away, but Reuben forced
her rein like mine.

Instantly, I saw why Ginger hated
it. I couldn't put my head down to
take the strain of pulling the
carriage. As the strength drained
out of us, Reuben whipped us on.

At last, we came to a grand courtyard crammed with horses and carriages. Ginger couldn't take it any more.

With a wild neigh she reared up, scaring all the horses who crashed into each other, kicking madly. Our carriage toppled over and broke to pieces.

Lady Richmore tumbled out, unharmed but furious.

Ginger was taken away forever. I longed to know what happened to her, but no one mentioned her name again.

I didn't trust Reuben. He oozed politeness to the Richmores, but secretly he drank too much.

One evening, he took me out for a ride on a road made of fresh-laid sharp stones. My shoe was loose, but Reuben was too drunk to notice.

He never heard the clatter of my shoe falling off. I don't think he even noticed me limping. My hoof split and – I couldn't help it! I fell onto my knees. Reuben shot to the ground, hit his head on the cobbles and lay there, not moving.

I stayed with Reuben all through the night. When morning dawned, a group of early walkers came by. They were shocked at the sight of us.

"That's Reuben," they shouted. "Dead, poor bloke. Thrown by that horse! Vicious brute! That'll be the end of him."

No one knew what really happened. And what would they do to me now?

Chapter 5

Life is a puzzle

"I'm going to sell that bad-tempered Black Beauty to any fool who wants him," Lord Richmore announced.

I was sorry for Reuben, but I couldn't help being thrilled to be leaving Lord and Lady Richmore.

I was put into a horse sale.
Buyers prodded me and stared at
me, but no one wanted me.

"Isn't he ugly with those nasty
knees?" I heard someone say.

And he's got a
bad temper.

Finally a kind-looking man paid
a small sum of money for me and
took me away.

The man's name was Jerry Barker and he lived in London with his wife and children – Harry and the twins, Polly and Molly.

"I want you to be my cab horse," Jerry told me. "I'll call you Jack."

It was strange to have a new name. My job was to be harnessed to Jerry's carriage, which he called his cab, and pick up passengers when they hailed us in the street.

We worked hard, out all day in all weather – rain, sleet, snow and ice – with hardly any rest.

I didn't mind anything because
Jerry was such a kind, honest man.
I wanted to do my best for him.

He made sure I was always
comfortable and had plenty of
food. He never whipped me to go
faster, even if customers in a hurry
bribed him with extra cash.

"You'll never be rich!" the other cab drivers jeered.

"I have enough, thanks," Jerry replied. "It's not fair on Jack to make him hurry all the time."

Other cab horses weren't so lucky. I often saw them exhausted and miserable, made old before their time with too much work.

Once I saw an old, worn-out chestnut, with a thin neck and bones that stuck out through a badly-kept coat. Its eyes had a dull, hopeless look.

I was wondering why the horse looked faintly familiar when I heard a whisper.

"Black Beauty, is that you?"

It was Ginger! Her beautiful
looks had completely vanished.

She told me she belonged to a
cruel driver who whipped her,
starved her and overworked her.

"You used to stand up for yourself if people were mean to you," I said.

"Yes, I did once, but now I'm too tired," she replied. "I just wish I could die."

"No, Ginger!" I cried. "Keep going! Better times will come."

"I hope they do for you, Black Beauty," she whispered. "Goodbye and good luck."

Soon after that meeting I saw a cart carrying a dead chestnut horse. It was a dreadful sight.

I think it was Ginger. I almost hope it was, for that meant her suffering was over.

53

Chapter 6

An unexpected ending

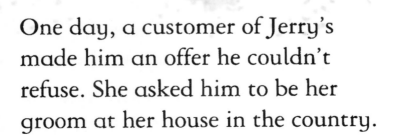

One day, a customer of Jerry's made him an offer he couldn't refuse. She asked him to be her groom at her house in the country.

"There's a little cottage for you and your family," she said. "I wish I could take Jack too, but I already have a horse."

"Sorry, old Jack," Jerry comforted me. "I hope someone kind will buy you."

55

But my new master was a cruel man. I had to pull his carts loaded with sacks of corn, and if I was too slow, he whipped me hard. He hardly fed me either, which made me weak.

In the end I simply collapsed in the street. "Stupid horse!" my master grunted. "Is he dead? What a waste of money."

I couldn't move. As I lay there barely breathing, someone came up and poured water down my throat. A gentle voice said, "He's not dead, only exhausted."

Take him. He's no use to me.

The gentle voice belonged to a horse doctor. I couldn't believe my luck! The doctor helped me to my feet, and led me to his stables, where he gave me a warm mash.

"I think you were a good horse once," said the doctor, "though you're a poor, broken-down old thing now. I'm going to feed you up and find you a nice home."

Rest, good food and gentle
exercise worked on me like magic.
But when the doctor said I was
ready to leave him, I trembled all
over. I dreaded to think what my
next home would be like.

The doctor took me to a pretty house in a small village. It had a pasture and a comfortable stable, and belonged to two grown-up sisters, Claire and Elspeth Lyefield.

"I'm sure we'll like you," they said, patting me. "You have such a gentle face." I nuzzled them, but I wasn't sure I could trust them.

Their groom led me to the stable and began to clean me. "That white star is just like Black Beauty's," he said, "and the glossy black coat. He's about the same height too. I wonder where Black Beauty is now?"

Soon he came to the tiny knot of white hair on my back. "That's what Squire Gordon called Beauty's patch. It is Black Beauty! It really *is!* Do you remember me? Young Joe who nearly killed you?"

I was so glad to see him! I've never seen a man so happy, either.

I've been here now for a year.
Joe is always gentle, Claire and
Elspeth are kind, and my work
is easy. All my strength has come
back and I've never been happier.

The sisters have promised never
to sell me. Finally I've found my
home, for ever and ever.

Anna Sewell, who lived from 1820-1878, adored horses. She suffered from a bone disease and, after spraining her ankle as a young girl, she became increasingly lame. For the last six years of her life she couldn't move from her house. She longed to make people more caring about horses, so she wrote "Black Beauty" (her only book), lying on her sofa. Anna died just after it was published, never knowing its success.

Series editor: Lesley Sims
Designed by Katarina Dragoslavic
Cover design by Russell Punter

First published in 2005 by Usborne Publishing Ltd., Usborne House, 83-85 Saffron Hill, London EC1N 8RT, England. www.usborne.com
Copyright © 2005 Usborne Publishing Ltd.
Printed in China. UE. First published in America in 2006.

HAMLET

Based on the play by
William Shakespeare

Adapted by Louie Stowell

Illustrated by Christa Unzner

Reading consultant: Alison Kelly
Roehampton University

Contents

Chapter 1

The dead king

It was a bitterly cold night in
Elsinore, in the kingdom of Denmark.
Three men huddled together on the
battlements of the King's castle.
They were waiting for someone.

3

A young man named Horatio
stood with two of the King's
guards. "I think you were seeing
things last night," he began.

I don't believe in
gho...

"Shh!" hissed one of the
guards. "It's here..."
Horatio gasped. A shadowy
figure had appeared beside them.

4

"It looks exactly like the King!"
cried Horatio, in terror. "The *dead*
King. Why are you here?" he
asked the figure. "Please, speak."

But the ghost shook its head and
did not reply. As the sun began to
rise, he faded away into thin air.

Cock-a-doodle-doo!

"I must tell Hamlet," said
Horatio. Hamlet was his best
friend, and the dead King's son.

5

Prince Hamlet had been utterly miserable since his father died. He kept to himself and dressed mostly in black.

Just one month after Hamlet lost his father, his mother had married the new King, his uncle. It made Hamlet's blood boil.

How could she forget his father so quickly? He was suspicious about his father's death, too. It had been so sudden. All these thoughts churned over and over in his mind.

When Horatio came to see Hamlet the next morning, his friend was sitting alone and looking very gloomy indeed.

"Hamlet," Horatio began, in a quiet voice. "I think I saw your father last night."

Hamlet leaped up. "What?"

Horatio told him about the ghost's visit the night before.

"I have to see this for myself," said Hamlet. That night, they went up to the battlements to wait.

8

Drunken yells echoed
around the castle courtyard.
"What's that noise?"
asked Horatio.

Hic!

"My uncle Claudius is having a
party to celebrate marrying my
mother," said Hamlet, bitterly.
"The guests came for my father's
funeral and stayed on."

9

As the clock struck midnight the ghostly figure appeared once more.

"Father?" cried Hamlet. "Speak to me! What do you want?"

The ghost beckoned to him and Hamlet stepped closer, trembling.

"Take revenge for my murder,"
said the ghost. His voice was like
the whistling of the wind.

Hamlet's eyes widened. "Who
murdered you?"

"Your uncle," said the ghost. "My
own brother did this dreadful thing."

11

Chapter 2

Revenge

The ghost told Hamlet the whole story. "I was dozing in the orchard when I felt something dripping into my ear. It burned me! So I opened my eyes... and the last thing I saw was Claudius, clutching a bottle of poison."

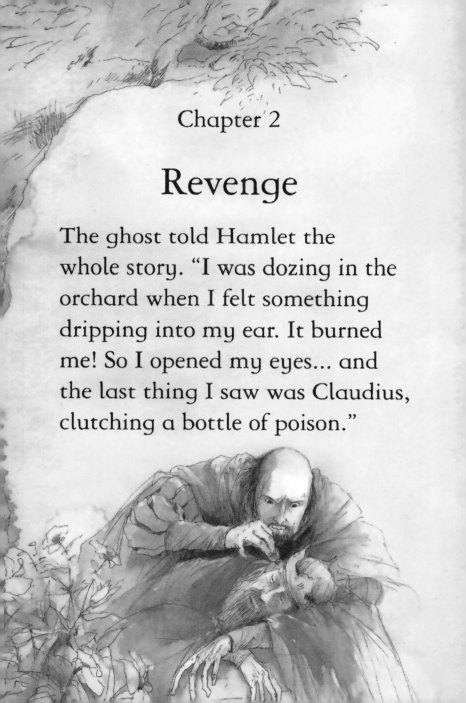

"I couldn't even beg forgiveness for my sins," added the ghost. His voice pierced Hamlet's heart. "So now I'm being punished."

"I'll avenge you!" said Hamlet. "I swear I will."

The ghost nodded. "Kill him for me," it said, and disappeared.

Horatio came up to Hamlet.
"Well, what did he want?"

Hamlet shook his head and
his eyes darted from side to side.
"You'll tell someone," he said.

"I swear, I won't tell a soul,"
promised Horatio.

"Very well," said Hamlet, and
told him what the ghost had said.

"If you see me acting as if I'm crazy," Hamlet added, "it's just part of my plan."

"What plan?" asked Horatio.

"I'm going to pretend to be mad," said Hamlet, "so my uncle won't guess what I'm really thinking."

Horatio saw a strange look in his friend's eye. He wasn't sure if Hamlet would have to pretend.

Chapter 3

A prince in love?

"King Claudius! King Claudius!" called a voice. It was Polonius, the King's adviser. He came rushing into the throne room. "Hamlet has gone mad," he announced. "And I know why."

The King started. "Mad?"

"Yes!" panted Polonius. "He came into my daughter Ophelia's chamber and ranted and raved."

"He's mad with love, you see," explained Polonius.

"Ah." The King sounded relieved. "I would like to see this for myself."

Polonius smiled smugly. "Let's send Ophelia to Hamlet's room, then hide and watch them. You'll soon see how the poor boy has lost his wits over my beautiful girl."

The King wasn't sure if he entirely believed Polonius, but he agreed to the plan. They hid behind a curtain to spy on Hamlet.

18

Ophelia went up to him and greeted him. Hamlet certainly started to rant and rave, but not like a man who was mad with love.

"Go away!" he screamed at her.

"You women are all the same!"
Hamlet spat. "You paint your
faces, you lie and you betray us."
When he'd finished yelling,
he stalked away, muttering to
himself. Ophelia stared after him
in shocked silence.

The King turned to Polonius.
"He doesn't *sound* like he's in love."

Secretly, the King was worried.
Was Hamlet angry with his
mother for remarrying so quickly?
Did he suspect something about his
father's death?

He should send Hamlet away,
just in case. But that might not
be enough. Perhaps he should get
Hamlet out of the way for good...

Chapter 4

The play

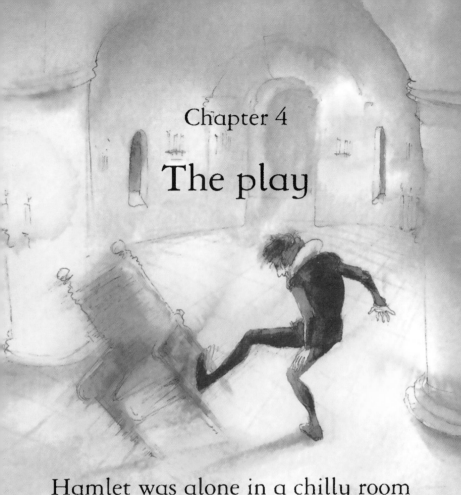

Hamlet was alone in a chilly room in the castle, cursing himself. "I'm useless!" he muttered. "I promised my father I would kill Claudius. What's stopping me?"

A voice of doubt was whispering in his ear. What if the ghost wasn't his father, but a devil in disguise? "I need proof that the ghost was telling the truth," he thought.

An idea struck him. A troop of actors was visiting the castle. "I'll ask them to put on a play about a man who poisons a king," he thought. "If Claudius looks guilty, I'll know he did it."

Hamlet went to see the leader of the troop and gave him a script. "Will you put on this play?"

"Of course, my lord," said the actor, with a bow.

That night, the King and Queen settled down to watch the play. Hamlet sat beside them, so he could keep an eye on the King.

Music struck up and the play began. An actor playing the villain crept up to the man who was playing the king. The fake king snored loudly and the villain poured poison in his ear.

Hamlet glanced at his uncle. He had gone pale.

"How do you like the play?"
asked Hamlet with a bitter smile.

The King did not reply. He
stood, stumbled over his chair and
left the room.

"The ghost told me the truth,"
thought Hamlet. "Now I can
have my revenge." He got up and
followed Claudius.

Chapter 5

A rat!

The King hurried along the castle
corridors to the chapel. His heart
was heavy with guilt. At the
chapel, he knelt before the altar
and tried to pray.

Hamlet was not far behind. He came into the chapel and watched his uncle.

"I could do it now," he thought. "He won't hear me coming."

But Hamlet shook his head. "If I kill him while he's praying, he'll go straight to heaven. That isn't a punishment. It's a reward." And he decided to wait.

When the King returned to his throne room, Polonius was waiting for him. "I've got another plan," he said, looking pleased with himself.

Claudius groaned.

"We should send Hamlet to talk to his mother," Polonius went on. "Perhaps she can get him to stop behaving like a lunatic? I'll hide and listen in."

So Hamlet was summoned to his mother's room. He strode in with a face like thunder.

"Hamlet, you've offended your step-father," his mother scolded.

"Mother, you've offended my father – by marrying my uncle," replied Hamlet. He grabbed her. His eyes flashed with fury.

"Help, help!" cried his mother.
There was a noise from behind
the curtain.

32

Hamlet whipped out his sword, crying, "What's that? A rat?" He plunged his sword through the curtain... and into Polonius.

There was a terrible groan.
"Was that the King?" said
Hamlet and he pulled the
curtain aside.

"Oh," he said, as Polonius's body
fell out. "It's you." He shrugged.
"I'm sorry I killed you, but it can't
be helped." He began to drag the
dead man out of the room.

"He's mad!" sobbed the Queen.

When the King heard what had
happened, he called for Hamlet.
"Where is Polonius's body?" he
asked. But no one knew
where Hamlet had hidden it.

"He's at dinner," said Hamlet.
He grinned. "With the worms.
Only they're eating him, not the
other way around."

The King saw his chance.
"Hamlet," he said. "My dear
son... You cannot possibly stay
in Denmark now. I'll send you to
England to keep you safe."

Hamlet agreed to go. But he
was sure that the King was up to
no good.

Chapter 6

The mad sister

The King and Queen were in the throne room some days later, when Polonius's daughter, Ophelia, drifted in. Her hair was wild and tangled. She looked as though she'd been dragged through a hedge.

She began to sing a song as she walked. Clutching bunches of wild flowers in her hands, she handed a bloom to the Queen.

Everyone watching realized that Ophelia had lost her mind.

A furious pounding on the door broke into her song. "Laertes is here!" called a guard.

Laertes was Ophelia's brother. He stormed into the throne room.

"Where is my father's body?"
Laertes demanded. "I heard he was
killed. Who did it?"

Before the King could answer,
Laertes saw Ophelia.

She gazed at him, hardly even
seeing him. Laertes was horrified.

"Oh, my dear sister, what's
happened to you?" he gasped.

"Would you like a violet?" she asked. Then she shook her head. "I can't give you a violet. They all withered when my father died."

"She's mad with grief," said the King. "I'm sorry to tell you, Laertes, Hamlet killed your father. It's all his fault."

"I'll kill Hamlet for doing this!" Laertes swore.

The King waved him close and whispered, "Don't worry. He will get what he deserves soon."

The King smiled. At any
moment, his men would be killing
Hamlet on board the ship to
England. Or so he thought...

"Prince Hamlet is here!" came
a cry from the courtyard. "Prince
Hamlet has returned from England."

The King's eyes widened with surprise. Laertes began to mutter under his breath about what he planned to do to Hamlet. The Queen rushed out to greet her son.

Hamlet's friend Horatio smiled.
He was standing quietly near the
King, holding a letter from Hamlet
that explained everything.

...The King's men turned on
me, as I suspected they would.
But at that very moment we
were attacked by pirates and I
managed to stow away on the
pirate ship. I am on my way
home. When I return, I will take
my revenge!

Yours ever,

Hamlet

The King spoke quietly to Laertes. "Hamlet might still be alive, but I have a plan to change that. You must challenge him to a duel."

"But what if I don't kill him?" said Laertes.

"I'll dip one of the blades in deadly poison," said the King. "Even if you merely graze his skin, he will die."

The King rubbed his hands. "If he wins without a scratch, I'll offer him a drink laced with poison."

Laertes thought about this for a moment. It seemed a dishonest way to get his revenge.

But his thoughts were interrupted by the Queen. She burst into the room, tears streaming down her face. "Ophelia has drowned herself!" she sobbed.

"They found her floating like a mermaid in the lake. Dead! Oh poor Ophelia!"

Laertes gripped his sword hilt. "I'm ready to challenge Hamlet," he told the King. "I will kill him, if it's the last thing I do."

Chapter 7

The duel

Hamlet was out walking with
Horatio. They passed through a
graveyard where two men were
hard at work, digging a grave.

One of the gravediggers threw an old skull up out of the grave.

Hamlet caught it. "Hey!" he called. "Whose skull is this?"

"A court jester who died years ago," the man replied. "His name was Yorrick."

Yorrick?

Hamlet felt sad. "Poor Yorrick. I knew him, Horatio — so full of fun when he was alive." He pointed at the skull. "Look, he's still grinning."

The sound of chanting floated across the graveyard. A funeral procession was coming closer. Hamlet recognized the King, the Queen... and Laertes.

"Oh, Ophelia," Laertes wept. Hamlet rushed over to the coffin. "That's Ophelia?" he said.

"You!" Laertes spat. "Go to the devil!" He leaped at Hamlet, pushing him into the empty grave and jumping after him.

"Hamlet, don't!" said Horatio, as guards pulled the pair out.
"You can settle this like gentlemen," the King declared. "I order you to fight a duel."

Chapter 8

The poisoned sword

That afternoon, the King, the Queen and their courtiers came to watch Hamlet and Laertes fight.

Two swords were laid out for them. Laertes knew which one to pick. "I'll take this one," he said.

The men faced each other, their shining swords held high.

"Good luck!" called the King. "And if you win, Hamlet, I have a delicious drink waiting, to toast your victory."

Hamlet and Laertes began to fight. With a quick thrust, Hamlet cut Laertes' arm with his blade.

"A hit!" everyone cried. "First blood! Well done Hamlet!"

The King was worried. He raised the poisoned cup. "Here, have a drink before you go on, Hamlet."

"No, I'll drink when the fight is over," said Hamlet.

The men circled each other. Hamlet struck again, this time on Laertes' shoulder.

Hurrah for Hamlet!

Before the King realized it was happening, the Queen had picked up the poisoned cup. "To my son!" she cried, and gulped down a mouthful of the deadly drink.

As the Queen drank, Laertes swiped with his sword and the blade bit into Hamlet's side. It wasn't a deep wound, but the poison was in Hamlet's blood.

Hamlet struck back and their blades clashed together. The force of the blow knocked both swords to the ground.

When they picked them up
again, Laertes had Hamlet's sword
in his hand and Hamlet was
clutching the poisoned blade.

With a grunt, Hamlet struck
Laertes. As the sword grazed
his arm, Laertes recognized the
weapon. "I'm dying," he thought.

Then the Queen began to groan in agony. "That drink... Oh my dear Hamlet, I've been poisoned."

"There's a traitor here," cried Hamlet. "Find him!"

"There *is* a traitor," said Laertes. "And it's me. I plotted with the King to kill you. My sword was poisoned. We're both dying. I... I am so sorry."

Hamlet looked down at the poisoned blade. Suddenly, everything became clear. He had nothing to lose now, and he knew what he had to do.

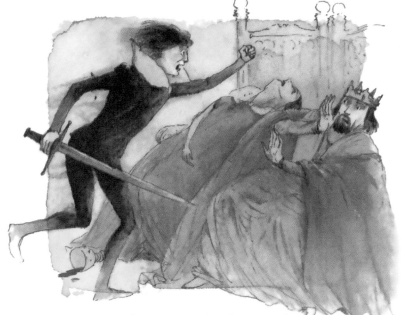

"This is for my father," he called. He rushed at the King, stabbing him with the poisoned sword. The King cried out.

The King and Queen slumped
in their thrones, life ebbing away.
Hamlet staggered and fell and
Horatio rushed to his side.

"If you are dying, I'll die with
you," cried Horatio. He picked up
the cup that the Queen had put
down. "I'll drink this poison."

Hamlet raised a hand. "Don't, please. I want you to tell the world my story," he said. His voice was growing weak.

"Remember me," he whispered. "The rest is silence."

William Shakespeare

1564-1616

William Shakespeare was
born in Stratford-upon-Avon,
England, and became famous
as an actor and writer when he moved to
London. He wrote many poems and almost forty
plays which are still performed and enjoyed today.

Internet Links

You can find out more about Shakespeare by
going to the Usborne Quicklinks website at
www.usborne.com/quicklinks and
typing in the keywords 'yr shakespeare'.
Please note that Usborne Publishing cannot be responsible
for the content of any website other than its own.

Designed by Michelle Lawrence
Series designer: Russell Punter
Series editor: Lesley Sims

First published in 2009 by Usborne Publishing Ltd., Usborne House,
83-85 Saffron Hill, London EC1N 8RT, England. www.usborne.com
Copyright © 2009 Usborne Publishing Ltd.

Stories of
Dragons

Christopher Rawson
Adapted by Lesley Sims

Illustrated by
Stephen Cartwright

Reading Consultant: Alison Kelly
Roehampton University

Contents

Chapter 1

All about dragons

Years ago, dragons were the terror of towns... or so it was said. They breathed in air and blew out flame. Just one puff of dragon breath could kill you.

Some dragons lived in caves, guarding stolen treasure.

Others lived under the sea. Sometimes, they popped up and scared sailors.

Dragons even lived in the sky. When they were angry, storms blew up.

Bolts of lightning were flames shot from a cross dragon's nose.

Most people kept as far
away from dragons as they
could. Only knights dared
go near them.

People offered huge rewards
to the brave knights who could
kill dragons. But dragons
weren't so easy to defeat.

Dragons had bumpy scales, flapping wings and pointed tails, and they came in all shapes and sizes.

Whatever they looked like, you wouldn't want to meet one.

8

Chapter 2

Stan and the dragon

Stan was a woodcutter. He
lived deep in the forest with
his wife. She was sad because
they had no children.

9

One day, a wizard appeared in the forest. "You're a good man, Stan," said the wizard. "I can grant you one wish."

Stan only wanted one wish. "I wish for as many children as my wife is thinking about now," he said.

Stan's wish came true! But they didn't have two... or ten... or even fifty children. They had one hundred.

Oh no!

"How will I afford to feed them all?" said Stan.

His friend
Sam had an
idea.

"A dragon
has been
scaring my
sheep," he
said. "If you can find its cave,
you might find treasure."

So, Stan
set off in
search
of the
dragon
and its
treasure.

Stan didn't find the dragon.
The dragon found him. When
he saw it, Stan knew he
couldn't fight the dragon.

Instead, he said, "I bet I'm
stronger than you. I can
squeeze a stone until it drips!"

Nnnnggghh!

"You are strong!" grunted the
dragon. He didn't know Stan's
stone was a lump of old cheese.

The dragon took Stan to meet his mother.

"It must have been a trick," she said. "If you really are stronger than my son, I'll give you our treasure."

You won't beat my son twice.

She found two clubs.
"See how far you can both
throw these."

"I'll throw mine over that
mountain," said the dragon.
"How about you?"

"I can't throw now," Stan
said. "The moon's in the way!"

Now, the dragons were scared. Stan was the strongest man they had ever met. They made a plan to kill him in the night.

I'll creep into his room when he's asleep...

...then you can bash him on the head!

But Stan heard them. He
decided to fool them and put
a log in his bed.

In the middle of the night,
the dragon crept to Stan's bed.

BAM! He whacked the bed
just where he thought Stan's
head was.

"That's killed him!" said
the dragon.

When Stan appeared next morning, the dragons were astonished.

"I have a little bump on my head," he said. "Perhaps a flea bit me in the night?"

Stan was much too clever for
the terrified dragons. They
took out their treasure.

"Here," they said. "Take
it! Just go away and leave
us alone!"

They even carried the treasure home for him. Stan had enough gold to buy his huge family all the food they could eat.

Chapter 3

The wicked worm

Tom loved fishing... until
the afternoon he caught
a worm instead of a fish.

22

An old man had seen him. "That worm is trouble," he warned Tom. "But don't throw it back in the river. You'll only make things worse."

You must get rid of it!

Tom didn't know what
to do. He tried to hide the
worm in a well.

But a week later, the worm
crawled out. It had grown
even bigger.

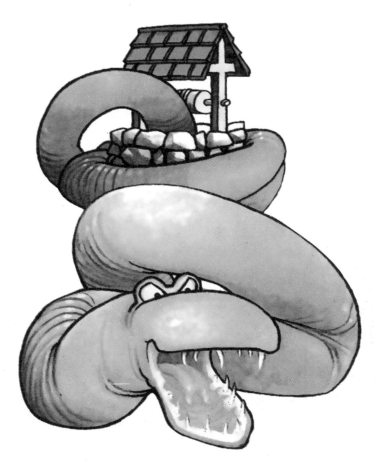

The worm was hungry and angry. It chased the cows around the fields. Then it chased the villagers around their houses.

Tom felt terrible. The worm was a menace – and it was all his fault.

Brave knights came from
miles around to kill the worm.
But it was too strong.

It curled itself around them
and squeezed them so they
couldn't fight.

Finally, Tom went to see a wise woman to ask for help.

"You caught it. You must get rid of it," she told Tom.

Tom wasn't sure about that. The dragon had never hurt anyone... because everyone left him alone.

But Tom had no choice. So, he dressed up like a brave knight and went to beg the dragon for help.

To his surprise, the dragon didn't look scary at all.

"What's wrong?" said Tom.

"I'm lonely," the dragon replied. "I have no friends."

"I know how you can have a hundred!" Tom told him. "But you'll have to look fierce."

Tom told the dragon about the worm. "If you eat the worm, everyone in the village will be your friend!" he said.

"I can't eat it," said the dragon. "I'm a vegetarian."

But I could scare it...

It was so hot, the worm was
swimming. The dragon stood
on the river bank, opened his
mouth and roared. "Yum!" he
cried. "Supper!"

The worm took one look at
the dragon and swam for its
life. It was never seen again.

Chapter 4

Victor saves the village

Victor made barrels, the best barrels in the country.

He made the best barrels
because he used the best wood.
He hunted hard to find the
tallest, straightest trees.

He was always looking out for the perfect tree. So he didn't always watch where he was going. One day, he tripped and fell...

...into a cave.

Try as he might...

...Victor couldn't climb out of the cave.

Suddenly, he heard a deep
growl. There was something
behind him! Victor looked.
He wished he hadn't.

"Please don't eat me!" Victor begged.

"We won't," said one of the dragons. "Not yet. We're going to sleep. Wake us up in the spring."

Victor was stuck. Soon, he was bored as well.

There was nothing he could do.

He had to wait until spring.

All he had to eat and drink
were grass and water. After
a while, he was no longer as
round as a barrel. He was as
thin as a twig.

Finally, the dragons awoke.
"We can't eat you!" said
one. "You're skin and bone."

"Grab my tail,"
the other dragon
said to Victor.
"We'll take
you home.
Perhaps
your
friends
will
make
a juicy
meal."

The villagers were amazed
to see Victor after so long,
and they were terrified to
see the dragons.

But before the dragons could
bite anyone, Victor invited
them to a huge feast.

Victor and the dragons ate
for a week. The dragons
enjoyed the food so much,
they decided they would never
eat people again.

The villagers were very pleased to hear it. They put up a statue of Victor in the market square.

Now, everyone who visits knows how Victor saved the village from two hungry dragons.

Now he always looks where he's going!

Try these other books in
Series One:

The Burglar's Breakfast: Alfie Briggs is a burglar, who discovers someone has stolen his breakfast!

The Dinosaurs Next Door: Mr. Puff's house is full of amazing things. Best of all are the dinosaur eggs — until they begin to hatch...

Wizards: One wizard looks after orphans, one sells cures and one must stop a band of robbers from taking the last sack of gold in the castle.

The Monster Gang: The Monster Gang is together for their first meeting in the tree house. But one of the monsters hides a secret.

Designed by
Katarina Dragoslavić

This edition first published in 2007 by Usborne Publishing Ltd.,
Usborne House, 83-85 Saffron Hill, London EC1N 8RT, England.
www.usborne.com
Copyright © 2007, 2003, 1980 Usborne Publishing Ltd.

Stories of
MONSTERS

Russell Punter

Illustrated by
Mike Phillips

Reading Consultant: Alison Kelly
Roehampton University

Contents

Chapter 1

The bed monster's secret

Ben Boggle lay awake in a cold sweat. How could he sleep with a monster under his bed?

3

Every evening it was the
same story. As soon as Ben
switched off his bedside light,
the monster woke with a snort.

Grrrgggh
Gruggluggle

All through the night, the
creature gurgled and growled
in the shadows.

Ben had never dared to look under his bed. He was too terrified of what he might see.

Perhaps the monster had ten eyes...

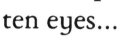

or long, slimy tentacles...

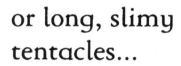

or huge, sharp teeth...

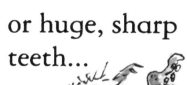

...or all of these!

At school, Ben could hardly keep his eyes open.

Wake up, Ben Boggle!

"That's the third time this week you've fallen asleep in class," yelled his teacher. Mr. Grizzle liked people to be awake in his mathematics lessons.

Even when he was wide awake, Ben was hopeless with numbers. They were even more difficult when he felt sleepy.

Get to bed earlier, young man!

Unless Ben could get rid of the monster, Mr. Grizzle would be shouting at him every day.

Tired and worried, Ben was walking home when he spotted something in a shop window.

"Maybe that book has something about bed monsters," Ben thought. He dashed inside.

8

As soon as he got home, Ben read the book from cover to cover. But there was no mention of monsters under the bed.

Chapter XII
What monsters eat

Monsters like to eat:
- little kids
- monster hunters
- small furry animals
- big furry animals
- chocolate chip cookies

"What a waste of money," thought Ben. Then he had an idea. Perhaps the book could help him after all...

Ben decided to build a
monster trap. He raided the
chocolate chip cookie jar and
took a net from his dad's
fishing box. In no time at all,
his trap was ready.

That night, he climbed into
bed, switched off the light and
waited.

At first, Ben's room was spookily silent. Then he heard a crunching, munching sound followed by a whoosh. His monster trap had worked!

Nervously, Ben crept over to the net. But nothing could have prepared him for what happened next...

"Please don't hurt me,"
squeaked a tiny voice. The
smallest monster in the world
was tangled in the net.

"I can't believe I was scared
of you," cried Ben.

12

"I know," the monster said sadly. "I'm too small to scare anyone. That's why I hid under your bed. I didn't want you to see me."

"I'm the most useless monster alive," she wailed and started to sob. Ben began to feel sorry for the strange little creature.

The monster sniffed.

"It's impossible to scare people when you only weigh fifteen ounces," she said. "I mean, that's less than half a kilo."

"Is it really?" said Ben.

"Oh yes," replied the monster. "I may be small, but I'm not stupid."

14

This gave Ben such a great idea that he grinned all night, even in his sleep.

He was still grinning the next day at school as Mr. Grizzle began the lesson.

"Ben Boggle," barked Mr. Grizzle. "What is nine times eight?"

"Seventy two," said Ben confidently.

Mr. Grizzle couldn't believe his ears. "Oh, that's correct," he said, shakily. He asked Ben problem after problem. Ben answered every one correctly.

Mr. Grizzle was amazed. "Well done, Ben," he said. "What an astonishing improvement!"

Luckily, no one but Ben had heard the tiny voice whispering the answers.

Ben smiled to himself. Mathematics is a lot easier when you have a monster in your pocket.

Chapter 2

Return of the ice monster

Frankie Frost was fed up. All her friends had gone to the mountains to ski and she had to stay behind and help her mother.

18

Frankie gazed sadly out of the
window.

"The gang will be drinking hot
chocolate in the log cabin, about
now," she thought. Bernie her
dog looked as sad as she did.

You were
looking forward to it
too, weren't you
boy?

Frankie sighed and swept up
another pile of frizzy hair.

19

Just then, one of Frankie's
friends rushed in. The look of
terror on his face made the
customers spill their coffee.

M...m...monster!

"What's the matter, Chip?"
asked Frankie. "Where are the
others?"

"The ice m...m...monster got
them," he stuttered.

"What a lot of nonsense, Chip Redwood," said Mrs. Frost. *"Ice monster*, indeed."

No one's seen it in years!

I think people just imagined it, anyhow.

"They're in trouble," insisted Chip. "I'm getting my dad."

"And I'm going to look for my friends," said Frankie, snatching her coat.

21

Frankie raced
out before
anyone could
stop her.

Come on,
Bernie!

Soon, she and her faithful
little dog were crunching
through the snow up the
mountain.

Frankie stared at the frozen mountainside. Her friends were nowhere to be seen.

Then she noticed a huge crater in the snow. Next to it was another, and another...

They look like...

They were ice
monster footprints.
Frankie's heart
thumped as she
ran for cover.

24

But Bernie was braver than he looked. He was determined to tackle the monster.

Unhappily for Bernie, the ice monster was in a very bad mood. He took one look at Bernie and let out an icy roar.

As Frankie watched
helplessly, Bernie was frozen
to the spot by the monster's
chilling breath.

26

The monster picked up the little dog like a lollipop and stomped on his way.

Frankie followed the massive creature across the mountain. "I've got to rescue poor Bernie," she thought.

It wasn't long before the
monster reached a sparkling
cave of ice.

Frankie wasn't sure if her
teeth were chattering with
cold or fear. She crept inside
and stared in horror.

There, glistening in the
corner, stood her friends —
frozen like icicles.

"You can join the rest of my
lunch," growled the monster,
sticking Bernie in the ground.

Unless Frankie acted quickly, her friends would be eaten alive.

As she sneaked outside to find help, Frankie noticed smoke rising from the gang's log cabin. She rushed over. The smoke had given her an idea.

The monster was just about
to take his first bite of lunch,
when a sweet, chocolatey
smell wafted into the cave.

Mmm!
Something
smells good.

He didn't know what it was,
but it certainly smelled better
than the little hairy creature
he'd found outside.

The monster followed the smell to the cabin and crashed through the wall.

He'd never eaten anything that wasn't ice-cold. But that didn't stop him from gulping down the steaming, chocolate drink.

In between gulps, the
monster spotted
Frankie.

Ah, something
chewy!

The creature tried to chase
her, but his legs wouldn't
move.

"Aagh!" he cried. There was
a puddle where his legs used to
be. He was melting.

33

The monster gave one last
desperate roar, but it was
too late.

Frankie watched as the
monster dripped and drizzled.
Soon, there was nothing left of
him but a pool of slushy water.

At that moment, Chip and his dad appeared.

"Where is everyone, Frankie?" asked Mr. Redwood.

"They're in the cave," she cried. "This way!"

The three of them loaded Bernie and the frozen children onto Mr. Redwood's truck and they drove back to town.

Back home, Frankie grabbed every hairdryer she could find.

"Set them to super warm!" she told the others, and they blasted her frozen friends with hot air.

As soon as everyone was back to normal, Chip's dad took them all out for burgers and colas – without ice!

Chapter 3

Attack of the swamp monster

Tom Smudge loved to listen to his Grandpa Jess tell creepy stories about the old days.

"Did I ever tell you about the swamp monster?" asked the old man one afternoon.

"No," gulped Tom nervously.

"It happened years ago," began Grandpa Jess. "I was a farmhand on Roy's ranch, when one of the cows went missing."

"I searched all day with no luck. As night fell, I spotted a muddy trail leading to the middle of the swamp..."

"What happened next?"
asked Tom, with a shiver.

"A terrible, slithering sound
filled the air, and I found
myself face to face with a
horrible, hideous..."

Tom, stop
bothering your
grandpa!

Mrs. Smudge suddenly burst
into the room waving a piece
of paper at Tom.

"I need you to go to the store and get these things!" she said.

"Can't I hear the end of Grandpa's story first?" begged Tom.

Grocery list
Soap for Grandpa
2 large bottles
of bubble bath
Lots of broccoli
Small cabbage
Peas

"No. Now, off you go," said Mrs. Smudge. "And hurry back," she added. "You haven't had a bath yet."

Tom groaned. He hated baths.

He was trudging back from
the store when his friends
asked him to play football.
Thinking of the waiting bath,
Tom quickly agreed.

By the time the game ended,
it was almost dark.
Tom decided to
take a shortcut
home across the
swamp.

He'd only been walking for a minute, when he heard a sinister, squelching sound. Green stalks seemed to be curling around him.

These weeds are very thick.

But they weren't weeds that Tom could feel tightening around his ankles...

Tom struggled in the slimy
creature's grasp. The more he
squirmed, the tighter the
monster squeezed.

43

Tom wished he'd never stopped to play football.

The monster dragged him closer to its huge, slimy, smelly mouth.

Suddenly there was a crack. The monster had smashed the bottles in Tom's bag.

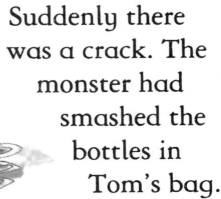

In seconds, the murky
swamp water became a mass
of sweet-smelling bubbles.

The monster choked and
spluttered on the foamy water.
Tom slipped from its grasp.
They were both getting the
bath of their lives.

By now, several people had heard Tom's shouts and come to help. They took one look at the new, squeaky-clean monster and burst out laughing.

The monster was so embarrassed, it swam off and was never seen again.

As for Tom, he had the best reward ever. He didn't need a bath for a week.

There are lots more great stories for you to read:

Usborne Young Reading: Series One
Aladdin and his Magical Lamp
Ali Baba and the Forty Thieves
Animal Legends
Stories of Dragons
Stories of Giants
Stories of Gnomes & Goblins
Stories of Magical Animals
Stories of Pirates
Stories of Princes & Princesses
Stories of Witches
The Burglar's Breakfast
The Dinosaurs Next Door
The Monster Gang
Wizards

Usborne Young Reading: Series Two
A Christmas Carol
Aesop's Fables
Gulliver's Travels
Jason & The Golden Fleece
Robinson Crusoe
The Adventures of King Arthur
The Amazing Adventures of Hercules
The Amazing Adventures of Ulysses
The Clumsy Crocodile
The Fairground Ghost
The Incredible Present
The Story of Castles
The Story of Flying
The Story of Ships
The Story of Trains
Treasure Island

Series editor:
Lesley Sims

This edition first published in 2007 by Usborne Publishing Ltd.,
Usborne House, 83-85 Saffron Hill, London EC1N 8RT, England.
www.usborne.com
Copyright © 2007, 2004 Usborne Publishing Ltd.

The Twelve Dancing Princesses

Retold by Emma Helbrough

Illustrated by
Anna Luraschi

Reading Consultant: Alison Kelly
Roehampton University

Contents

Chapter 1

Family trouble

There were once twelve
beautiful princesses, all with
long, flowing hair and short,
fiery tempers.

3

Their father, the king, was a grumpy old man who didn't believe in having fun.

In fact, he believed that princesses should be seen and not heard.

Ballroom →

NO ENTRY

The princesses strongly disagreed.

The thing they argued about most was dancing. Their father hated it, but the princesses loved it...

so whenever he wasn't looking, they danced anyway.

Chapter 2

The sisters' secret

The girls slept in a tall tower
with their beds side by side.

7

Every night, the king locked the tower door, so that they couldn't sneak out.

Sleep well, my dears.

8

One morning, when the door
was unlocked, the princesses
were still asleep.

As the maid went to wake
them, she noticed their shoes
were lying in a soggy pile on
the floor.

How
strange!

The shoes were worn out.

When the king heard about
the shoes, he was furious.
"Those girls have been out
dancing," he spluttered.

Bring my
daughters
here... NOW!

Yes, sire.

"Princesses should not be out dancing all night!" he yelled at them. "You need your beauty sleep. You should all be ashamed of yourselves."

The girls weren't ashamed in the least. What's more, they wouldn't tell him how they had escaped or where they had been.

11

The next morning, it was clear that the princesses had been out again. The same thing happened seven nights in a row.

The king didn't know what to do.

Then he had a brilliant idea.

He decided that the first man to discover where his daughters went each night could marry one of them. Posters went up across the land.

Fed up with your job? Feel like a challenge?

Solve a royal mystery and win big prizes!!

Win your own kingdom and marry a genuine princess!

Interested? Drop in to the castle for further details.

No time wasters please.

Chapter 3

Taking the challenge

The first man to take up the
king's challenge was brave
Prince Marcus.

"By the way, there is one small catch," the king told him. "If you fail, I'll cut off your head!"

That night, Prince Marcus
was taken to the tower and put
in a room next to the princesses.

Very
comfortable
indeed!

They made him
very welcome.
One even
brought him
a cup of hot,
milky cocoa.

16

As Prince Marcus drank the cocoa, he began to feel sleepy.

He tried splashing cold water on his face, but that didn't work.

Soon he was fast asleep and snoring loudly.

17

Next morning, the princesses'
shoes were worn out again.
Prince Marcus had failed – and
the king wasn't joking about
chopping off his head.

Take him
away!

Many more princes and
noble knights came forward.
But they were all fooled by the
princesses' sweet smiles...

and their offer
of hot cocoa.

Chapter 4

Ralph and Rascal

One day, a magician named
Ralph and his pet dog, Rascal,
were passing the castle.

20

Ralph noticed one of the king's posters and decided to find out more.

This could be interesting, Rascal!

When he saw Ralph, the king looked doubtful. But he was desperate to know what the girls were up to, so he agreed to let Ralph try.

I'll chop off your head if you fail, you know.

Yes, but I won't fail...

Night came and Ralph was put in the same room where the others had stayed.

"Hello! I'm Amy," said the youngest. "He's nice," she whispered to her sisters. "I don't want him to die because of us. Maybe we shouldn't go out tonight..."

Her sisters ignored her.

A few minutes later, Annabel, the eldest sister, brought Ralph a cup of cocoa. But Ralph was a wise magician. He knew what she was up to.

He pretended to drink the cocoa. Then, when Annabel wasn't looking, he poured it into Rascal's bowl. Rascal was delighted.

Ralph yawned. "I think I'll just put my feet up for a few minutes," he told Annabel.

Then, with an even bigger
yawn, he pretended to fall
fast asleep.

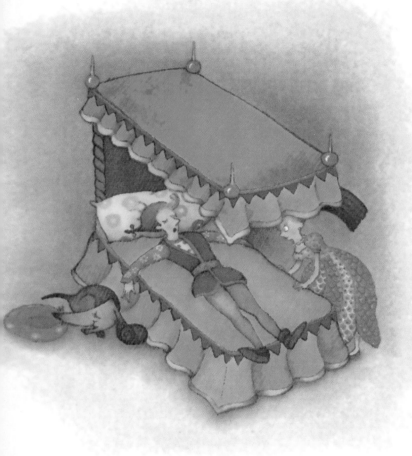

Annabel crept back to
her sisters. "He's asleep,"
she whispered.
"Let's get ready!"
They put on
their sparkliest
ball dresses...

and new
shoes. The
princesses
shimmered
like a rainbow.

27

With the last button buttoned and the last bow tied, the girls stood by their beds. Annabel pulled back a dusty, old rug in the corner of the room to reveal a secret trap door. The hinges creaked as she pulled it open.

One by one the girls disappeared down some steps and into a long, dark tunnel.

28

Chapter 5

Ralph on the trail

When the princesses were out of sight, Ralph quickly entered their room.

29

He clicked his
fingers and a
cloak appeared.
With a second
click, Ralph
vanished.

Carefully, he
tiptoed down the
steps into the tunnel.

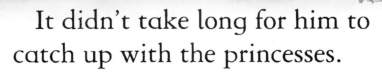

It didn't take long for him to
catch up with the princesses.

Ralph tried to walk quietly,
but it wasn't easy. At one
point he stepped on Amy's
dress. She jumped and turned
around, but there was no
one there...

A few moments later Ralph stepped on a twig. Now Amy was convinced that someone was following them. Her sisters didn't believe her.

At the end of the tunnel they came to an astonishing row of trees.

Some of the trees glistened with silver...

some with gold...

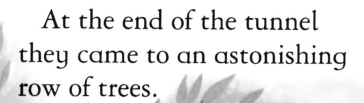

and some with sparkling diamonds.

Ralph had never seen trees
like them. While the princesses
carried on, he gently broke
off a twig from each tree.

Up ahead, the princesses had
stopped before a lake. It stood in
the shadow of a beautiful castle.

Twelve boats were waiting at the edge of the lake and in each boat sat a handsome prince.

Each prince rowed a princess across the lake.

35

Ralph sneaked into the boat carrying Amy. When they reached the other side, a band began to play.

The princesses danced until
their feet were sore and
the soles of their shoes
were worn through.

As the sun rose, they limped home. "Our nights of dancing are still safe – unlike poor Ralph's head!" said Annabel, yawning. Amy looked upset.

Chapter 6

A shock for the king

The king was having breakfast
when Ralph strolled in. "Good
morning, your majesty," said
Ralph brightly.

"I suppose you've come to tell me you failed too," sighed the king.

"Ah, but I didn't, sire," Ralph replied. Waving the twigs, he told the king what he'd seen.

The mystery is solved!

"This all sounds very unlikely," grumbled the king, when Ralph had finished. "Are you sure you're not just making it up to save your head?"

He decided to call for Annabel. When she saw the three twigs in his hand, she looked horrified.

One look at her face told the king all he needed to know. "Dancing is banned!" he declared.

The princesses sobbed and wailed when they heard their secret had been discovered.

"What will we do?" they cried. "Life is so dull without dancing."

This is the worst day of my life.

But there was nothing they could do.

True to his word, the king let Ralph marry one of his daughters. "I'd like Amy," Ralph said, "if she'll have me. She's the sweetest of all."

I'm sure you'll both be very happy.

Amy and Ralph's wedding
was a joyful occasion. Even
the king couldn't stop smiling.
"I have a surprise for you," he
whispered to Amy.

The king led her to the
ballroom and Amy gasped.
Hundreds of candles lit up
the dance floor and in
the corner a band was
playing a lively tune.

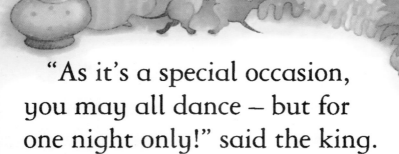

"As it's a special occasion,
you may all dance – but for
one night only!" said the king.

"Oh, how wonderful!" cried Amy and her sisters, grabbing partners. They were all still dancing the following night.

"I thought I said one night only!" said the king, but he smiled. Ralph had worked some more of his magic.

The Twelve Dancing Princesses was first
written down by two brothers, Jacob and
Wilhelm Grimm. They lived in Germany
in the early 1800s and together they
retold hundreds of fairy tales.

Series Editor: Lesley Sims

Designed by Russell Punter
and Natacha Goransky

This edition first published in 2009 by Usborne Publishing Ltd.,
Usborne House, 83-85 Saffron Hill, London EC1N 8RT, England.
www.usborne.com Copyright © 2009, 2004 Usborne Publishing Ltd.